CORPORATE MILITARY INTELLIGENCE

CORPORATE MILITARY INTELLIGENCE

Edited by

SHANTANU K. BANSAL
MONOJIT DAS

KW Publishers Pvt Ltd
New Delhi

ISBN 978-81-986658-0-5 Hardback

Published in India by Kalpana Shukla

KW Publishers Pvt Ltd
4676/21, First Floor, Ansari Road
Daryaganj, New Delhi 110 002
Phone: +91 11 43528107
Marketing: kw@kwpub.in
Editorial: production@kwpub.in
Website: www.kwpub.in

Printed and bound in India
Quiinkit Infotech Pvt. Ltd., Gurugram

Contents

Acknowledgement

It is with immense gratitude that we extend our heartfelt appreciation to all those who contributed to the successful completion of this book. This work would not have been possible without the unwavering support and expertise of scholars, practitioners, and thought leaders from across the globe.

First and foremost, we extend our sincere thanks to KW Publishers for their trust and collaboration in bringing this important volume to life. Their commitment to publishing works of strategic significance has provided us with a platform to explore the evolving nexus between corporate intelligence and military strategy. A special note of gratitude goes to Ms. Kalpana Shukla, Managing Director, KW Publishers Pvt Ltd, whose guidance and support throughout the publication process have been invaluable. Her vast experience, spanning half a decade, is an inspiration for the book.

We would also like to express our deep appreciation to all the contributors whose expert insights have shaped this book into a comprehensive and thought-provoking analysis. Their diverse perspectives, spanning Australia, France, Georgia, India, Kenya, Lebanon, Lithuania, Nepal, New Zealand, Nigeria, Poland, Russia, and Turkiye, have enriched the discourse, making this volume truly global in its scope and relevance. The cross-national collaboration underscores the universal importance of corporate intelligence in modern warfare and the need for international dialogue on this critical issue.

A special mention is due to the well-wishers and dedicated readership of Indian Aerospace Defence News (IADN). Since its inception in 2012, IADN has grown to become one of the most trusted sources for analysis and reporting on aerospace, defence, and strategic affairs. The unwavering support from our readers and contributors has played a crucial role in making IADN a leading news portal, recognised for its in-depth coverage and analytical rigour.

We also extend our gratitude to our mentors, colleagues, and friends who have supported this endeavour in many ways, both big and small. Your encouragement and belief in the significance of this work have been a driving force behind its completion. Lastly, we would like to thank Mr Manish Jaiswal, Research Assistant, IADN, for his timely support.

With deep appreciation,

Shantanu K. Bansal
Monojit Das

Introduction: Corporate Military Intelligence in a Complex World

The Convergence of Corporate and Military Intelligence

In an era defined by geopolitical shifts, economic competition, and technological advancements, the intersection between corporate strategies and military intelligence has emerged as a crucial domain of study. Traditionally seen as separate spheres, the military and corporate sectors are increasingly intertwined, influencing global security, economic warfare, and political power structures. This book, *Corporate Military Intelligence*, explores the evolving relationship by examining how corporate actors engage with military intelligence, influence conflicts, and shape security landscapes across the world.

The concept of corporate military intelligence encompasses the role of private entities in security operations, economic warfare, cyber intelligence, and geostrategic manoeuvres. From private military companies (PMCs) to intelligence-driven economic policies, the corporate world has become an active participant in shaping military strategies and intelligence practices. This book provides a comprehensive analysis of these themes, highlighting historical precedents, contemporary challenges, and future trajectories.

Scope and Objectives of the Book

The purpose of this volume is to provide a multidisciplinary perspective on how corporate and military intelligence converge in the modern world. It seeks to:

1. examine the historical foundations of corporate involvement in military intelligence and strategy;
2. analyse contemporary case studies demonstrating corporate influence on military engagements and intelligence operations;
3. assess the impact of private military security companies (PMSCs) in conflict zones and economic warfare;

4. explore the role of emerging technologies, such as artificial intelligence (AI) and big data, in intelligence gathering;
5. investigate the geoeconomic implications of intelligence warfare and corporate-military alliances; and
6. understand the ethical and regulatory challenges posed by the increasing privatisation of military functions.

Chapter Overview

Part I: Strategic Foundations and Economic Warfare

The first section of the book delves into the historical and strategic aspects of corporate-military interactions.

- Chapter 1: From Sea to Strategy (Hasim Turker) applies naval command principles to modern intelligence operations, illustrating how maritime strategies influence both corporate and military intelligence.
- Chapter 2: Economic Warfare: The Corporate Involvement (Oloke Moses Olalekan) examines how corporations act as key players in economic warfare, shaping financial and trade policies that impact national security.
- Chapter 3: Private Military Security Companies in Pacific Island Countries (Sasha Gillies-Lekakis) explores how PMSCs operate in the Pacific region, assessing their impact on development and security structures.

Part II: Political Influence and Intelligence in Foreign Policy

This section focuses on the role of intelligence in global politics and corporate lobbying in military engagements.

- Chapter 4: Intelligence and Foreign Policy (Sureyya Yigit) discusses the intersection between intelligence agencies and diplomatic decision-making.
- Chapter 5: The Business of War (Mohamad Hassan Soueidan) highlights how corporate entities influence military strategies and interventions for political gain.
- Chapter 6: Tangled Power Game (Sampa Kundu) investigates the role of Myanmar's military in the jade industry, showcasing corporate-military entanglements in resource economies.

Part III: Technology, AI, and the Future of Intelligence

The advancement of technology has significantly altered intelligence-gathering methodologies and military-corporate relations.

- Chapter 7: From Fossil Fuels to Chips (Shushant Vc Parashar) examines how intelligence strategies have evolved in the era of Big Tech.
- Chapter 8: Economic Warfare as a Component of Geoeconomic Strategy (Greg Simons) contextualizes economic intelligence in the broader framework of global power shifts.
- Chapter 9: The Issue of Regulating Artificial Intelligence (AI) (Simant Shankar Bharti and Saroj Kumar Aryal) maps the divide between the Global North and South in cybersecurity and AI governance.

Part IV: Private Military Forces and Security Dynamics

As military operations become increasingly privatised, this section analyses the role of mercenaries and private forces in contemporary warfare.

- Chapter 10: Why Wagner Wins (Aaryaman Nijhawan) explores the operational success of Wagner Group, illustrating the growing role of mercenary organisations in statecraft.
- Chapter 11: The Nexus Conundrum (Antoine Renaux) unpacks the complex relationship between military intelligence and corporate interests in modern warfare.
- Chapter 12: Civil-Military Fusion in Artificial Intelligence (Niranjan Marjani) examines India's AI-driven military strategies and the integration of AI into defence.

Part V: Ethical and Regulatory Challenges

The final section addresses the political and ethical dimensions of intelligence and warfare in modern statecraft.

- Chapter 13: An Analysis of Russia's Counter-Terrorism Efforts in The Sahel (John Mwangi Githigaro) discusses intelligence and military strategies in Africa, particularly Russia's counterterrorism policies.
- Chapter 14: Political Ethics and the Politicisation of Intelligence Services (David Shakarishvili) explores the ethical dilemmas associated with intelligence agencies and political decision-making.

- Chapter 15: Increasing Role of Private Military and Security Companies (PMSCs) (Anuradha Oinam and Monojit Das) evaluates the future trajectory of private military companies and their influence on global security.

As this book illustrates, the future of warfare will not be solely military-driven but increasingly shaped by corporate influence. From intelligence gathering and cybersecurity to private military operations and economic warfare, corporations are becoming central players in global security dynamics. Each chapter in this volume unpacks different facets of this evolving landscape, analysing how financial power, technological advancements, and privatised security forces are redefining traditional military strategies. By bridging historical insights with contemporary case studies, *Corporate Military Intelligence* provides a critical foundation for understanding this transformation, offering researchers, policymakers, and security professionals the necessary tools to navigate the complex interplay between corporate and military intelligence in the 21st century.

Tables and Figures

Tables

Figures

Abbreviations

APIs	Application Programmable Interfaces
ACLED	Armed Conflict Location and Event Data Project
AI	Artificial Intelligence
BNPL	Basic Needs Poverty Line
BRA	Bougainville Revolutionary Army
BP	British Petroleum's
FACA	Central African Armed Forces
CAR	Central African Republic
CDS	Chief of Defence Staff
CASTC	China Aerospace Science and Technology Corporation
CETGC	China Electronics Technology Group Corporation
CCP	Chinese Communist Party
CPC	Coalition for Patriots for Change
CAGR	Compound Annual Growth Rate
CPC	Corporate Political Connections
CSR	Corporate Social Responsibility
COIN-CT	Counter-Insurgency and Counter-Terrorism Cooperation
DDoS	Damage and Denial-of-Service Attacks
DAIC	Defence AI Council
DAIPA	Defence AI Project Agency
DPSUs	Defence Public Sector Undertakings
DRDO	Defence Research and Development Organisation
DDIL	Denied, Degraded, Intermittent, and Limited
DoD	Department of Defense
DPI	Digital Public Infrastructure
ECOWAS	Economic Community of West African States

ELINT	Electronic Intelligence
ECSR	Environmental Corporate Social Responsibility
EU	European Union
GDPR	General Data Protection Regulation
HDI	Human Development Index
IIoT	Industrial Internet of Things
IW	Information Warfare
IFRI	Institut Français des Relations Internationales
IC	Intelligence Community
ISR	Intelligence, Surveillance & Reconnaissance
IDPs	Internally Displaced Persons
IHL	International Humanitarian Law
IPE	International Political Economy
IoT	Internet of Things
ISIS	Islamic State's
KIO	Kachin Independence Organisation
LLM	Large Language Model
LDCs	Least Developed Countries
LAWS	Lethal Autonomous Weapons Systems
MGOs	Mercenary-Governmental Organisations
MSMEs	Micro, Small and Medium Enterprises
MSTIC	Microsoft Threat Intelligence Centre
MIC	Military Industrial Complex
MPRI	Military Professional Resources Inc.
MCF	Military-Civil Fusion
MOIS	Ministry of Intelligence and Security
MINUSMA	Multidimensional Integrated Stabilization Mission in Mali
MEHL	Myanmar Economic Holding Limited
MGE	Myanmar Gems Enterprise
NGOs	Non-Governmental Organisations
OSINT	Open Source Intelligence
P/CVE	Preventing and Countering Violent Extremism
PMCs	Private Military Companies
PSCs	Private Security Companies
PSYOPS	Psychological Operations

R&D	Research and Development
FPA	School and the Foreign Policy Analysis
SIGINT	Signal Intelligence
SOF	Special Operations Forces
SIO	Stanford Internet Observatory
SIPRI	Stockholm International Peace Research Institute
UFC	United Fruit Company
UAVs	Unmanned Aerial Vehicles
CENTCOM	US Central Command

1

From Sea to Strategy: Applying Naval Command Principles to Corporate and Military Intelligence

Hasim Turker

Introduction

In the evolving landscape of global security, the integration of time-honoured naval command principles into corporate and military intelligence operations emerges as a potent strategy for navigating the complexities of future warfare. This chapter explores the application of fundamental naval command guidelines—unity of command, decentralisation and delegation, purpose and direction, efficiency, readiness and preparedness, discipline and cohesion, adaptability and flexibility, ethical conduct and integrity, and continuous improvement—to enhance strategic decision-making and operational effectiveness in the realms of corporate and military intelligence.

Drawing upon a synthesis of historical naval leadership practices and contemporary intelligence challenges, the chapter elucidates how these principles, traditionally designed to govern the leadership, management, and operation of naval forces, are remarkably applicable and beneficial to the strategic imperatives of modern intelligence frameworks. By leveraging case studies and theoretical analysis, the chapter demonstrates the transformative potential of naval command principles in fostering a culture of discipline, excellence, and innovation within intelligence operations—critical attributes for success in the information-driven society at large.

This chapter showcases a paradigm shift in how intelligence strategies are formulated and executed, advocating for a deeper integration of naval command principles to cultivate resilience, foster ethical leadership, and enhance operational efficiency. In doing so, it contributes to a broader discourse on the strategic alignment of military heritage with future security endeavours, offering insightful perspectives for both practitioners and scholars in the field of security and strategic studies and management.

Foundations of Naval Command: An In-Depth Examination

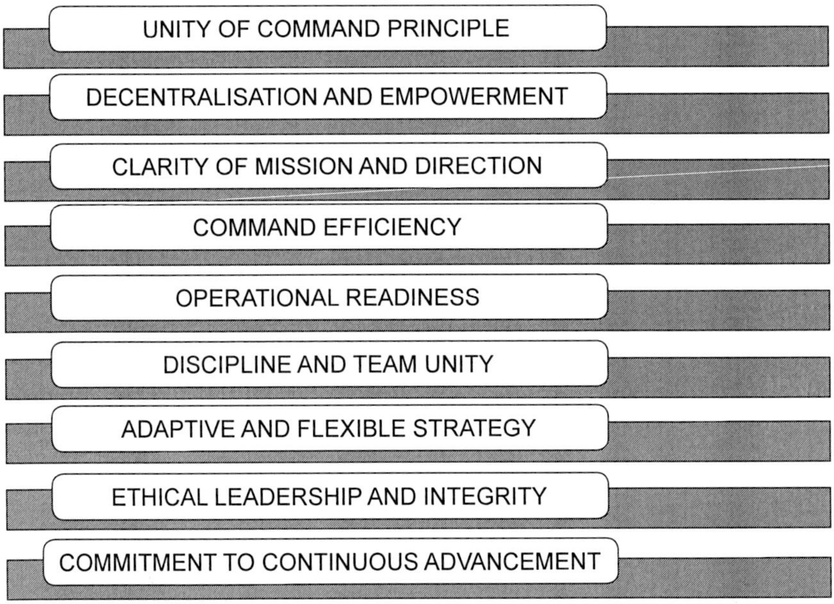

At the heart of naval leadership, management, and operational tactics across the globe lie the enduring principles of naval command. These principles, deeply rooted in a rich maritime legacy, offer a strategic framework for command and control, aimed at fostering discipline, efficiency, and superior performance. While nuances exist among the doctrines of various naval forces, the essence of these principles is universally esteemed and forms a cornerstone of naval education. This section seeks to elucidate these pivotal principles, underscoring their relevance and application in the naval arena (Till, 2013).

Unity of Command Principle

Central to naval operations is the principle of Unity of Command, which posits that every individual within the naval architecture should be answerable to a singular superior. This principle is instrumental in delineating clear lines of authority and accountability, thereby obviating the potential for confusion and duplicative directives. It stands as a fundamental pillar in preserving order within the naval hierarchy and enhancing the efficacy of decision-making and operational execution (Jones, 2000).

Decentralisation and Empowerment

Balancing the principle of Unity of Command, the principles of decentralisation and empowerment emphasise the significance of entrusting authority to the lower echelons of the command structure. This strategic delegation is pivotal for nurturing initiative, expeditious decision-making, and adaptability, particularly crucial in the fluid and often unpredictable maritime operational contexts (Jones, 2000).

Clarity of Mission and Direction

The articulation of clear missions, objectives, and anticipated outcomes to all members is a hallmark of adept naval leadership. This clarity ensures that every participant is cognisant of their role and the broader objectives at stake, fostering a collective sense of purpose and dedication essential for unified and motivated operations (Sinek, 2011).

Command Efficiency

The exigencies of naval operations necessitate judicious use of resources and personnel, as well as time management. The principle of Command Efficiency mandates commanders to strive for unparalleled operational efficiency, optimising resource allocation and strategic implementation to achieve mission objectives with minimal waste (Bungay, 2011).

Operational Readiness

The inherently unpredictable milieu of maritime operations mandates a perpetual state of readiness and preparedness among naval forces. This principle is a testament to the imperative of ensuring that units are consistently equipped, trained, and mentally fortified to embark on missions at a moment's notice, encapsulating the naval ethos of relentless vigilance and service readiness (Olson, 2009).

Discipline and Team Unity

Discipline, the bedrock of naval efficacy, ensures the meticulous execution of commands and the seamless conduct of operations. Coupled with the principle of Team Unity, which cultivates an ethos of solidarity and collaborative endeavour, these principles engender an environment where individuals synergise seamlessly under the established command hierarchy (Willink & Babin, 2017).

Adaptive and Flexible Strategy

The dynamic and often volatile nature of naval engagements necessitates an adaptive and flexible strategic posture. Commanders and their forces are thus enjoined to exhibit versatility in tactics and planning, allowing for the agile recalibration of strategies and the seizing of emergent opportunities (Freedman, 2015).

Ethical Leadership and Integrity

The expectation that naval leaders exemplify the highest standards of ethical conduct and integrity is paramount. This principle not only ensures operations are conducted with honour but also upholds the Navy's esteemed standing as a principled force in the international arena (Ciulla, 2014).

Commitment to Continuous Advancement

A culture of continuous learning and development is advocated through the principle of Continuous Advancement. This ethos encourages the pursuit of innovation in tactics and technology, underscoring the criticality of adaptability and foresight in sustaining naval superiority (Tidd & Bessant, 2020).

These structured principles of naval command, while anchored in age-old maritime traditions, impart timeless insights into the art of leadership and strategic foresight. Their applicability transcends the confines of naval operations, offering invaluable lessons for any venture that demands disciplined leadership, strategic depth, and operational acumen. Future discussions will delve into the application of these principles to bolster corporate and military intelligence strategies, preparing them to navigate the challenges that lie ahead.

Intelligence in Modern Warfare and Corporate Strategy

In the current global landscape where security concerns and business competition intersect, intelligence plays a crucial role in shaping strategic directions and decision-making. The realms of both modern warfare and corporate strategy, while differing in objectives, depend heavily on intelligence to navigate through complexities, mitigate risks, and capitalise on opportunities (Cronin & Crawford, 1999). This discussion explores the evolution of intelligence within these areas, spotlighting the challenges faced and underscoring the imperative for innovative intelligence practices in gathering, analysing, and applying information.

Transformative Dynamics in Intelligence Strategies

The sphere of modern warfare has undergone a profound shift in intelligence strategies, transitioning from conventional espionage and reconnaissance to advanced cyber operations and information warfare. The advent of the digital era has extended the battlefield from tangible territories into the vast, intangible realm of cyberspace, where dominance in information can critically sway conflict outcomes (Gilad et al., 2021). Similarly, in the corporate arena, competitive intelligence has progressed from simple market research to intricate data analytics and artificial intelligence algorithms, which predict market movements and identify business opportunities (Chandan, 2017).

Technology: A Double-Edged Sword

Technology is at the vanguard of this transformation, presenting both novel capabilities and vulnerabilities. In the military domain, technologies, such as satellite imagery, Unmanned Aerial Vehicles (UAVs), and signal interception, yield vital real-time data for strategic planning and action (Dupont, 2013). In the corporate world, the utilisation of big data analytics, machine learning, and blockchain technologies is crucial for understanding market trends and safeguarding assets. However, this dependency on technology also introduces risks, with cyber threats and information warfare tactics targeting these systems, potentially undermining security and operational integrity (Tao et al., 2019).

The Convergence of Cyber and Information Warfare

Cyber and information warfare epitomise the merging challenges of military and corporate intelligence. Actors, both state and non-state, utilise cyber operations to disrupt, degrade, or deceive adversaries, aiming at military assets and critical civilian infrastructure alike (Gilad et al., 2021). In the corporate sphere, cyber espionage attempts to pilfer intellectual property and sensitive data, while information operations manipulate public perceptions and erode trust in brands or products. These strategies underscore the increasingly blurred lines between military and corporate intelligence efforts, highlighting the necessity for resilient and robust intelligence frameworks (Buchan & Navarrete, 2021; Chandan, 2017; Vashisth & Kumar, 2013).

Challenges in Corporate and Military Intelligence

Navigating an environment marked by swift technological progress and changing geopolitical dynamics poses a significant challenge. The overwhelming volume and pace of information call for advanced analytical tools to filter actionable intelligence from mere noise. Furthermore, the ethical considerations surrounding surveillance, data collection, and psychological operations warrant a balanced approach, ensuring efficacy while respecting privacy and legal standards (Wasilow & Thorpe, 2019).

The Imperative for Innovative Approaches

Confronting these challenges demands innovative solutions that harness both human expertise and technological advancements. Artificial intelligence and machine learning hold promise for improving predictive analytics and streamlining routine tasks, allowing analysts to concentrate on more intricate evaluations (Tamang et al., 2021). Nonetheless, technology cannot supplant the nuanced comprehension and critical thinking provided by seasoned intelligence professionals. A synergistic approach, blending technological sophistication with human insight, stands as an effective strategy for the future of intelligence in both warfare and corporate competition (Wang et al., 2023).

The convergence of intelligence roles in modern warfare and corporate strategy underscores the indispensable nature of information in achieving strategic goals. As the landscape of threats and opportunities evolves, so too must intelligence methodologies. Embracing technological innovation and fostering a culture of continuous learning and ethical conduct, military and corporate entities can bolster their strategic postures, ensuring adaptability and success in the dynamic challenges ahead (Lin et al., 2020). The forthcoming discussion will examine the application of naval command principles to these intelligence strategies, offering a distinctive lens through which to view leadership and strategic management in the digital era.

Applying Naval Principles to Corporate and Military Intelligence

The integration of naval command principles into the realms of corporate and military intelligence operations presents a strategic paradigm for navigating the intricacies of today's multi-domain threat environment. Leveraging these enduring principles can significantly bolster decision-making processes, operational efficacy, and strategic vision. This discourse aims to elucidate the application of each naval command principle within the context of intelligence operations, drawing on both hypothetical scenarios and real-world case studies to illustrate their impact on enhancing intelligence-driven strategies.

Unity of Command in Intelligence Operations

The principle of Unity of Command, which underscores the importance of clear, singular lines of authority, is indispensable for the streamlined execution of intelligence operations (McDowell et al., 2024)fast-paced, ill-structured, and demanding conditions. C2 will be further complicated by operational challenges such as Denied, Degraded, Intermittent, and Limited (DDIL). In a corporate setting, this principle ensures that intelligence units report directly to top-tier decision-makers, enabling rapid responses to critical intelligence insights (Wixom & Watson, 2010). For military endeavours, it facilitates the efficient flow of actionable intelligence to the appropriate units, thereby eliminating delays (Xiyu et al., 2024).

Hypothetical Scenario: A global enterprise institutes a centralised intelligence division with direct reporting lines to the CEO, markedly enhancing the organisation's agility in responding to market threats and opportunities.

Decentralisation and Delegation for Agile Intelligence

The principles of decentralisation and delegation recognise the value of empowering lower echelons to make informed decisions based on immediate intelligence. In military contexts, this autonomy allows field operatives to swiftly adapt to unfolding situations, potentially tipping the scales towards mission success (Kolwicz, 2020). Similarly, in the corporate world, granting regional managers the authority to act on competitive intelligence fosters a nimble adaptation to market fluctuations.

Hypothetical Scenario: A naval fleet operating in a volatile region delegates decision-making power to individual vessel commanders, enabling them to respond instantaneously to intelligence inputs, thereby enhancing operational flexibility and safety.

Purpose and Direction for Strategic Intelligence Alignment

Articulating the purpose and direction of intelligence efforts ensures they are in lockstep with overarching organisational objectives. This alignment is crucial in both military and corporate spheres to ensure that intelligence activities are strategically focused and impactful (Agor et al., 2023; Jewell, 2003).

Hypothetical Scenario: A leading tech company steers its competitive intelligence initiatives towards its ambition of dominating the renewable energy market, concentrating on tracking sector innovations and disruptions, thereby securing a competitive edge.

Efficiency in Command for Optimised Intelligence Utilisation

The principle of Efficiency in Command advocates for the strategic allocation of intelligence resources to maximise coverage without resource dilution. This approach is vital for both military and corporate entities to ensure that intelligence gathering is comprehensive and focused (Belfares et al., 2007).

Hypothetical Scenario: A defence organisation refines its satellite reconnaissance efforts to prioritise areas with heightened insurgent activity, enhancing the effectiveness of intelligence collection while conserving satellite resources.

Readiness and Preparedness in Intelligence

Maintaining a perpetual state of readiness within intelligence operations is critical for pre-empting threats and capitalising on opportunities (Junor, 2017). This principle demands continuous vigilance and the ability to mobilise intelligence capabilities at a moment's notice, a necessity in both military and corporate arenas.

Hypothetical Scenario: A multinational retail chain employs real-time social media monitoring to swiftly adapt marketing strategies to emerging consumer trends, demonstrating the value of constant intelligence readiness.

Discipline and Cohesion for Effective Intelligence Collaboration

The principles of Discipline and Cohesion are fundamental in ensuring the reliability and integrity of intelligence outputs. Through disciplined analytical methodologies and cohesive team dynamics, both military and corporate intelligence entities can provide accurate, actionable intelligence insights (Chiocchio & Essiembre, 2009).

Hypothetical Scenario: An intelligence agency's adoption of stringent cross-validation techniques for data analysis fosters a disciplined, cohesive environment, significantly enhancing the accuracy of intelligence reporting.

Adaptability and Flexibility in Intelligence Operations

The capacity for Adaptability and Flexibility is essential in the rapidly evolving landscape of intelligence, allowing entities to pivot in response to new information or changing operational contexts. This agility is crucial for maintaining strategic advantage in both military and corporate settings (Alnoukari et al., 2016).

Hypothetical Scenario: In the wake of an unexpected geopolitical event, a corporation's intelligence team swiftly redirects its focus to gather critical information affecting its operations in the region, exemplifying the strategic benefit of adaptability.

Ethical Conduct and Integrity in Intelligence Gathering

Adhering to ethical standards and maintaining integrity in intelligence operations are paramount for building trust and credibility. This principle ensures that military intelligence respects the laws of warfare and human rights, while corporate intelligence operations adhere to legal and ethical guidelines (Wasilow & Thorpe, 2019).

Case Study: A finance corporation's commitment to ethical intelligence practices, aligned with international norms, bolstered its reputation and stakeholders' trust, underscoring the importance of ethical integrity.

Continuous Improvement for Advanced Intelligence Capabilities

Embracing the principle of Continuous Improvement is vital for the evolution of intelligence capabilities, necessitating ongoing investment in training, technology, and methodologies (Gonzalez & Martins, 2016). This commitment ensures that military and corporate intelligence operations remain cutting-edge and responsive to the dynamic global landscape.

Hypothetical Scenario: A naval intelligence unit's regular training on advanced digital forensics techniques enhances its capability to extract actionable insights from enemy communications, demonstrating the value of continuous skill and knowledge enhancement.

The strategic application of naval command principles to intelligence operations across military and corporate sectors offers a robust framework for enhancing strategic decision-making and operational effectiveness. By embracing these principles, organisations can adeptly navigate the complexities of the contemporary world, grounded in agility, ethical integrity, and strategic acumen.

Case Studies

The practical application of naval command principles in shaping strategies for military and corporate intelligence operations is vividly illustrated through real-world case studies. These examples not only showcase the direct impact of naval principles on intelligence activities but also provide insightful lessons for their future implementation.

Case Study 1: Operation Neptune Spear and Unity of Command

Operation Neptune Spear, which culminated in the elimination of Osama Bin Laden, exemplifies the Unity of Command principle in a military intelligence context. This operation was marked by a streamlined command structure, with all participating units reporting through a unified hierarchy directly to the President of the United States. This clear chain of command was instrumental in integrating diverse intelligence inputs, facilitating precise decision-making and the mission's successful execution (Govern, 2012).

Outcomes: The operation's triumph underscored the critical role of a singular command line in orchestrating complex operations, ensuring rapid communication and implementation of actionable intelligence.

Lessons Learned: Operation Neptune Spear highlights the effectiveness of the principle of Unity of Command in coordinating efforts across various intelligence and operational units, proving its essential value in executing high-stakes military missions.

Case Study 2: Toyota's Lean Manufacturing and Continuous Improvement

Toyota's adoption of lean manufacturing principles, mirroring the naval principle of Continuous Improvement, transformed its production processes and corporate strategy. By perpetually striving to minimise waste and enhance efficiency, Toyota not only optimised its operations but also cultivated a culture of innovation and adaptability, significantly bolstering its global standing (Haley, 2013).

Outcomes: The implementation of the principle of Continuous Improvement led to marked improvements in production efficiency, product quality, and customer satisfaction, cementing Toyota's position as an automotive industry leader.

Lessons Learned: Toyota's experience demonstrates the benefits of applying the principle of Continuous Improvement in a corporate setting, highlighting its potential to foster operational excellence and strategic competitiveness in the business realm.

Case Study 3: The Battle of Midway and Decentralisation and Delegation

The Battle of Midway during World War II serves as a testament to the effective use of the principle of Decentralisation and Delegation. Armed with intelligence from decrypted Japanese communications, Admiral Nimitz empowered his commanders with the authority to make tactical decisions based on the battle's evolving dynamics (Shultz, 1997).

Outcomes: The strategic empowerment of commanders was a decisive factor in the U.S. Navy's victory, significantly influencing the Pacific War's trajectory in favour of the Allies.

Lessons Learned: The Battle of Midway underscores the strategic advantage of enabling commanders to act on intelligence and adapt to changing conditions, showcasing the value of decentralisation and delegation in military engagements.

Case Study 4: British Petroleum and Adaptability and Flexibility

British Petroleum's (BP) handling of the Deepwater Horizon oil spill in 2010 highlights the principles of Adaptability and Flexibility in managing corporate crises. Confronted with an environmental catastrophe of unprecedented scale, BP had to swiftly adjust its strategies, from containment and cleanup efforts to public relations campaigns, based on the continuously evolving situation and intelligence regarding the spill's impact (Kanso et al., 2020).

Outcomes: BP's adaptable approach mitigated some effects of the disaster, though the company endured substantial financial and reputational losses. The crisis emphasised the necessity for prompt adaptability and flexibility in response to unexpected challenges.

Lessons Learned: The BP incident illustrates the imperative for corporations to maintain agility and quickly adapt to crises, guided by timely intelligence and environmental assessments.

These case studies vividly demonstrate the tangible benefits of integrating naval command principles into military and corporate intelligence frameworks. The insights gleaned from these instances affirm the universal relevance of these principles in enhancing decision-making, operational efficiency, and strategic agility across diverse scenarios.

Future Implications and Challenges

The forward integration of naval command principles into the fabric of future warfare and corporate intelligence strategies presents a visionary approach to steering through the increasingly intricate global scenario. This discourse explores the ramifications of such integration, spotlighting the potential hurdles and underscoring the imperative for continuous adaptation and innovation to surmount these challenges.

Future Warfare: Strategic and Operational Enhancements

In the evolving landscape of warfare, the infusion of naval command principles promises to significantly bolster strategic and operational agility. As adversaries harness cutting-edge technologies like artificial intelligence (AI), unmanned systems, and cyber capabilities, the principles of Unity of Command alongside Decentralisation and Delegation become pivotal in sustaining a unified yet flexible force architecture. This integration ensures military operations are primed to rapidly counter dynamic threats through the leverage of instantaneous intelligence and autonomous decision-making frameworks (Fazekas, 2023; Zak et al., 2023) without those it cannot be fully applied. These principles are the mutual trust between participants, the understanding, the clearly articulated intent of the superior, the decentralized execution and the timely-made decisions. As Artificial Intelligence is progressing and gaining ground it will influence the entirety of the military command and control process: new decision situations will arise and human-machine cooperation may create new relationships. This paper scrutinizes whether the identified principles of mission command can be applied in the same way in the Artificial Intelligence-infused operational environment as it can be among traditional circumstances.

Furthermore, the adherence to the principles of Continuous Improvement and Adaptability and Flexibility is vital for crafting doctrines that assimilate the forefront of technological progress, positioning military forces at the spearhead of warfare capabilities. Such a proactive posture not only amplifies deterrence but also guarantees readiness across a broad spectrum of conflict scenarios, ranging from hybrid engagements to significant state confrontations (Finkel, 2011; Kilic & Celmeli, 2014).

Corporate Intelligence Strategies: Building Resilience and Agility

For the corporate sphere, embedding naval command principles within intelligence strategies can cultivate more robust and nimble business mechanisms. Amidst swift technological shifts and geopolitical fluxes, principles like "purpose" and "direction", coupled with "efficiency" in command, direct corporations to synchronise their intelligence endeavours with overarching business aims. This strategic congruence is crucial for manoeuvring through market instabilities and seizing nascent opportunities.

Additionally, the focus on the principle of Ethical Conduct and Integrity gains augmented relevance in today's corporate governance landscape where ethical can inflict severe reputational harm. Upholding these principles ensures responsible conduct of intelligence activities, nurturing trust among stakeholders and the broader community.

Navigating Potential Challenges

While the advantages are manifest, the path to integrating naval command principles into future strategic frameworks is fraught with obstacles. A significant barrier is the entrenched resistance to change within established organisational cultures. Both military and corporate entities may exhibit deep-rooted operational traditions, and introducing novel paradigms may face scepticism and resistance (Kasemsap, 2017; Kelly, 2008).

The rapid pace of technological advancement also poses a challenge in sustaining a workforce proficient in the latest innovations. Ensuring continuous education and skill development is essential but demands substantial investment and strategic vision (Beer & Mulder, 2020).

Overcoming Challenges Through Continuous Innovation

To transcend these challenges, a steadfast commitment to continuous innovation and adaptation is essential. This requires cultivating an organisational culture that values learning and flexibility, encourages innovation, and views setbacks as growth opportunities. Leadership plays a critical role in catalysing this cultural transformation, exemplifying adaptability, and advocating for innovation (Imran et al., 2016).

In tackling the technological hurdle, forging partnerships with academia and industry pioneers can offer avenues to stay updated on emerging trends and technologies (Wohlin et al., 2011). Moreover, dedicating resources to research and development, especially in domains like AI, cyber defence, and data analytics, can elevate operational competencies and intelligence analytical capabilities.

The strategic incorporation of naval command principles into the blueprint of future warfare and corporate intelligence strategies delineates a guide for navigating the 21st-century complexities. While challenges are inevitable, they can be addressed through a dedication to continuous adaptation, ethical integrity, and innovation. By adopting these principles, leaders in both military and corporate realms can ensure their organisations are not merely equipped to confront the present challenges but are also strategically positioned to leverage future opportunities.

Conclusion

This chapter has navigated the complex terrain where the enduring principles of naval command intersect the evolving strategies of modern military and corporate intelligence. Through a detailed examination of these foundational principles—Unity of Command, Decentralisation and Delegation, Purpose and Direction, Efficiency in Command, Readiness and Preparedness, Discipline and Cohesion, Adaptability and Flexibility, Ethical Conduct and Integrity, and Continuous Improvement—we have revealed their sustained significance and transformative impact in addressing the multifaceted challenges of contemporary warfare and corporate competition.

The case studies showcased herein vividly demonstrate the practical implementation and profound influence of these principles across a spectrum of scenarios, ranging from critical military operations to intricate corporate crisis management situations. These instances highlight the adaptability and efficacy of naval command principles in bolstering strategic decision-making, enhancing operational efficiency, and promoting ethical leadership across varied environments.

Reflecting upon the assimilation of these timeless principles into current intelligence frameworks, it becomes clear that their integration cultivates an organisational ethos marked by resilience, innovation, and ethical stewardship. Amidst the swiftly changing technological arenas and geopolitical landscapes, these principles stand as a reliable beacon for navigating the complexities and uncertainties that define our era. They not only amplify the strategic acumen of military and corporate bodies but also contribute to fostering a more secure and stable global milieu.

Looking forward, the confluence of naval command principles with intelligence strategies opens vast avenues for future inquiry and innovation. Promising areas for further exploration include leveraging these principles within cyber warfare and information security, advancing AI and machine learning technologies in alignment with these command doctrines, and addressing the ethical dilemmas posed by their application in novel contexts. Additional research could venture into a cross-cultural and organisational analysis of these principles, shedding light on their universal relevance and adaptability.

In sum, the voyage from maritime command to the forefront of intelligence operations encapsulates the enduring wisdom of naval traditions. By tailoring these age-old principles to meet the exigencies of the modern world, leaders are equipped to steer through the tumultuous seas of the 21st century with assurance, charting a course toward success and security in an intricately connected and dynamic global landscape.

References

Agor, S. D., Kanesie, D. A., Boateng, P. A., & Yamoah, P. (2023), "Formulating Strategies that Align Corporate Goals with Organisational Capabilities", *International Journal of Research and Scientific Innovation*, 10(11), pp. 620–633.

Alnoukari, M., Razouk, R., & Hanano, A. (2016), BSC-SI, "A framework for integrating strategic intelligence in corporate strategic management", *International Journal of Strategic Information Technology and Applications (IJSITA)*, 7(1), pp. 32–44.

Beer, P. & Mulder, R. H. (2020), "The effects of technological developments on work and their implications for continuous vocational education and training: A systematic review", *Frontiers in Psychology*, 11, 535119.

Belfares, L., Klibi, W., Lo, N., & Guitouni, A. (2007), "Multi-objectives Tabu Search based algorithm for progressive resource allocation", *European Journal of Operational Research*, 177(3), pp. 1779–1799.

Buchan, R. & Navarrete, I. (2021), "Cyber espionage and international law". In *Research Handbook on International Law and Cyberspace*, pp. 231–252. Edward Elgar Publishing.

Bungay, S. (2011), "The Art of Action: How Leaders Close the Gaps between Plans", *Actions and Results (London: Brealey, 2011)*, pp. 26–53.

Chandan, H. C. (2017)," Blurred lines between competitive intelligence and corporate espionage". In *Corporate Espionage, Geopolitics, and Diplomacy Issues in International Business*, pp. 1–12. IGI Global.

Chiocchio, F. & Essiembre, H. (2009), "Cohesion and Performance: A Meta-Analytic Review of Disparities Between Project Teams, Production Teams, and Service Teams", *Small Group Research*, 40(4), pp. 382–420. https://doi.org/10.1177/1046496409335103

Ciulla, J. B. (2014),*Ethics, the heart of leadership*, 3rd Ed. ABC-CLIO.

Cronin, B. & Crawford, H. (1999), "Raising the intelligence stakes: Corporate information warfare and strategic surprise",*Competitive Intelligence Review*, 10(3), pp. 58–66. https://doi.org/10.1002/(SICI)1520-6386(199933) 10:3<58::AID-CIR9>3.0.CO;2-N

Dupont, A. (2013), "Intelligence for the twenty-first century". In *Twenty-First Century Intelligence*, pp. 15–39. Routledge.

Fazekas, F. (2023), "Mission Command and Artificial Intelligence", *Land Forces Academy Review*, *28*(2), pp. 69–79. https://doi.org/10.2478/raft-2023-0010

Finkel, M. (2011), *On Flexibility: Recovery from Technological and Doctrinal Surprise on the Battlefield*. Stanford University Press.

Freedman, L. (2015),*Strategy: A History*. Oxford University Press.

Gilad, A., Pecht, E., & Tishler, A. (2021), "Intelligence, Cyberspace, and National Security", *Defence and Peace Economics*, *32*(1), pp. 18–45. https://doi.org/10.1080/10242694.2020.1778966

Gonzalez, R. V. D. & Martins, M. F. (2016), "Capability for continuous improvement: Analysis of companies from automotive and capital goods industries", *The TQM Journal*, *28*(2), pp. 250–274.

Govern, K. H. (2012), "Operation Neptune Spear: Was Killing Bin Laden a Legitimate Military Objective?", *Targeted Killings: Law and Morality in an Asymmetrical World*, pp. 347–373.

Haley, M. (2013), *Lean principles and defense information technology acquisition: An investigation of the determinants of successful application* [PhD Thesis, Capella University].

Imran, M. K., Ilyas, M., & Aslam, U. (2016), "Organisational learning through transformational leadership", *The Learning Organisation*, 23(4), pp. 232–248.

Jewell, D. P. (2003), "Transforming the Core Function of Military Intelligence to Knowledge Management", *School of Advanced Military Studies, United States Army Command and General Staff*. https://apps.dtic.mil/sti/citations/ADA416035

Jones, L. (2000),*Toward the Valued Ideal of Jointness: The Need for Unity of Command in US Armed Forces*. Naval War College. https://apps.dtic.mil/sti/citations/ADA378445

Junor, L. J. (2017),*Managing military readiness*. Government Printing Office.

Kanso, A. M., Nelson, R. A., & Kitchen, P. J. (2020), "BP and the Deepwater Horizon oil spill: A case study of how company management employed public relations to restore a damaged brand", *Journal of Marketing Communications*, *26*(7), pp. 703–731. https://doi.org/10.1080/13527266.2018.1559218

Kasemsap, K. (2017), "The roles of organisational change management and resistance to change in the modern business world". In *Organisational culture and behavior: Concepts, methodologies, tools, and applications*, pp. 1034–1062. IGI Global.

Kelly, J. W. (2008), *Resistance to organisational cultural change in the military: A JFO case study*. US Army War College. https://apps.dtic.mil/sti/citations/ADA479711

Kilic, Y. & Celmeli, M. (2014), "Adapting Military Leadership in a Changing Warfare Environment", *Journal of Management and Information Science*, 2(4), pp. 88–95.

Kolwicz, T. (February 1, 2020), *The Side Effect of Tech for Decentralised Command*. U.S. Naval Institute. https://www.usni.org/magazines/proceedings/2020/february/side-effect-tech-decentralized-command

Lin, W. L., Yip, N., Ho, J. A., & Sambasivan, M. (2020), "The adoption of technological innovations in a B2B context and its impact on firm performance: An ethical leadership perspective", *Industrial Marketing Management*, *89*, pp. 61–71.

McDowell, K., Novoseller, E., Madison, A., Goecks, V. G., & Kelshaw, C. (2024), *Re-Envisioning Command and Control* (arXiv:2402.07946). arXiv. http://arxiv.org/abs/2402.07946

Olson, C. R. (2009), "Naval Leadership: Developing Operational Leaders for the 21st Century", *Newport, RI: Naval War College*. https://apps.dtic.mil/sti/citations/ADA503030

Pfeffer, J. & Sutton, R. I. (2006), *Hard facts, dangerous half-truths, and total nonsense: Profiting from evidence-based management*. Harvard Business Press.

Shultz, L. K. (1997), *A Comparative Analysis of the Operational Leadership of Admiral Isoroku Yamamoto and Admiral Chester W. Nimitz at the Battle of Midway* (ADA328219). Naval War College. https://apps.dtic.mil/sti/citations/tr/ADA328219

Sinek, S. (2011), *Start with why: How great leaders inspire everyone to take action*. Penguin.

Tamang, M. D., Shukla, V. K., Anwar, S., & Punhani, R. (2021), "Improving business intelligence through machine learning algorithms". 2021 2nd International Conference on Intelligent Engineering and Management (ICIEM), pp. 63–68. https://ieeexplore.ieee.org/abstract/document/9445344/

Tao, H., Bhuiyan, M. Z. A., Rahman, M. A., Wang, G., Wang, T., Ahmed, M. M., & Li, J. (2019), "Economic perspective analysis of protecting big data security and privacy", *Future Generation Computer Systems*, *98*, pp. 660–671.

Tidd, J. & Bessant, J. R. (2020), *Managing innovation: Integrating technological, market and organisational change*. John Wiley & Sons.

Till, G. (2013), *Seapower: A guide for the twenty-first century* (Vol. 51). Routledge Oxon.

Vashisth, A. & Kumar, A. (2013), "Corporate espionage: The insider threat", *Business Information Review*, 30(2), pp. 83–90. https://doi.org/10.1177/0266382113491816

Wang, Z., Mao, S., Wu, W., Ge, T., Wei, F., & Ji, H. (2023), "Unleashing cognitive synergy in large language models: A task-solving agent through multi-persona self-collaboration", *arXiv*, *1*(2), p. 3.

Wasilow, S. & Thorpe, J. B. (2019), "Artificial intelligence, robotics, ethics, and the military: A Canadian perspective", *AI Magazine*, 40(1), pp. 37–48.

Willink, J. & Babin, L. (2017), *Extreme ownership: How US Navy Seals lead and win.* St. Martin's Press.

Wixom, B. & Watson, H. (2010), "The BI-based organisation", *International Journal of Business Intelligence Research (IJBIR)*, 1(1), pp. 13–28.

Wohlin, C., Aurum, A., Angelis, L., Phillips, L., Dittrich, Y., Gorschek, T., Grahn, H., Henningsson, K., Kagstrom, S., & Low, G. (2011), "The success factors powering industry-academia collaboration", *IEEE Software*, 29(2), pp. 67–73.

Xiyu, W., Yuanbo, X., Rong, Y., Xuefei, N., Yongliang, T., & Hu, L. (2024), "Meta-Battlefield: Concept Design of Multi-Domain Man-Machine Cooperative Operation". In Chinese Institute Of Command And Co (Ed.), Proceedings of 2023 11th China Conference on Command and Control, Vol. 1124, pp. 638–649. Springer Nature Singapore. https://doi.org/10.1007/978-981-99-9021-4_59

Zak, Y., Parmet, Y., & Oron-Gilad, T. (2023), "Facilitating the Work of Unmanned Aerial Vehicle Operators Using Artificial Intelligence: An Intelligent Filter for Command-and-Control Maps to Reduce Cognitive Workload", *Human Factors: The Journal of the Human Factors and Ergonomics Society*, 65(7), pp. 1345–1360. https://doi.org/10.1177/00187208221081968

2

Economic Warfare: The Corporate Involvement

Oloke Moses Olalekan

Introduction

The international community observes economic warfare as a recurring phenomenon that significantly impacts a country's capacity to sustain economic stability. Likewise, due to its frequent use as a means to advance governmental objectives, the business sector also contributes substantially to economic warfare. With the advent of nuclear weapons,international conflicts were relegated to the periphery and a new balance of power was established, which profoundly altered the global order. Developments in economic techniques have supported the development of new economic analyses of warfare to explain these changes (Goldgeier & McFaul, 1992).

To gain a competitive edge in the international arena, corporates across nations employ economic warfare, i.e., economic tactics to damage the economy of a target nation(s) for strategic benefit. In recent years, there has been an increase in corporate involvement in economic warfare as corporations use their financial influence to influence trade agreements, public policy, and other economic initiatives. It is imperative that economic warfare is indirect and permanent, including negotiations, transactions, and specialised institutions created to restrict, isolate, or control the financial and economic capabilities of the adversary. It has historically proven to be more effective than direct and temporary forms that rely on coercion or legal mechanisms (Coulomb & Dunne, 2008). Established in 1757, the doctrine of economic warfare allows the use of economic strategies as a strategic tool to wage conflict, even during periods of peace (Bowen, 1998).

Johnson, Scholes, and Whittington (1988) asserted that for a business to engage in economic warfare, it must have a comprehensive understanding of its environment and the factors that influence it in order to formulate an effective business strategy. In the context of economic warfare, corporations must comprehend the political, social, and economic dynamics that impact the global market and their operations. There are numerous ways in which corporations can employ the economy as a weapon. The imposition of economic sanctions, which restrict commerce and other economic activities, is one such method. The term "economic sanctions" often denotes measures implemented by one country as economic instruments to impose trade barriers on another country to advance specific political objectives. Sanctions may be levied against a nation, a collective of individuals, or a corporation if it is determined that the actions of such entities pose a danger to the harmonious coexistence of another nation. Additionally, sanctions may be levied against any nation or group of individuals with ties to the government of the targeted nation. In the targeted nation, sanctions may induce political disturbance, social unrest, and significant economic devastation (Müller-Stewens and Brauner, 2021).

Definition of Economic Warfare

Organisations employ economic warfare strategies, such as market manipulation, unfair trade practices, and public opinion influence, to gain a competitive edge over their adversaries. The act of corporations employing their economic influence to achieve strategic objectives is known as "corporate involvement in economic warfare". Corporate strategy delineates an organisation's approach to achieving its goals and objectives, often including economic warfare. Since the Great War, military and legal discourse has employed the phrase "economic warfare" (Della Torre, 2017). While the phrase "economic war" has been in usage since the 16th century, its connotation has evolved in recent times to encompass heightened levels of global economic competition among nation-states.

However, an inherent limitation of the definition of economic warfare is its failure to differentiate between economic competition and economic warfare. Economic warfare, when initiated by one country against another, invariably results in adverse economic consequences for the implementing nation. For example, the imposition of an embargo results in financial losses for the imposing nation and detrimental consequences for the target nation. There have been numerous evaluations of the implementation of power policy since the end of World War II. By conducting a comprehensive examination of the global balance of power, they offer valuable strategic insights into all international economic relations (Ibid.).

An extensive scholarly consensus holds that the phrase "economic warfare" is frequently applied synonymously with "trade wars" or that it merely denotes an all-encompassing classification of economic instruments employed within the framework of a particular economic policy strategy, predominantly trade sanctions or investment limitations. There is a common misunderstanding that trade conflicts and economic warfare are synonymous (Farrell & Newman, 2019). However, although they have an intimate connection, they are, in fact, two separate concepts. People frequently employ the phrase "trade war" to refer to the expansion of market share or the monopolistic control of a market. This objective is achieved by implementing trade war strategies, such as import bans, tariffs, dumping export licences, quotas, currency restrictions, and transitory price reductions below production costs. Economic warfare is characterised by the systematic and cohesive implementation of the complete range of these tactics and methods. Consequently, meticulous monitoring is applied to every supply and acquisition in the target nations, encompassing not only the domestic market but also those of allies and neutral nations (Krc & Hynkova, 2022).

In other words, economic warfare acts as a tool for achieving certain strategic objectives previously attained through the use of military force. Economic warfare is a type of conflict that utilises economic instruments to achieve strategic objectives. Nations once employed economic sanctions to damage the economies of their adversaries; this marked the beginning of the strategic application of economic power. Presently, corporations assume a pivotal role in the economic warfare strategy, an increasingly intricate tactic. Economic warfare involving corporations consists of a variety of strategies designed to destabilise the economies of adversaries or seize market share from competitors (Dicken, 2003).

Historical Examples and Tactics Employed by Corporate Actors in Economic Warfare

Economic warfare is the practice of utilising economic instruments to advance the objectives of foreign policy. Economic sanctions, trade embargoes, and other forms of economic pressure, imposed to achieve ideological, political, or military goals, illustrate this. Since 1950, North Korea has been subject to economic sanctions imposed by the United States. The severity of these sanctions escalated after North Korea's 2003 withdrawal from the Nuclear Non-Proliferation Treaty (1968). Generally, economic sanctions consist of monetary restrictions that impede the target's ability to engage in commercial activities or transmit funds. Furthermore, suspicions of North Korea conducting nuclear weapons tests during that period led to the discovery of non-North Korean individuals, institutions, and companies aiding the country in evading trade sanctions. Sanctions levied against these companies have facilitated the disruption of North Korea's international transactions. The United States represents an additional approach adopted by commercial organisations. The Countering America's Adversaries via Sanctions Act (2017) prohibits U.S. financial institutions from providing financial services to North Korea and restricts U.S. assistance to foreign governments that do so (Park, 2014).

The British Navy employed numerous economic strategies against the Germans during World War I, including port blockades, to prevent Germany from importing food and basic materials. This represents one of the earliest historical instances of economic warfare. By employing this form of economic warfare, the British sought to undermine the German war efforts. Germany experienced extensive starvation and civil unrest as unintended consequences. British maritime corporations actively participated in this economic conflict by providing financial support and aiding in the enforcement of the blockade (Ansoff, 1965).

Furthermore, economic warfare by corporate entities has a significant historical background, tracing its origins to the mercantilist practices of European nations during the colonial era (Sharman, 2019). Israeli restrictions on the entry of civilian goods into the Gaza Strip serve as a prominent example of contemporary economic warfare strategies, raising several ethical concerns intricately linked to military ethics regarding blockades, sanctions, and sieges (Gross, 2023). Additionally, some argued that Israel's initial restrictions on

Gaza, as a preliminary measure to prevent terrorism without resorting to military conflict, were not inherently unjustifiable. However, due to their failure to achieve these goals, the devastation they inflicted upon civilians grew in magnitude and was entirely unnecessary. Israel ultimately realised that it was illogical to maintain the restriction on the flow of civilian products into Gaza (Nijim, 2023). Nevertheless, for the protection of its citizens, Israel retains the power to monitor and regulate the ingress and egress of humanitarian assistance into Gaza, irrespective of its mode of transport (Amir, 2021).

Sanctions imposed by the EU on Russia constitute a unique example of economic warfare. The European Union (EU) levied economic sanctions against Russia since the start of the Russia-Ukraine war in retaliation of the actions of the Russian government in Ukraine. The penalties in question were implemented in July 2014 and were further enforced on September 8 of the same year. Full implementation of the Minsk Agreement was contingent on the duration of sanctions imposed on Russia by the European Council in 2015 (Nieder, 2023).

The European Council indefinitely enforced sanctions against Russia from March 2018 until their extension in March 2019. In 2022, seven amendments to the sanctions further strengthened the restrictions imposed on Russia (Chernousov, 2016). The execution of a variety of restrictive actions served to reinforce the sanctions against Russia. Sanctions imposed on Russia include restrictions on freezing assets, issuing visas, importing products, and providing travel services. Also prohibited from importation into Russia were products and technologies associated with the energy, transportation, telecommunications, and transportation industries, as well as those utilised in the exploration of mineral, hydrocarbon, or gas deposits (Cui, Yue, Nghiem, & Duan, 2023). The EU further stated that EU nationals and businesses were not allowed to purchase or sell new bonds or collaborate with certain Russian state banks, big energy corporations, or Russian defence firms.

Economic warfare has a cost to be paid, just like any other kind of warfare. Examples include embargoes on the import and export of weapons, exports of specific energy equipment and technology to Russia, and exports of dual-use technology. The invasion of Russia in Ukraine has caused a dramatic increase in the prices of most commodities and energy. The primary cause of the price increase was the fear, confirmed in certain cases, that the ongoing conflict would lead to severe shortages of essential raw materials. As per Bloomberg's Commodity Index, there has been an 18 per cent increase in commodity prices since the beginning of 2022. The surge in commodities markets, particularly in energy and grains, with wheat leading the way, dominated the first half of the year (Gilbert, 2023).

Throughout the Cold War, the United States and the Soviet Union were embroiled in intense economic competition. The 1960 implementation of the United States embargo on Cuba is an example of economic warfare that occurred at this time. Extensive trade sanctions imposed by the United States against Cuba were intended to destabilise the economy of the island nation and isolate the communist regime. The embargo had substantial economic consequences for American companies as well, particularly those operating in the travel and agriculture industries (Sharma and Vredenburg, 1998).

The United States Joint Chiefs of Staff (1994) noted that Iran faced one of the most severe sanctions in history during a period when economic warfare primarily used sanctions instead of violent and costly military conflict (Bajoghli, Nasr, Salehi-Isfahani, & Vaez, 2024). A powerful instrument for the security of the United States and its allies, sanctions stigmatise and discourage adversaries from engaging in undesirable conduct. Today, we perceive sanctions as a tool of economic denial, aiming to harm multiple actors and force the targeted state to reevaluate the benefits and drawbacks of its policies. Additionally, they aim to impede the progress of adversaries, be it other states or terrorist establishments, and the attainment of international support by the former (Rosenberg, Goldman, Drezner, & Solomon-Strauss, 2016).

In the Middle East, economic warfare has become an increasingly prevalent tactic used to advance geopolitical goals. As an illustration, the United States and its allies have imposed economic sanctions on Iran to compel the Iranian government to cease its nuclear programme and financing terrorism. Particularly in the energy industry, the Iranian economy has been severely impacted by these sanctions.

Analysis of How Corporations Use Economic Warfare Strategies

Economic warfare refers to the strategic and calculated utilisation of economic instruments to undermine or eradicate the economic capabilities of the adversary. Governments often employ such tactics to advance their objectives within the realm of international relations. To gain a competitive advantage and exert influence over market conditions, corporations have heavily engaged in economic warfare with their economic might.

To combat their competitors, corporations employ a diverse array of strategic warfare tactics from their arsenal. Corporations employ predatory pricing as a strategy in their economic warfare. Predatory pricing is the act of setting prices below the cost of production with the intent of driving competitors from the market. As stated (Bera, 2022), the United States singled out nearly 4,000 politicians, oligarchs, businesses, institutions, and other entities to impose numerous sanctions on Russia in retaliation of Moscow's incursion into Ukraine. Among the over 2,000 individuals and organisations that the European Union has singled out are associates of Russian President Vladimir Putin. Despite not yet proving to be a fatal blow to Putin's objectives, President Joe Biden asserts that the sanctions aim to "impose an even greater cost on Putin for his aggression abroad and repression at home" (Nichol, Cooper, Woehrel, Woolf, Hildreth, & Morelli, 2014).

Fligstein (2002) identifies exclusive transaction arrangements as an additional economic warfare strategy that businesses employ. Furthermore, the terms of exclusive dealing arrangements stipulate that manufacturers or suppliers require purchasers to purchase all or most of their products exclusively from them. In contrast to other foreign policy instruments, such as military statecraft (involving the use or threat of force), diplomacy (involving negotiation), and propaganda (involving the manipulation of spoken or visual symbols), corporations distinguish themselves through the implementation of economic warfare strategies. In some fashion, the preponderance of foreign policy approaches combines these strategies.

Several tactics are used in economic warfare, including positive and negative sanctions. Harmful sanctions consist of tangible or threatened punishments, whereas positive sanctions consist of incentive promises. The objective of adverse sanctions is to impede the entry of competitors into the market and bolster the incumbent's market dominance. Exclusive dealing agreements have the potential to impede the entry of competitors, thereby impeding competition and potentially resulting in increased consumer prices (Arora et al., 2000). Illustrative instances of negative sanctions comprise embargoes, asset freezes, expropriation, punitive taxes, covert trade restrictions, and purchases to prevent products from reaching target countries.

Types of Economic Warfare

Financial Surveillance

Corporate espionage poses a significant risk to the investment, development, growth, and innovation of businesses, as well as to the global economy as a whole. Foreign governments or corporations engage in economic espionage when they steal proprietary information and trade secrets for the purpose of gaining a strategic economic advantage. Corporate espionage also includes stealing or misappropriation of trade secrets,business plans, and intellectual property in order to acquire competitive advantages(Van Arnam, 2001). Economic warfare often involves the use of hacking, cyberattacks, and other illicit methods while the two objectives of the compromised information are to either bring about the demise of the competitor's enterprise or to gain a market advantage. Economic espionage has become a prevalent phenomenon, resulting in significant financial setbacks for organisations worldwide (Arora et al., 2002).

Sanctions on Commerce

Economic sanctions are a form of economic warfare that achieve political objectives by imposing monetary fines or trade limitations on a specific nation or corporation. The United Nations Security Council and many states have placed greater emphasis on targeted sanctions, also known as "smart sanctions". These sanctions now consist of travel restrictions for specific individuals, financial asset blocking orders, and export restrictions on strategic goods and services (Alexander, 2009). Sanctions can be imposed by a government or international organisation to restrict trade with a nation or company that is deemed to be a threat to international peace and security. Companies may be subject to penalties levied by governments to restrict their utilisation of financial facilities, basic materials, and markets. Campbell and Goold (1995) assert that the implementation of economic sanctions could significantly jeopardise the profitability and market share of a business.

Corporate Social Responsibility (CSR) in Military Strategy

Corporate Social Responsibility (CSR) warfare is a type of economic strategy where businesses implement social responsibility initiatives to gain a competitive edge in the market. To bolster their standing and attract fresh clientele, businesses engage in CSR endeavours, such as philanthropic contributions, community service, and environmental preservation. CSR warfare aims to out manoeuvre the rivals who demonstrate a lesser commitment to social responsibility. The integration of CSR into business strategy, according to Gazzola and Colombo (2014), has become widespread and has a significant effect on the market share and financial performance of a company.

Economic Coercion

Economic coercion or economic warfare refers to the use of monetary incentives or sanctions to influence the conduct of other countries or organisations. Economic coercion includes investments, trade agreements, and other forms of financial assistance that are used to influence the policies of other countries. Conversely, it could involve the implementation of financial sanctions, including currency manipulation, tariffs, or quotas, to impede the economic operations of foreign countries or corporations. Stalk et al. (1992) assert that economic coercion, a common strategy in economic warfare, can significantly impact the growth and progress of an economy.

Environmental Corporate Social Responsibility (ECSR)

The strategic use of environmental conservation initiatives to gain a market advantage is referred to as Environmental Corporate Social Responsibility (ECSR) warfare. Businesses profit from carbon offsetting, pollution reduction, and energy efficiency, among other ECSR initiatives, and engage in them to improve their image and attract new customers. ECSR warfare aims to outmanoeuvre or outgun competitors who demonstrate a lesser commitment to environmental responsibility. According to Han et al. (2019), ECSR is increasingly prevalent in the aviation industry and has a significant impact on the market share and profitability of a business.

Ethical Considerations of Corporate Involvement in Economic Warfare

The utilisation of economic instruments to gain a competitive advantage in the marketplace, also known as economic warfare, has become pervasive among numerous organisations. As businesses engage in economic warfare, numerous stakeholders debate the legitimacy of utilising monetary sanctions to advance economic objectives, thereby giving rise to ethical concerns.

It is of the utmost importance to acknowledge that economic warfare possesses the capacity to severely cripple the economy of the targeted nation and inflict suffering upon defenceless civilians, and as a result of economic sanctions, the targeted nation will experience an economic slowdown, as well as a higher unemployment, inflation, and destitution rate. Businesses that engage in economic warfare must consider the repercussions of their actions on the entire nation's populace, particularly the most vulnerable segments of society, such as children, women, and other dependents. Glass et al. (2016) argues that to promote sustainability, businesses must consider the social and environmental impacts of their operations on the surrounding communities. Moreover, implementing financial sanctions calls into question the legitimacy of economic warfare. Katz (2017) argues that international law does not recognise monetary sanctions and that countries may engage in a financial war of retaliation by employing comparable tactics.

Consequently, businesses engaged in economic warfare must consider the legal consequences of their actions as they may expose their brands to the risk of litigation and reputational harm. As argued by Katzenstein and Park (2023), economic warfare may precipitate a political crisis in which the targeted nation retaliates to protect its sovereignty. Diplomatic relations are of paramount importance in facilitating economic and commercial connections for companies that conduct business on a global scale. Hence, businesses that engage in economic warfare must consider the long-term repercussions of their actions on the nation's diplomatic relations and their business operations. Unanticipated consequences may result from financial sanctions, including the proliferation of illicit markets and organised criminal activities. As Trigeorgis (1996) notes, criminals may establish a shadow economy in response to economic warfare, which is characterised by a scarcity of goods and services. Hence, enterprises participating in economic warfare must consider the potential unintended consequences of their conduct, particularly those concerning the stability and security of the country.

Consequences of Economic Warfare Strategies on Nations

Economic warfare is the use of economic instruments to undermine or disrupt the economy of another nation in order to gain an advantage over it. Organisations that seek to increase their profits through unethical methods often employ such strategies. The objective of this essay is to examine the manner in which corporations engage in economic warfare strategies and the resulting impact on nations. A decline in economic development due to economic disruption is among the repercussions of economic warfare on nations. Economic warfare strategies frequently target agriculture, energy, finance, and other vital economic sectors. For instance, firms may engage in unscrupulous practices, such as sabotage, trade barriers, and pricing manipulation, to gain a competitive advantage over their rivals (Farwell, 2012). Consequently, the targeted nation often responds with retaliatory measures that intensify its economic instability.

This vicious cycle of economic warfare, according to Godfrey et al. (2009) and Johnson et al. (2008), can have lasting effects on nations, including a decline in economic development and social instability. Russia serves as an illustrative case in point, having been subjected to a multitude of international economic sanctions and presently bearing the unfavourable distinction of being the most sanctioned country on a global scale. Russia was subjected to several sanctions as the Russia-Ukraine conflict entered its second year. To curtail Russia's ability to engage in international transactions denominated in dollars and euros, the European Union and the United States imposed restrictions on its gold reserves and assets (Foss, 2023). As Russia's isolation increased, its economy became increasingly reliant on trade with its limited number of allies, the most significant being China. A considerable number of economists have predicted that the cumulative effects of the sanctions will cause a fundamental transformation in the Russian economy (Carlsson, Oxenstierna & Weissmann, 2015).

Unemployment is an additional consequence that economic conflict imposes on countries. To gain a competitive edge, organisations may employ economic warfare strategies, including workforce downsizing, compensation adjustments, or extended workweeks, to reduce production expenses. As a consequence, the standard of living of the inhabitants of the targeted nation declines. Moreover, in times of heightened economic conflict, corporations might opt to relocate their activities to countries offering more affordable labour, thereby leading to the elimination of employment opportunities in the nation being targeted (Landrum & Ohsowski, 2018; Westphal & Fredrickson, 2001).

Analysis of The Impact of Unethical Corporate Involvement in Economic Warfare

Economic warfare, according to Fenaroli (2016), is the application of financial instruments to exert pressure on nations. The repercussions that unethical corporate involvement in economic warfare has on nations have transformed in recent years into a tool utilised by nations to achieve strategic objectives and cannot be ignored. Acknowledging the significance of corporate participation in this form of warfare is crucial. From an economic standpoint, unethical conduct by corporations significantly impacts entire nations and could lead to political turmoil, social discord, and economic instability. Corporations' involvement in economic conflicts is a significant contributor to economic instability. Companies are now key players in the financial sector, and their decisions can have a significant impact on economies, according to Myers (2013). This holds especially true for multinational corporations that conduct business on a global scale. Katz (2014) asserts that global corporations possess the capacity to influence governmental decisions by their substantial financial resources. This may give rise to conflicts of interest. Under specific circumstances, it may lead to regulatory capture.

Corrupt corporate conduct, which leads to monetary penalties, influences economic warfare. Jones (2015) asserts that these sanctions could potentially yield adverse consequences and exert a significant impact on the economies of the affected countries. For instance, sanctions against oil exports could result in a decline in oil prices, which could be detrimental to oil-producing nations. According to Zarate (2013), financial sanctions may also be employed to single out specific individuals and organisations. This would result in a decline in economic activity, which would be detrimental to the nation's economy.

The contribution of unethical corporate conduct to social instability is indisputable. Economic disparity is a significant source of societal discontent, according to Peetz (2013). Multinational corporations possess the capacity to exacerbate this matter through their unscrupulous conduct, thereby fostering economic inequality. This may give rise to protests and various forms of social unrest. As posited by Varnalii and Tomashevskyi (2019), within the context of economic warfare, multinational corporations possess the capacity to instigate economic instability. This may give rise to social unrest, which could potentially be leveraged to advance strategic objectives.

Summary

Economic warfare is a recurring occurrence that has a profound impact on a nation's capacity to maintain economic stability. State and multinational corporations employ various economic strategies, including market manipulation, unfair trade practices, and the shaping of public opinion, to gain an advantage in the global arena.

Sanctions can be imposed on a nation, a group of people, or a company if it is deemed that their actions pose a significant threat to the peaceful coexistence of another nation. The term "economic warfare" is commonly used interchangeably with "trade wars" or as a broad categorisation of economic tools used in a specific economic policy approach, such as trade sanctions or investment restrictions. Economic warfare is a strategic conflict that utilises economic instruments to accomplish strategic objectives, with its origin in the application of military force to ensure compliance and has since developed into a more intricate strategy involving corporations. Notable instances of economic warfare encompass the enduring sanctions imposed on North Korea by the United States since 1950, the British Navy's blockades against Germany during World War I, and the European Union's sanctions targeting Russia. Economic warfare has a rich historical background, stemming from the practices of European mercantilism during the colonial era.

For instance, the EU's sanctions against Russia, which were first imposed in 2014 and later extended in 2019, have served as a remarkable illustration of economic warfare. Sanctions imposed on Russia include restrictions on freezing assets, issuing visas, importing products, and providing travel services. Products and technologies related to energy, transportation, telecommunications, and mineral, hydrocarbon, or gas deposits are also prohibited. EU nationals and businesses are prohibited from engaging in the purchase or sale of new bonds or collaborating with specific Russian state banks. Economic warfare can be projected in the varied manner and ways through which nations try to achieve their strategic goals that may or may not seem feasible to the global order at large.

References

Alexander, K. (2009), Introduction in *Economic Sanctions*. Palgrave Macmillan, London.

Amir, M. (2021), "Post-occupation Gaza: Israel's war on Palestinian futures", *Geografiska Annaler: Series B, Human Geography*, 103(4), pp. 283-300.

Bajoghli, N., Nasr, V., Salehi-Isfahani, D., & Vaez, A. (2024), *How Sanctions Work: Iran and the Impact of Economic Warfare*. Stanford University Press.

Bera, R. K. (2022), *Putin's Dilemma: Weighing the Risk of Defiance*. Available at SSRN 4092044.

Bowen, H. V. (1998), *War and British society 1688-1815*. Cambridge University Press.

Chernousov, P. (2016), *Economic sanctions and international conflicts: The case of Russia in comparative perspective* (Doctoral dissertation, Université d'Ottawa/University of Ottawa).

Coulomb, F. & Dunne, J. P. (2008), "Economics, conflict and war", *Real-World Economics Review*, Peacon, pp. 147-157.

Cui, L., Yue, S., Nghiem, X. H., & Duan, M. (2023), "Exploring the risk and economic vulnerability of global energy supply chain interruption in the context of Russo-Ukrainian war", *Resources Policy*, 81, 103373.

Della Torre, Giuseppe. (2017), *Theorizing Economic Warfare. Economic Warfare, storiadell'armaeconomica, Quaderno SISM.*

Dicken, P. (2003), *Global shift: Reshaping the global economic map in the 21st century.* Sage.

Farrell, H. & Newman, A. L. (2019), "Weaponized interdependence: How global economic networks shape state coercion", *International Security*, 44(1), pp. 42-79.

Farwell, J. P. (2012), *Persuasion and power: The art of strategic communication*. Georgetown University Press.

Fligstein, N. (2002), "Markets as politics: A political-cultural approach to market institutions", *Readings in economic sociology*, pp. 197-218.

Foss, M. J. (2023),*The Sanctions Weapon: The Dual-Sided Policy Shaping the Russo-Ukrainian War.*

Gilbert, C. L. (2023), *The impact of the Ukraine conflict on world grains prices.*

Gross, A. (2023), "Reducing the Friction: A Functional Analysis of the Transformed Occupation of the Gaza Strip". In *Prolonged Occupation and International Law*, pp. 69-103. Brill Nijhoff.

KRC, M. & HYNKOVA, V. (2022), "Aspects of Economic Warfare—Causes and Consequences",*Journal of Conflict, Defense, and Security*, 1(1), p. 40.

Nichol, J., Cooper, W. H., Ek, C., Woehrel, S., Woolf, A. F., Hildreth, S. A., & Morelli, V. (2014), *Russian political, economic, and security issues and US interests*, p. 0107. Washington, DC: Congressional Research Service.

Nieder, A. (2023), *The EU actorness-sanctions nexus and the wars in Ukraine 2014-2023* (Master's thesis, NTNU).

Nijim, M. (2023), "Genocide in Palestine: Gaza as a case study", *The International Journal of Human Rights*, 27(1), pp. 165-200.

Park, J. S. (2014), "The key to the North Korean targeted sanctions Puzzle", *The Washington Quarterly*, 37(3), pp. 199-214.

Rao, A. R., Bergen, M. E., & Davis, S. (2000), "How to fight a price war", *Harvard Business Review*, 78(2), pp. 107-120.

Rimpiläinen, E. (2020), "Victims, villains, or geopolitical tools? Representations of Donbas displacement in Ukrainian and Russian government media", *Europe-Asia Studies*, 72(3), pp. 481-504.

Rosenberg, E., Goldman, Z., Drezner, D., & Solomon-Strauss, J. (2016), *The new tools of economic warfare: Effects and Effectiveness of Contemporary US Financial Sanctions.* Centre for a New American Security, April.

Sharman, J. C. (2019), "Power and profit at sea: the rise of the West in the making of the international system", *International Security*, 43(4), pp. 163-196.

Tarkhanova, O. (2023), "Shades of protracted displacement: reconciling citizenship and the status of internally displaced in Eastern Ukraine",*Journal of Ethnic and Migration Studies*, 49(19), pp. 4809-4827.

Thompson, I., Nurse, L., & Fazel, M. (2023), "Tensions in Cultural Identity and Sense of Belonging for Internally Displaced Adolescents in Ukraine", *Child Care in Practice*, 29(3), pp. 319-334.

United States Joint Chiefs of Staff (1994), *Department of Defense Dictionary of Military and Associated Terms (Vol. 1, No. 2).* Joint Chiefs of Staff.

Van Arnam, R. C. (2001), "Business war: Economic espionage in the United States and the European Union and the need for greater trade secret protection", *NCJ Int'l L. & Com. Reg.*, 27, p. 95.

3

Private Military Security Companies in Pacific Island Countries: Impacts on Development

Sasha Gillies-Lekakis

Introduction

The operations of Private Military Companies (PMCs) and Private Security Companies (PSCs) in diverse situations of instability and insecurity have ancient origins, with the practice having existed in some form or other since antiquity. While PMCs are "groups hired to provide services to train, replace, reinforce or enhance an army or armed group", PSCs "provide services to governments, businesses or individuals aimed at protecting property from criminal activity" (Piney, 2021). Though there are nuanced differences to these operations, often times the work of PMCs and PSCs converge, combining to create unique security dynamics. As such, the term "Private Military Security Company" or PMSC has come to be used extensively to refer to both organisations, and hence, this chapter utilises "PMSC" when referring to either of these organisations going forward.

Modern conceptions of PMSCs as playing a vital role in safeguarding the security of the nation-state, corporate projects, and even war objectives are a recent development in need of greater attention and study. More specifically, the activities of these private organisations in securitising economic, social, and political processes throughout the Global South should be a priority area of focus. This is significant given the operation of PMSCs throughout Africa,

Asia, Latin America, and the Pacific. Even though most PMSCs themselves are based in Western nations, their presence in Global South nations is extensive, often controversial, and provides the bulk of PMSC financial returns (Kanemasu and Molnar, 2017).

The region of Oceania and, in particular, Pacific Island countries, have a surprisingly long history with PMSCs dating back to the 1950s. Notably, this has included an export aspect, with Fiji, in particular, providing a significant number of PMSC employees who have served globally in various conflict zones and for numerous corporate interests throughout the Global South. Conversely, the grave insecurity and instability present in several Pacific countries, particularly those of Melanesia such as Papua New Guinea and the Solomon Islands, have contributed to an outsized and often controversial presence of PMSCs within the region—either filling the gaps left by an absent state or security service or directly serving foreign corporate interests, often violating national legal norms to do so.

This chapter will focus on the history and impact of PMSCs in the Pacific region, with an evaluation of the ways in which these organisations have contributed to the development and, often, 'mis-development', of several Pacific nations. After a review of the literature that has covered the issue of PMSC operations throughout the Global South and in Oceania specifically, two case studies will be utilised to evaluate the role that PMSCs play amidst the socio-economic and political changes that have taken place in Pacific Island countries in the 20th and 21st centuries.

Fiji will constitute the first area of focus, and in particular, the island's export of thousands of ex-military personnel and the unemployed to work in PMSCs around the world—chiefly those based in Western countries. The economic benefits that this work can provide for Fijians, which are substantial, will be evaluated through a comparison with the adverse social, political, and health consequences of involvement in these private security organisations.

The second case study will focus on Papua New Guinea, which, since the 1970s, has come to rely heavily on PMSCs as a means of re-establishing and then maintaining, with varying degrees of success, the integrity of the state. The arguably positive role that PMSCs thus play in stabilising Papua New Guinea's crisis-prone state will be juxtaposed with the deeply controversial and negative impact that PMSCs have played when serving the interests of foreign multinational corporations in the country—exemplified by the Sandline affair—that has contributed to violent confrontation and economic exploitation of Papua New Guinea's populace. Moreover, the role of local political figures and foreign actors in promoting certain PMSCs and their influence has left the state prone to corruption, and its legitimacy has been significantly weakened as a result.

Ultimately, the role of PMSCs will be shown to be a complex and ambiguous one, with diverse and often contradictory impacts on social and economic development. On the one hand, communities benefit economically from the work of PMSCs in Oceania, well beyond what domestic opportunities can provide. However, this short-term incentive to accept private security and military work is often overshadowed by more damaging consequences, ranging from health impacts on Pacific individuals and communities to the erosion of state authority and foreign multinational penetration of national economic and political life.

Literature Review: PMSCs, The Global South, and Implications for Development

Given the sensitive and often confidential nature of PMSC work around the world, it is perhaps not surprising that academic focus on this area has been limited and, though growing, in need of far greater cultivation. In particular, the significant role played by PMSCs during the illegal US invasion of Iraq first saw academic interest in this area of security studies emerge. Some authors,such as Whyte (2003), tied PMSC operations to Western geostrategic and geoeconomic projects of control over parts of the Global South. Others, like Krahmann, chose to focus on the legal frameworks underpinning PMSC operations and their often-dubious legality (2012). These studies, while important to understanding the general mechanisms of PMSCs, which remain opaque and poorly understood, tend to focus on the Western-based organisations themselves and neglect the impact that these companies have in the Global South.

The emphasis placed by scholars on the complex relationship between PMSCs and Global South nations and communities is a far more recent phenomenon and is increasing. A particularly innovative approach to these studies was introduced by Kanemasu and Molnar (2017), utilising PMSC recruiting practices to demonstrate the ways in which the industry is a microcosm of wider North-South and 'periphery'—'core' divides. Others, including Chisholm (2014) and Eichler (2015), have reflected upon the ways in which PMSC recruitment and operational practices reinforce the gender and racial biases inherent in North-South post-colonial relationships. The relatively recent and scarce nature of these publications speaks to the need for research into the relationship between PMSCs and the Global South.

In the context of the Pacific region specifically, the body of literature available is even smaller. Indeed, the only two substantial documents focussing on the case of Fijian military migration for work in PMSCs are Maclellan's (2006) early seminal work and Kanemasu and Molnar's (2017) most recent, updated attempt to detail this phenomenon. As for the presence of PMSCs in Papua New Guinea, only Dinnen (2020) and Walton (2021) have presented any sustained analysis of their role in their capacity as employees of the Australian Defence Force. Though some of these more recent additions to the academic literature body are encouraging indications of a greater interest in PMSC operations in the Pacific region, this newfound research focus is still very much in its infancy.

The literature on PMSCs, whether it is their history, legal frameworks, or role in peacekeeping efforts, is an understudied and under appreciated area of research. Even less of a focus is the link between PMSC operations and the Global South and specifically, the Pacific region. This chapter, in part, aims to address this gap by highlighting the impacts that PMSC operations have on Pacific development, evaluating the benefits and drawbacks of an increasing economic and sometimes political, dependence on PMSC contractors in Oceania. The first area of focus, fittingly, will be the case of Fiji's PMSC exports and its ramifications for the nation and its people.

FIJI: International and Local Dimensions of a PMSC Export Economy

Despite the country's reputation as a quiet, welcoming tourist destination, Fiji boasts of a remarkably long history of military activity, both domestically and abroad. This trend originated with the formation of the Republic of Fiji Military Forces under the auspices of the British colonial administration, which culminated in some 8000 Fijians participating in World War II in the Solomon Islands, on the side of the Allies (Kanemasu and Molnar, 2017). Fiji further cemented the professionalism and influence of its military through involvement in the Malayan war from 1948-1960, where 1600 Fijian personnel were dispatched to bolster the brutal British colonial response to Malayan independence movements (Kanemasu and Molnar, 2017). Since independence in 1970, Fiji has seen its military maintain an outsized and, often, controversial sway over the nation's development, having been involved in numerous coups since that time. Since independence, Fiji's military personnel have continued to participate in conflicts around the world through service to PMSCs, and additionally, as part of UN peacekeeping forces—though in this latter instance, PMSCs can be contracted to undertake UN projects (Maclellan, 2007). This new trajectory for Fijian military forces was initiated through participation in the 1978 UN mission to Lebanon. Since that time, Fijian PMSC personnel have served across the world, in places as diverse as Sinai, Cyprus, Timor Leste, and Iraq. As of 2016, 1040 Fijians were working for foreign PMSCs in war zones and other crisis areas (Kanemasu and Molnar, 2017).

The participation of Fijians in PMSC work abroad is the result of local Fijian socio-economic conditions. PMSC contract work is, therefore, a result of, yet also an influence on, local Fijian development through a complex interplay of various processes. The poverty and socio-economic exclusion caused by neoliberal economic doctrines in Fiji have led to the inability of the most vulnerable sections of society to access necessary services or obtain sustainable and secure work to provide economic security for their families and communities. According to the Basic Needs Poverty Line (BNPL) assessment, as of 2022, at least 30 per cent of Fijians are living in extreme poverty, with little prospect for socio-economic improvement or advancement (Gounder, 2022). As a result, at least one in three Fijians is excluded from the gains of national development and the necessities required to live a fulfilling and dignified life. Often, survival is the norm, with social security benefits non-existent in Fiji and formal education to achieve new qualifications difficult to access (Maclellan, 2007).

Notably, when other poverty indicators and measurements are used instead of the BNPL, the results suggest an even higher share of Fijians living in extreme poverty. With significant portions of the Fijian populace excluded from economic and social opportunities and little visible or tangible development, the allure of PMSC work becomes quite easy to understand. Indeed, contract work with Private Military Companies is a lucrative opportunity for many Fijians struggling in the aforementioned situation. With an average wage of 1500 USD per month working in PMSCs compared to a meagre 130 USD per month as the average (insufficient) Fijian wage (Kanemasu and Molnar, 2017), the choice is clear for most Fijians.

From a development perspective, the option to work with PMSCs results in several complex impacts on Fijian communities. On the one hand, there is undoubtedly an objective economic, and, ultimately, social benefit for those families and communities that can capitalise on the employment of one or more Fijian men through PMSC contract work. Amidst a bleak socio-economic landscape, the significant financial returns of PMSC work are a boon for struggling Fijian communities and can provide important pathways for socio-economic advancement and, potentially, prosperity in Fiji's context. However, the economic benefits of such work do not overshadow the several concerning impacts of PMSC work on Fijian individuals, communities, and the development of the country.

The heavy involvement of Fijians in PMSC contract work in international conflict zones, often at the behest of dubious actors, has contributed to serious challenges for these Fijians, physically, mentally, and economically. Most notably, this took place during the Fijians' involvement in the Iraq War, which coincided with the US occupation of that Middle Eastern nation in 2003. In particular, Fijians found employment in a wide range of US and UK-based PMSCs, including Control Risks, SOC, Triple Canopy, and Reed (Kanemasu and Molnar, 2017). Fijians were often engaged in military services directly in conflict zones, personal security work, as well as protecting Iraq's (then US-controlled) currency exchange (Kanemasu and Molnar, 2017). By 2006, over 4000 Fijians were operating in Iraq. However, their treatment was less than fair. In particular, Fijians were subject to extreme financial inequalities as compared to their fellow Western PMSC workers in what can only be described as an example of racism rooted in the socio-economic disparities—and hence, limited negotiating power—of the Fijian mercenaries. Indeed, one anonymous Fijian PMSC worker indicated that while he received 1500 USD per month for security work in Iraq, US citizens undertaking the same work were receiving 10,000 USD per month (Kanemasu and Molnar, 2017).

The development challenges faced by Fiji, and in particular, the desperate socio-economic situation in the country, have exposed many Fijians to mistreatment and exploitation in PMSC work, with most contractors based in Western, developed economies. Financial insecurity is another challenge facing Fijians. While the comparatively lucrative returns of PMSC work are helpful to Fijian communities, there is little guarantee that this type of employment will be sustainable. PMSC contracts for Fijians and many others are characterised by fixed-period employment that can be terminated at any time (Kanemasu and Molnar, 2017). Such economic realities have resulted in many Fijians suddenly losing work, often for years at a time, before the next PMSC contract becomes available. Economic challenges are just as numerous as the financial benefits to be garnered from PMSC work for Fijians.

As far as Fiji's national development is concerned, PMSC work has now become one of the largest avenues for migration from Fiji to other countries, either on a permanent or semi-permanent basis (Maclellan, 2007; Kanemasu and Molnar, 2017). For a country already struggling with migration outflow and the loss of skilled workers, the further withdrawal of Fijians from the country perpetuates the nation's economic stagnation and presents little possibility for genuine, sustainable development relying on Fijian capital and resources, which continue to steadily leave the country. At a national level, too, PMSC work has had significant ramifications for Fiji's development.

Beyond the financial and development impacts on Fiji, PMSCs are notorious for leaving their former workers with little or no psychological/counselling support upon their return from active duty. In the specific case of Fiji, former PMSC employees are provided with no psychological or physical support in place in the event of trauma during operations abroad (Kanemasu and Molnar, 2017). The symptoms of this post-traumatic stress disorder, which is never treated adequately, are felt throughout Fijian communities—ranging from anger and violence to impulsive fast driving and extreme anxiety and paranoia on the part of those affected. These ramifications should also be considered when evaluating the role of PMSC work in Fiji's socio-economic development, at the personal, community, and national levels.

The significant involvement of Fijians in PMSC work has a long history dating back to Fiji's military involvement in World War II. The impacts of this phenomenon on Fijian development—both in terms of local community socio-economic advancement and wider national processes—have been complex and multifaceted. While an objective economic benefit undoubtedly exists for those involved in PMSC work and their families, serious risks to individuals, communities, and Fiji as a nation have also emerged from PMSC involvement in Fiji's economy. Economic discrimination, unsustainable emigration, and important health challenges are all difficulties that will need to be recognised and addressed if PMC work is to be properly integrated into Fiji's economic and development agenda. Similar challenges exist in nearby Papua New Guinea, the next focus of this chapter.

PMSC Operations in Papua New Guinea: Economic and Security Impacts

Since independence from Australia in 1975, Papua New Guinea has consistently struggled with structural weaknesses in state legitimacy and state security. Tribal conflicts, the so-called Raskol criminal gangs in urban centres, as well as clashes with regional independence movements, such as those in Bougainville, have characterised Papua New Guinea's recent history. A combination of socio-economic crises, often caused by the nation's neoliberal economy, has led to Port Moresby, Papua New Guinea's capital, gaining the dubious distinction of being one of the most dangerous cities in the world, and the nation is one of the most dangerous in the world for women. Amidst such a situation, it is hardly surprising that the activities of PMSCs have increased over the decades. Particularly since the turn of the century, PMSC operations in Papua New Guinea have skyrocketed. The number of licensed PMSCs operating in the country grew from just 174 in 2006 to 566 in 2018 (Dinnen and Walton, 2021), representing a significant boost to the industry's relevance and importance in Papua New Guinea's economic landscape.

Over 30,000 people are directly employed by these private organisations, exceeding in number the nation's police force, military, and prison staff combined (Dinnen and Walton, 2021). Papua New Guinea's PMSCs range from small operations involving just a handful of staff and security vehicles to multinational outfits with global reach (Dinnen and Walton, 2021). Chiefly, the two principal actors driving PMSC expansion in Papua New Guinea are foreign business interests eager to protect their assets and projects in the country, as well as local political elites with a vested economic interest in particular PMSCs.

When considering Papua New Guinea's economic development, it is clear that PMSC operations play a significant role in safeguarding the viability of lucrative mineral and other resource extraction projects in the country. While this officially provides Port Moresby with significant fiscal returns, the reality is that most financial benefits are pocketed by Australian, US, or UK multinational corporations. However, PMSCs are considered important to maintain the stability of these economic projects. This is particularly significant in the context of Papua New Guinea's numerous mineral extraction projects in rural areas, which remain, in many cases, completely outside the purview of state control (Dinnen and Walton, 2020). Even commercial projects in the capital are protected through the use of PMSC personnel, who are much needed in light of a 2012 survey that indicated 80 per cent of businesses in the country, both domestic and foreign-led, have suffered the impacts of crime or insecurity (Dinnen and Walton, 2021). As such, many in Papua New Guinea believe PMSC involvement in the country to be necessary.

Just because PMSC operations are deemed necessary does not necessarily mean that they are desired, nor should the desperate need for security in Papua New Guinea overshadow the many problematic consequences of extreme economic and political power exercised by these private organisations. Indeed, several instances have demonstrated the regressive impacts of PMSC operations in Papua New Guinea, linked chiefly to their independent operations outside of national legal norms. The ability of PMSCs to operate independently of state authorities has diluted Port Moresby's authority and legitimacy, and concerns have been expressed that the growth of private security influence at the expense of the state will seriously undermine sustainable future development goals and prospects. This has manifested in several ways, including through influence peddling and the corrosion of state integrity through the involvement of domestic political actors in the PMSC industry (Dinnen and Walton, 2021). To provide just one glaring example, John Rosso, MP for Lae Open region and a police chief sergeant, owns Executive Security Services, a 1500-strong Private Security Company that has deliberately been utilised at the expense of domestic state law enforcement and is permitted to encroach upon state security initiatives as a result of this political connection (Dinnen and Walton, 2021).

On occasion, the intervention of PMSCs in domestic political and economic development has directly clashed with Papua New Guinea's authorities, leading to conflict and casualties. This was most obvious during the Sandline affair of 1997. Following the defeat of Port Moresby's security forces by the Bougainville Revolutionary Army (BRA), a secessionist movement opposed to foreign control over the lucrative Panguna copper and gold mine, then Prime Minister Julius Chan solicited the aid of a UK-based Private Security Company, Sandline, to hire a mercenary outfit to eliminate the rebels (May, Regan, and Dinnen, 1997). The contract, signed without the knowledge of Papua New Guinea's Defence Force and worth an estimated USD 36 million, enraged Papua New Guinea's nascent civil society, members of the military, as well as the BRA at Papua New Guinea's government having essentially signed an agreement with a foreign multinational to murder its citizens in Bougainville (Ivarature, 2023). The Sandline affair fuelled a conflict that had already claimed more than 10,000 lives and ultimately brought down the Chan administration.

Despite requesting foreign PMSC assistance, Papua New Guinea saw its insecurity crisis aggravated and tensions linger between Bougainville and the central government over the question of independence and the Panguna mine's operations. In this case, it became clear that PMSC penetration of national political and economic life contributed to serious damage to development in the country: the country's economy remained precarious following the inability of Sandline to reclaim Panguna mine from the BRA rebels; serious fractures emerged between the central government and armed forces; and a long-disgruntled civil society erupted in anger at Port Moresby's inability to guarantee security and the viability of arguably the country's most lucrative economic project (Ivarature, 2023). The activities of Sandline can be more broadly generalised to warn against the excessive powers granted to PMSCs in states such as Papua New Guinea, which are not yet strong or legitimate enough to hold these foreign actors accountable.

The operation of PMSCs in Papua New Guinea has provided much-needed security amidst an insecurity crisis, both in urban and rural settings.

Commercial businesses in the capital, Port Moresby, and important economic projects in rural areas have been safeguarded through PMSC operations. In this sense, the development shortfalls of Papua New Guinea's state and security apparatus have in some ways been mitigated. However, it is equally important to discuss the adverse impacts of PMSC work in the country linked to the influence and power play these companies come to exercise in the face of Papua New Guinea's weak and, sometimes, non-existent state. The abuses of power, corruption, and even direct conflict with state institutions and citizens during the Sandline affair reflect the negative consequences of reliance on PMSCs—particularly concerning the country's economic development and the strengthening of state institutions.

Conclusion

The operation of PMSCs throughout the Pacific region is an important and controversial, though remarkably understudied, phenomenon, with great importance for the economic, security, and development prospects of the region. Despite this significance, the literature to date has been rather limited in scope and quantity as concerns PMSC operations, even in the broad sense. When attempting to search for journal articles or books dedicated to PMSC operations in the Global South or the Pacific region specifically, this becomes even more difficult. Nonetheless, enough research has been produced to allow for an appraisal of the development impact that PMSCs have in Pacific Island countries.

Fiji's heavy reliance on the export of its ex-servicemen and unemployed to serve in PMSCs and peacekeeping operations around the world has, in many ways, been a double-edged sword for the country. While the lucrative financial returns of even a small stint with a PMSC can provide important monetary relief and even prosperity for some Fijian communities, this should not detract from the adverse consequences of PMSC recruitment. Racism, financial exploitation, untreated post-traumatic stress, and large-scale emigration all complicate the long-term development of Fiji.

Similarly, Papua New Guinea has come to rely heavily on PMSC operations to maintain basic levels of security and state integrity, amidst a long history of instability, violence, and an absent state apparatus. While the financial and social stability provided in some areas by PMSCs and the protection of economic projects are important, there are often far more complex consequences to these operations in Papua New Guinea. Corruption, influence peddling, and direct conflict with the state have all characterised PMSC activities in Papua New Guinea, seriously threatening the future progress of what is very much a nascent state.

Ultimately, it is clear that the PMSC operations have produced mixed results for Pacific development and security. While in some cases, Pacific Islander communities and nations have benefitted, either economically or in terms of safety, there are also clear and significant drawbacks that should not be ignored. Violence, exploitation, and the threat of replacing the state or forcing it into dependency on PMSCs are all factors that need to be considered as the operations of private organisations of this nature continue to grow in the region.

References

Chisholm, A. (2014), "Marketing the Gurkha security package: Colonial histories and neoliberal economies of private security", *Security Dialogue*, 45(4).

Dinnen, S. and Walton, G. (2021), "Private Security in Papua New Guinea: A Networked Approach", viewed March 30, 2024. https://www.acmc.gov.au/sites/default/files/2021-08/PNG%20Publication%20Electronic%20web%20Version.pdf

Dinnen, S. and Walton, G. (2020), "PNG's private security industry: what role for international regulation?", viewed March 30, 2024. https://devpolicy.org/pngs-private-security-industry-what-role-for-international-regulation-20201203-2/

Eichler, M. (eds) (2015), *Gender and Private Security in Global Politics*, Oxford University Press, Oxford.

Ivarature, H. (2023), "A matter of conscience? Jerry Singirok, Sandline and Bougainville", viewed March 31, 2024. https://devpolicy.org/a-matter-of-conscience-jerry-singirok-sandline-and-bougainville-20230614/

Kanemasu, Y. and Molnar, G. (2017), "Private Military and Security Labour Migration: The Case of Fiji", *International Migration*, 55(1), viewed March 29, 2024. https://www.researchgate.net/publication/313623662_Private_Military_and_Security_Labour_Migration_The_Case_of_Fiji

Krahmann, E. (2012), "From "Mercenaries" to "Private Security Contractors": The (Re) construction of armed security providers in International Legal Discourses", *Millennium: Journal of International Studies*, 40(2).

Maclellan, N. (2007), "Fiji, Iraq and Pacific island security", *Race & Class*, 48(3), viewed March 30, 2024. https://journals.sagepub.com/doi/epdf/10.1177/0306396807073857

May, R.J., Regan, A., and Dinnen, S. (1997), *Challenging the state: The Sandline Affair in Papua New Guinea*, ANU Press, Canberra.

Neuhaus, S. and Keys, G. (2010), "Private Military Companies in the Operational Health Care Environment: pragmatism or peril?", *Australian Defence Force Journal*, viewed March 30, 2024. https://search.informit.org/doi/pdf/10.3316/ielapa.201008917

Piney, J. (2021), "A Fistful of Dollars: The Changing Paradigm of the PMSC and Mercenary in the Modern Battlespace", viewed March 30, 2024. https://theforge.defence.gov.au/article/fistful-dollars-changing-paradigm-pmsc-and-mercenary-modern-battlespace

Whyte, D. (2003), "Lethal regulation: state–corporate crime and the United Kingdom government's new mercenaries", *Journal of Law and Society*, 30(4).

4

Intelligence and Foreign Policy

Sureyya Yigit

Introduction

Today's political leaders wield immense power over their state, whether they display the traits of Plato's philosopher king, Machiavelli's Prince, or Hobbes' Leviathan. With an unyielding focus on grandeur and ambition, these leaders make consequential decisions that shape the course of nations and impact the lives of their citizens. Hence, the modern political leader is a force to be reckoned with.

Empowered by the exercise of supreme sovereign power, they maintain a broad authority that shapes the nation's politics. This power embodies the state within its borders and ensures the proper functioning of various public authorities, which it has the ability to summon, adjourn, dissolve or seize, and who, on the international stage, within this great concert of fellow Leviathans, are presumed to represent their own country, maintaining diplomatic relations, negotiating treaties, ensuring peace, or, failing that, declaring war. This is a power to which the constituents have lent a name of choice, thereby bringing the entirety of all its activities to the modest execution of laws; this is, of course, the Executive (Heclo, 1977).

This Executive, particularly its head, is, by nature, the supreme power of the state and possesses decision-making power. Being at the top, the head of state or government and their closest collaborators, both political and administrative, have real and significant decision-making power. Due to acting in the name of the common good, the Executive is the decision-making power of the ordinary and the extraordinary, the power, which, as a depositary of public force, must prepare for all eventualities and respond, in all circumstances, to the unexpected. It is, in essence, the master of exceptional execution.

As such, whether its actions are part of the ordinary management of the nation's life or in extraordinary circumstances, carried out by reasons of state and responding to necessities, the head is, by nature, a decision-maker. S/he seeks so much to preserve the regime that s/he embodies and acts on behalf of the national interest. Moreover, according to their functions and responsibilities, the statesperson is responsible for all or part of the nation's policy and is active in a given sphere of influence. Thus, the political leaders intervening at the international level try to preserve the favourable situations and modify the unfavourable ones. They use the instrument by which a state attempts to shape its international political environment: foreign policy. Hence, foreign policy decision-makers are particularly interested in international relations. As it is at the heart of the decision-making process that punctuates relations between states, it is an essential subject of study for anyone who wants to understand these relations.

Foreign Policy Decision- Making and Uncertainty

Waltz's (1954) contributions to understanding foreign policy in the 1960s featured the distinction between three levels of analysis and their introduction as a problem in international relations. These three levels reflect three political-economic spaces, proposing an explanation relevant to global questions: the individual, the state level, and finally, the international system on a global scale. Waltz studied the causes of war, paying particular attention to structural factors that could explain the emergence and end of conflicts. For him, it was necessary to be cognizant of the international system itself, the balance of power, and the interstate interactions to draw palpable conclusions about the causes of war and peace.

Waltz (1996) believes that an analysis of foreign policy is radically distinct from this structural level. Singer (1961) points out that the international system and the national level of the state allow us to understand decision-makers' behaviour according to causal factors. According to him, the choice at the state level or that of the international system to interpret the behaviour of the state differs according to the kind of questions that one asks.

This separation between the levels of analysis is a distinctive feature of the traditional approach to the discipline of international relations, which was widely criticised by the heterodoxy of the International Political Economy (IPE) school and the Foreign Policy Analysis (FPA) approach. The former focuses on areas of intersection between politics and the economy and the latter on internal and external factors.

Keohane and Nye (1973) see it as a continuum of international relations studies and a complementary or critical contribution to classical interpretations while emphasising reciprocal interactions of internal and external dynamics. Their foreign policy analysis looks like a funnel, going from the most general and observable to the more particular and implicit. They are primarily interested in objectives and intentions, more particularly in the causes of these intentions, and finally, more specifically in the preference of an intention over the others. This combination of the analysis of the international system and the analysis of foreign politics demonstrates that the presuppositions of each level of analysis are not necessarily competitive but can be complementary. Each value is inevitably part of one of the foreign policy dimensions, whether at the level of domestic or international determinants.

The foreign policy analysis exemplified by Allison (1971), Brezinski (1974), or Snyder et al. (2002) integrates internal stakeholders into the decision-making process. One can distinguish three approaches qualifying the relationship between their foreign policy and the international system to reconcile the different levels. The first postulates that foreign policy depends on the international system and is interested in something other than foreign politics. A second trend, referred to as"foreign policy analysis", constructs links between foreign policy's outputs and the inputs that intervene in the decision-making process at internal and external levels. Thirdly, a final current brings together those interested in a single actor or network forming foreign policy.

Research on analysis of their foreign policy trends has focused on explaining the decisions of the government in foreign policy through specific factors at different levels of analysis. Due to Nye and Keohane (1972), the domestic factors also gained importance in the field of IPE through their analysis of the interdependence complex. A strong commitment between the two disciplines, IPE and FPA, becomes an inevitable consequence of the scientific decline of the sharp separation between the various paradigms.

Hence, a systemic theory does not say why a particular state acted in such a way at a given point. Implicitly, foreign policy analysis reveals why a particular state has implemented specific decisions regarding foreign policy at certain times. Like Allison (1971) in his analysis of the Cuban Missile Crisis of 1962, one must understand why and how the decisions have been made.

According to some perspectives, asking "how" about an event could be perfectly reasonable from the leaders' outlook at the time and in the circumstances in which the decision was made. However, the main objective of this work is not to evaluate the decisions normatively, whether they are bad or good, but rather to understand why and how decision-makers reached a certain decision. All decision-making models have developed as a counterargument to the explanation of the rational actor. The latter assumes that the state is a single, rational actor that chooses foreign policy decisions according to a set of ordered preferences. By calculating costs and benefits, the state develops its policy to maximise benefits or minimise losses. The decision-making analyses diverge according to one essential point: many domestic actors contribute to foreign policy making.

Consequently, rationality, as the partisans of rational choice which perceive it, is called into question. If one mistakenly thinks that conflict is a core assumption of realism, one might conclude that wherever states are agreeable to each other, realist theories must not apply. However, this is not necessarily so because realist theories explain war and peace. For realists, peace results when the key causes of war are absent (Höglund & Kovacs, 2010).

The bureaucratic model assumes that the organisations and the state's bureaucratic government prioritise their survival and interests when forming foreign policy (Rosenthal, 1998). This survival is measured in terms of relative influence on other entities. The question remains how a foreign policy guided by realist principles influences the economic relationships in a system characterised by neoliberal cooperation.

However, it operates in an uncertain world, changing the world's conception since humanity accepted that the future is more than a whim of the gods and that men and women are not passive before nature. According to Beck (2006), man has given uncertainty a new dimension by passing from a world of enemies to a world of risks. Beck's identification of risk here clearly demonstrates the fundamental place occupied by the idea of the unknown.

Therefore, the international sphere comprises situations that are not fixed in advance, indeterminate, and variable, which can fail or deceive. At the heart of this environment steeped in uncertainty, the decision-maker is confronted with some measurable and immeasurable risks. The decision-maker may not know the existence of a situation that could become uncertain, or a risk may become a factor with the addition of ignorance (Knight, 1960). Informed in this way, it can be seen as a stage before uncertainty. From then on, those involved in international relations face ignorance, uncertainty, and risk; ultimately, the risk factor can become tangible and threatening. In short, foreign policy decisions are intrinsically characterised by high stakes, enormous uncertainty, and substantial risk.

In practice, this general uncertainty can just as easily relate to an event as to another state's motivations, beliefs, intentions, or calculations. It becomes the framework of decision and human action as it is an intrinsic component. Any decision would then be made in an ambiguity of variable intensity and acting in uncertainty. Thus, evolving as a Clausewitzian fog of war, international actors must, like the strategist, tame their environment and take advantage of it or, at least, avoid its disadvantages. To do this, they deal with the uncertainty specific to their actions and decide to accept the existence of uncertainty.

Hence, the political leader must be able to decide despite uncertainty. In an ideal theoretical model, s/he seeks to clarify her/his decision so that it is optimal for the objectives s/he is pursuing. To do this, they seek to collect, process, and use information in a dynamic of central importance to general and particular knowledge. Information, consequently, is essential in the decision-making process, and knowledge systems constitute what Deutsch calls the nerves of government (Deutsch & Model, 1983). The decision-maker has a set of tools to feed this nervous system, among which intelligence figures prominently. For Handel (2012), using accurate and timely intelligence can significantly reduce uncertainty, enabling political and military leaders to improve the quality of their decisions and develop more effective strategies including conducting more successful military operations.

Therefore, it is a question of clarifying the decision, as intelligence makes it possible to reduce uncertainty as long as it is precise and timely. If the practice of espionage has accompanied this quest for information, conferring a strategic advantage since antiquity, the institutionalisation of real intelligence services began in the 19th century,

Intelligence

The professionalisation of intelligence found its meaning at the start of the Cold War (Yigit, 2023). To this end, intelligence is also understood as a practice carried out by professionals within dedicated services. It can be defined by its method, usually summarised by the figure of the intelligence cycle. Lowenthal modernised this cycle and widely discussed it since it can be summarised in a seven-phase programme: orientation, collection, treatment, analysis, dissemination, consumption, and feedback (Voutilainen & Kari, 2020).

In this respect, it is more than a relationship to information alone; intelligence, to be useful, must be shaped through a logical process. As per the orientation given, the service is busy collecting, processing, and analysing information, which, through this refinement, becomes information intended for use with a material dimension formed with information creating a relationship with reality specific to intelligence (Berg, 2021). Indeed, by distinguishing between the raw fact and the analysed fact, intelligence acts as an agent of transmutation, moving from tacit to explicit. It allows the transformation of data into information and then into knowledge.

There is, therefore, a substantial relationship between intelligence and knowledge. It can be seen as an anthropological foundation that proceeds from a cognitive process that inhabits every individual or every organisation, bringing it closer to science (Hayez, 2010). However, it is not easy to consider it as such. Intelligence is also of real practical significance because it inherently has a goal of action. Indeed, it is based on a teleological dimension by the nature of its recipient.

As demonstrated, intelligence intervenes to reinforce political authority; it is, therefore, at the service of the state, and decision-makers resort to it because they are vulnerable, prey to uncertainty or need to inform a decision. Intelligence involves identifying problems and threats, but it has other functions, too. Accordingly, there are four reasons for information being complementary to contemporary intelligence: firstly, it aims to avoid strategic surprise by monitoring risks and threats; secondly, it provides long-term expertise that decision-makers, anchored in the daily reality of state administration, cannot obtain by themselves; thirdly, by extension, it generally supports the political process, particularly at the decision-making level; and finally, it maintains the secret nature of information, needs and methods, due to the particular or special nature of its activities and its intrinsic relationship to secrecy (Lowenthal, 2017).

Moreover, intelligence goes beyond the sole framework of advantageously collected information. As such, to be considered intelligence, the information processed must, according to the four cumulative criteria traditionally retained, be accurate, insightful, tailored, and timely. These additional criteria confirm the idea that one would like precise and timely information and that the vision of tailored information, shaped to suit a client, is found in both the orientation and consumption of that client (Handel, 1987). Suppose intelligence services respond to a consumer. In that case, it is because intelligence is defined in terms of information that responds to the stated or understood needs of policymakers and which has been collected, refined, and reduced to meet these needs (Lowenthal, 2013).

In this conception, intelligence exists to serve and support the policymaker, and any other activity is illegal or superfluous. It is, therefore, information designed for action, and, in an even more absolute way, one can consider that information is only useful to the extent that it can influence a decision. If it does not concern any decision, it is not, strictly speaking, information. One may summarise this relationship in the following manner breaking through ignorance and uncertainty and gaining sufficient knowledge and understanding to identify and assess risks, thus providing an analysis/warning that will enable timely policy intervention (Phythian, 2009).

To do this, the services have a range of means, including the transmission of raw intelligence, which is collected and processed to be usable. Intelligence concerning daily events comprises an element of analysis—current intelligence—or even estimated intelligence that addresses the unknown and offers conjectures on the potential development of situations—estimative intelligence (Laur, 2019). One, therefore, understands the importance of intelligent action, which allows one to optimise action by reducing ignorance.

Thus collected, the action of intelligence seems translucent and mechanical. However, as it evolves in the same environment deeply marked by uncertainty, it experiences difficulties specific to this world of risks. Suppose it is organised to meet decision-makers' needs and ensure monitoring of threats weighing on the state. In that case, it remains constrained by the indeterminacy, inconstancy, and unpredictability specific to international action.

Therefore, intelligence is inscribed in time as a situation in which a service analysis will likely change before being processed and integrated into the decision-making process. It is also doubly linked to it in that decision-making has a timetable that is often specific to it and whose deadlines come to an end faster than it takes time for intelligence to collect, process, and analyse information. Hence, this need for speed in the decision-making process is a constraint on intelligence and can facilitate error, if not cause it. Indeed, the quantity of information that intelligence is capable and likely to collect has grown considerably with the advent of new information and communication technologies. Collection methods linked to technical and human intelligence make gathering and processing an incredible amount of information possible. However, these are only sometimes capable of obtaining the information useful for analysis and decision-making. These methods can, therefore, require more information. Through such a massive collection, there can be an information overabundance and it is up to the services to manage to develop timely and precise intelligence.

Moreover, because some of its missions relate to the enemies or adversaries of the nation, it faces harmful actions that aim to make it difficult, or even prevent, access to information and its processing. Just as external actions can fuel the general confusion resulting from the fog of international relations, domestic constraints on intelligence also exist. As intelligence is not an exact science, it is prone to error and mistakes, and even if it were quasi-scientific, it would nonetheless be a human science whose practice is organised around services composed of necessarily fallible and imperfect personnel.

In short, at all levels of services, the action of intelligence practitioners can be limited or disrupted by a set of elements likely to deceive the process of manufacturing intelligence to pervert it as it generates information. Suppose intelligence depends on the orientation of the political decision-maker and serves to inform his decision. In that case, it is also based on a method of collection, processing, and careful analysis inspired by scientific practice.

Therefore, it is just as important to protect it from excessive external and internal influences while allowing it to know and understand the needs of statesmen and respond to them without neglecting the work of in-depth, long-term analysis, monitoring, and protection of specific secrets (Piaget, 2005). In this perilous configuration, intelligence can easily become its enemy in that its action can be interfered with by a set of internal elements, just as it can be subject to the external action of harmful elements.

Thus, this set of parameters reflects the complex and perilous situation in which intelligence finds itself as it attempts to inform the decision, and this gives rise to a problem which contradicts the very reason for the existence of intelligence. Indeed, while it is considered a tool for reducing uncertainty in the service of political leaders, the nature of its actions and objectives, the composition of its structures, and the environment in which it works could contribute to a paradoxical increase in uncertainty (Javorsek & Schwitz, 2014).

Henceforth, it is appropriate to question the nature of this potential paradox, the concordance of its theoretical reason for being, and the effective consequences of its action. In this sense, it is necessary to restrict oneself to the study of an action integrated into the relationship that drives the producers of intelligence and their primary consumers, that is to say, the services and political decision-makers. As such, it is advisable to avoid considering situations in which intelligence would increase the uncertainty of the political decision-maker by acting independently, outside of its relationship with the consumers of intelligence.

Conclusion

In conclusion, it is essential to recognise situations in which intelligence operates outside the spectrum of this relationship. Understanding the increase in uncertainty as a potential consequence of the natural limits of intelligence action is key (Griffiths, 2020). These limits must be acknowledged and managed to harness the full potential of intelligence. The action of the services, as much as it can be a normal or even expected mechanism of the decision-making process, is understood in the broadest sense. Questioning the existence of this seemingly paradoxical dynamic then amounts to exploring intelligence, its action and limits, and the nature of its reason for being, that is, its relationship with political leaders and the service brought to them.

In the context of intelligence action, it is crucial to consider the possibility of heightened uncertainty that may arise as a paradoxical outcome of its fallibility. This contradictory character of intelligence action can be overcome by critically examining the necessity and usefulness of this mechanism in the relationship between intelligence providers and their consumers. This requires a deep understanding of the complexities involved in intelligence work, which consist of gathering and analysing information, assessing risks, and making informed decisions. It also requires a careful consideration of the potential consequences of intelligence action, including unintended consequences and increased uncertainty, and a commitment to transparency and accountability in the intelligence process. Thus, it is crucial to analyse the potential rise in ambiguity due to intelligence action, which can have an unexpected outcome because of its imperfection. It is important to address this paradoxical situation by questioning the need and effectiveness of this mechanism in the relationship between intelligence and the decision-maker. Ultimately, the goal of intelligence action should be to provide decision-makers with accurate and reliable information while minimising the risks and uncertainties associated with this process.

References

Allison, G. (1971), *Essence of decision*.

Beck, U. (1996), "World risk society as cosmopolitan society? Ecological questions in a framework of manufactured uncertainties", *Theory, Culture & Society*, 13(4), pp. 1-32.

Beck, U. (2006), "Risk Society Revisited: Theory, Politics and Research Programmes". In *The sociology of risk and gambling reader*, pp. 68-90. Routledge.

Berg, E., Jean-Claude Cousseran, and Philippe Hayez (2021): *New lessons on Intelligence;* Odile Jacob (2021); 518 pages. *Revue Defense Nationale*, (7), pp. 146-150.

Brzezinski, Z. (1974), "The Deceptive Structure of Peace", *Foreign Policy*, (14), pp. 35-55.

Deutsch, K. & Model, A. C. (1983), *Of Governmental Learning. Toward a general model of collective learning: a critique of existing models of specific social systems and a sketch of a model for social systems in general*, p. 16.

Griffiths, T. L. (2020), "Understanding human intelligence through human limitations", *Trends in Cognitive Sciences*, 24(11), pp. 873-883.

Handel, M. (1987), "The politics of intelligence", *Intelligence and National Security*, 2(4), pp. 5-46.

Handel, M. I. (2012), "Leaders and intelligence". In *Leaders and Intelligence*, pp. 3-39. Routledge.

Hayez, P. (2010), "'Renseignement': The new French intelligence policy", *International Journal of Intelligence and Counterintelligence*, 23(3), pp. 474-486.

Heclo, H. (1977), "Political executives and the Washington bureaucracy", *Political Science Quarterly*, 92(3), pp. 395-424.

Höglund, K. & Kovacs, M. S. (2010), "Beyond the absence of war: the diversity of peace in post-settlement societies", *Review of International studies*, 36(2), pp. 367-390.

Javorsek II, D. & Schwitz, J. G. (2014), "Probing uncertainty, complexity, and human agency in intelligence", *Intelligence and National Security*, 29(5), pp. 639-653.

Keohane, R. O. & Nye Jr, J. S. (1973), "Power and interdependence", *Survival,* 15(4), pp. 158-165.

Keohane, R. O. & Nye, Jr, J. S. (Eds.) (1972), *Transnational relations and world politics*. Harvard University Press.

Knight, F. H. (1960), *Intelligence and democratic action*. Harvard University Press.

Laur, T. M. (2019), "Principles of Warning Intelligence". In *The Military Intelligence Community*, pp. 149-168. Routledge.

Lowenthal, M. M. (2013), "A disputation on intelligence reform and analysis: my 18 theses", *International Journal of Intelligence and Counter Intelligence*, 26(1), pp. 31-37.

Lowenthal, M. M. (2017), "My take on teaching intelligence: why, what, and how", *Intelligence and National Security*, 32(7), pp. 986-994.

Phythian, M. (2009), "Intelligence analysis today and tomorrow", *Security Challenges*, 5(1), pp. 67-83.

Piaget, J. (2005), *The psychology of intelligence*. Routledge.

Rosenthal, U. (1998), "Reappraising bureaucratic politics", *Mershon International Studies Review*, 42(2), pp. 233-240.

Singer, J. D. (1961), "The level-of-analysis problem in international relations", *World Politics*, 14(1), pp. 77-92.

Snyder, R. C., Bruck, H. W., Sapin, B., Hudson, V., Chollet, D., &Goldgeier, J. (2002), *Foreign policy decision making*. New York: Palgrave Macmillan.

Voutilainen, J. & Kari, M. (2020), "Strategic cyber threat intelligence: Building the situational picture with emerging technologies". In Proceedings of the European conference on information warfare and security. Academic Conferences International.

Waltz, K. N. (1954), *Man, the State, and the State System in Theories of the Causes of War*. Columbia University.

Waltz, K. N. (1996), "International politics is not foreign policy", *Security Studies*, 6(1), pp. 54-57.

Yigit, S. (2023) 2022: "Unipolar Delusion, Bipolar Illusion and Multipolar Aspiration", ДИПЛОМАТИЈА И БЕЗБЕДНОСТ, *Diplomacy and Security*, Volume VI, Number 1/2023, pp. 79-99.

5

The Business of War: Corporate Political Influence on Military Engagement

Mohamad Hassan Soueidan

Introduction

The relation between politics and war has been entwined in human history, and many political scientists and foreign policy makers view war as an instrument of politics. According to Carl von Clausewitz, a leading social theorist of war, war is an instrument of policy. It is, in fact, the policy itself, which takes up the sword in place of the pen (Orts, 2001). Clausewitz (1968) also argued that the role of the military leader is to assist in the crafting of a policy that makes strategic sense, but the final choice rests with the statesman, meaning that it is the role of the politics which sets the goals of the military. Another political theorist, Niccolò Machiavelli, treats war as a profoundly political practice and the military as the site of potential political upheaval and popular revolt (Winter, 2014). Machiavelli argues that the end justifies the means, and thus, war is justified when the goal is achieving political gains.

To understand the forces affecting the decisions of war, it becomes essential to understand the drivers of the politics in a state. In other words, understanding the drivers of politics is crucial for analysing the decisions which lead to war. The motivations, structures, and dynamics of politics are fundamental to comprehending why and how decisions to engage in war are made. Politics not only sets the goals of the war which it seeks to achieve but also defines the scope and limitations of military engagement. As such, any comprehensive analysis of war cannot be separated from the political context in which it occurs. This connection highlights the importance of political analysis in understanding not only why wars are fought but also how they are conducted and concluded.

In this perspective, corporate political activities, or corporate attempts to shape government policies in ways favourable to the firm, become an important factor to be studied in today's globalised world. Micaela Faccio (2006) observed that political participation by firms is widespread, existing in 35 of the 47 countries she studied in the year 2006. Corporations today are feared to "have not only become prominent actors in society, but they may have become the only kind of actor with significant cultural and political influence" (Stern & Barley, 1996).

Research has shown that corporations, especially multinational companies, not only compete in a market environment but also engage with political actors in both their home and host societies. This engagement aims to have Corporate Political Connections (CPC). Corporate political connections are the boundary spanning personal and institutional linkages between firms and the constituent parts of public authorities (Cui et al., 2018). The CPC covers a wide range of interactions between actors in business and government for mutual benefits. Businesses may, for example, use CPC to network with powerful political actors, to obtain preferential access to information on forthcoming regulatory changes, or to influence the interpretation of such rules in their favour (Cui et al., 2018).

In this way, by influencing politics, corporations try to play a significant role in shaping government policies related to warfare (Mikler, 2018). By leveraging their economic power, global corporations could influence and even dictate government decisions on matters of security and war. They do so by utilising their financial resources to lobby policymakers, establish relationships with influential politicians and decision-makers, and fund political campaigns (Bonica, 2016). This influence allows corporations to shape policy agendas that align with their interests, such as securing lucrative defence contracts or gaining access to valuable resources in conflict zones. In addition, corporations often have close ties and partnerships with military-industrial complexes, providing them with privileged access to information and decision-making processes. This enables corporations to effectively influence government decisions on warfare, influencing everything from defence budgets and procurement strategies to military interventions and the use of private military contractors.

These corporations can also shape public opinion through their control over media outlets and advertising campaigns (Croteau & Hoynes, 2006). They can shape public narratives about warfare, promoting certain ideologies and perspectives that serve their interests. By doing so, corporations not only shape government policies related to warfare but also perpetuate a cycle of militarism with profit-driven motives.

Companies: A Driving Force for Warfare Decisions

In the 20th century, concerns began to arise about the possibility of corporate "war merchants" influencing national politics in a belligerent direction (Orts, 2021). The issue of companies influencing state decisions, including decisions related to war, became more valid with the increasing number of companies over the years reaching a phase where many large multinational corporations have become much larger, in terms of overall economic wealth and political influence—as large as some nation-states. In 2001, a study showed that 51 of the 100 largest integrated economic entities in the world were business corporations; the remaining 49 entities were nation-states (Hertz, 2001). The gap between corporations and nation-states increased over time, and in 2015, a report showed that 69 of the world's top economic entities were corporations rather than countries (Global Justice Now, 2015). The same study discovered that the world's top 10 corporations—a list that includes Walmart, Shell, and Apple—have a combined revenue of more than the 180 'poorest' countries combined in the list, which included Ireland, Indonesia, Colombia, Greece, South Africa, Iraq, and Vietnam (Global Justice Now, 2015).

Moreover, the globalisation era has transformed many multinational enterprises (e.g., Amazon and Alphabet) into highly efficient and productive entities that outweigh small countries and grow in power and control (Barrios et al., 2005). This gave corporations the ability to interfere in state politics by funding those who serve their interests, lobbying politicians, or controlling narratives in media that direct the public opinion. This led to the appearance of an opinion which states that "significant decisions affecting people everywhere are increasingly made by corporate managers, not political officers" (Orts, 2001).

Corporate goals in warfare decisions are typically driven by a blend of factors mainly related to profit motives and strategic business interests. The desire to maximise financial gains is a crucial part of the corporate mindset (Edmans, 2021). For that, it is paramount for companies that all decisions result in a net financial gain and preferably one that is significant in comparison to the resources invested. This is what wars in certain situations offer companies by providing them with new areas of resources, facilitating foreign direct investments or increasing their market share.

One significant example where corporate interests may have played a role in initiating war is the involvement of the United Fruit Company in the 1954 coup in Guatemala. The United Fruit Company (UFC) was a powerful American corporation with extensive banana plantations in Central America, particularly in Guatemala. During the early 20th century, UFC had developed substantial control over local economies and even infrastructure within the region.

In 1951, Guatemalan President Jacobo Árbenz initiated an agrarian reform programme that included redistributing uncultivated land to impoverished peasants (Bowen, 1983). A significant portion of the land targeted by this reform belonged to the United Fruit Company. In response, UFC lobbied intensively in Washington, D.C. to counter these reforms. It leveraged its connections within the U.S. government—several key officials, including Secretary of State John Foster Dulles and CIA Director Allen Dulles, had direct or indirect ties to the company (Schlesinger & Kinzer, 1982). UFC portrayed Árbenz's policies as leaning towards communism, playing on the U.S. government's fears during the Cold War era.

In 1954, the CIA launched Operation PBSUCCESS, a covert operation that supported a coup led by Colonel Carlos Castillo Armas. The operation involved psychological warfare, economic pressure, and paramilitary activities, ultimately leading to Árbenz's resignation. Schlesinger and Kinzer (1982) argue that "the takeover of United Fruit land was probably the decisive factor pushing the Americans into action".

It is important to mention that not only do economic actors strive to increase profit and power through war, but in certain situations, they act to maintain peace and push against wars. Addressing which groups in society benefit from international markets, which groups are harmed by commercial openness, and the political influence of these respective segments of society is crucial to understanding what drives companies to influence war and peace decisions (Brooks, 2013).

Lobbying

Economists and political scientists have long been interested in the role of special interests in the policymaking process. Scholars frequently portray special interests as motivated actors with specific policy preferences who lobby politicians to advance them (Brooks, 2013). By pursuing lobbying objectives that favour them, economic actors are seen as having the potential to secure benefits for themselves, perhaps at the expense of the collective interests of the public and/or other economic actors that are less able to engage in effective lobbying (Brooks, 2013).

Economic analysis often commences with the premise that corporations behave as rational actors, engaging in activities only when the anticipated benefits surpass the expected costs. This perspective pervades a substantial corpus of scholarship that seeks to elucidate the variability in corporate political activities, such as campaign contributions. Corporate efforts to influence politics are perceived by managers to produce benefits for the firm, such as a friendlier regulatory environment or additional government contracts (Drutman, 2015). In other words, if corporate managers think that lobbying will benefit their company, then they will lobby; if not, then they won't.

Politics is like a marketplace in which interests and prices are ever shifting (Drutman, 2015). If it is a market, it most resembles a byzantine bazaar which is marked by unpredictability, both in terms of availability of goods and their pricing. The goods in this market are frequently obscure, and their value is often unknown ahead of time—it is only upon learning what one has actually purchased that one can determine the value of it. Access to these goods largely depends on the relationships one cultivates with the vendors, which are relationships that require time to develop. Transactions often take place within an auction-like setting where losing bidders forfeit their stakes. The number of competitors, the extent of their bids, and even the stability of the marketplace itself, which can be disrupted by unexpected upheavals, remain unknown factors. Such a market is not for the inexperienced and uninitiated.

The complexities of this environment typically necessitate guidance from one or more knowledgeable insiders, who can navigate the intricate dynamics and help secure the desired outcomes. This is where lobbying companies come in. They are the professional advisors that guide companies on what to do politically and when to do it.

In the U.S. political system, for example, lobbying is par for the course. Like other interest groups, major industries and leading corporations actively endeavour to shape legislative and regulatory outcomes. For these businesses, this involves articulating their interests clearly to lawmakers to ensure that any enacted legislation and regulations are optimally aligned with their financial objectives. This strategic engagement is designed to maximise favourable conditions for their operations, thereby enhancing their bottom line. From 1998 till 2023, companies paid around US$ 75.79 billion for lobbying companies (Open Secrets, 2023). Of the 100 organisations that spend the most on lobbying in the US, 95 represent businesses (Drutman, 2015).

Total Spending and Lobbyists in the U.S. (Open Secrets, 2023)

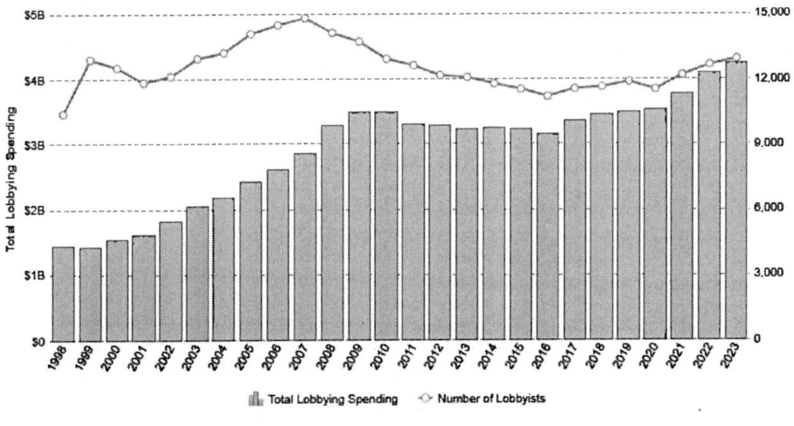

A clear example of companies lobbying for benefitting from wars is the British companies before the war in Iraq in 2003. In the year leading up to the Iraq War, British government officials engaged in discussions with major oil companies, including BP and Shell, about the potential for accessing Iraq's vast oil reserves (Bignell, 2011). Britain's involvement in the war divided Tony Blair's cabinet and was voted through only after his claims that Saddam Hussein had weapons of mass destruction. According to documents revealed by *The Independent*, five months before the March 2003 invasion, Baroness Symons, then the trade minister, told BP that the government believed British energy firms should be given a share of Iraq's enormous oil and gas reserves as a reward for Tony Blair's military commitment to US plans for regime change (Curry, 2016). The papers show that Lady Symons agreed to lobby the Bush administration on BP's behalf because the oil giant feared it was being "locked out" of deals that Washington was quietly striking with the US, French, and Russian governments and their energy firms.

The Foreign Office invited BP on November 6, 2002, to talk about opportunities in Iraq "post regime change". The minutes of the meeting state: "Iraq is the big oil prospect. BP is desperate to get in there and anxious that political deals should not deny them the opportunity." After another meeting in October 2002, the Foreign Office's Middle East director at the time, Edward Chaplin, noted: "Shell and BP could not afford not to have a stake in Iraq for the sake of their long-term future... We were determined to get a fair slice of the action for UK companies in a post-Saddam Iraq."

Whereas BP was insisting in public that it had no strategic interest in Iraq, in private, it told the Foreign Office that Iraq was "more important than anything we've seen for a long time" (Bignell, 2011). BP was concerned that if Washington allowed French oil company TotalEnergies' existing contract with Saddam Hussein to stand after the invasion, it would make the French conglomerate the world's leading oil company.

Over 1,000 documents were obtained under Freedom of Information over five years by the oil campaigner, Greg Muttitt (Bignell, 2011). They reveal that at least five meetings were held between civil servants, ministers, and BP and Shell in late 2002. In 2009, BP's efforts gave results by the signing of a 20-year contract with the Iraqi government, and this was Iraq's first major new oil deal since the 2003 invasion (Rasheed, 2009).

Political Funding

Money is ubiquitous in politics. Election campaigns, political parties, interest groups, non-profit organisations, and the media depend heavily on money, or more broadly speaking, on material resources (OECD, 2013). Both coordinating collective efforts and engaging with voters, journalists, or politicians require financial resources for staffing, office rentals, and communication services to effectively connect with the public. This threatens to have parties and politicians answerable to donors who will have the power to shape policies, mould legislation, and even sway public opinion. In the field of political science, this phenomenon is called "regulatory capture".

Regulatory capture reflects a phenomenon whereby a regulatory agency, which was established initially to serve the interests of the public, formulates a policy based on private or special interests. Actors within the legislative process are influenced by external parties or may even fall for regulatory capture as they have engraved a mindset that sides with the regulated industry (Prihandono & Widiati, 2023).

Since money is an essential of politics, political theorists found it important to study the effect of corporate funding on power. Starting at the beginning of the 20th century, political scientists offered a view of politics as a conflict among plural interests emanating from both the state and private associations, all considered to be at the same level (Yumatle, 2015). Pluralist theorists concluded that power is distributed among various groups in society, each with its own interests and levels of influence. They emphasise the role of non-state actors, including multinational corporations, non-governmental organisations (NGOs), and international institutions, in shaping global politics. They suggest that the international system is not merely governed by the unilateral actions of sovereign states but is influenced by a multitude of actors, each contributing to the formation of international norms and policies.

While pluralists define corporations as part of the decision-making process, elite theorists state that a small number of wealthy and powerful individuals or organisations dominate policymaking. The doctrine of elite theory goes as far back as the end of the 19th century through an argument that in every society, there is inevitably a minority who dominate decision-making, and that this dominant minority cannot be controlled by the majority regardless of the democratic checks on power that exist (Nouri, 2021).

Corporate political funding usually occurs in different ways. It starts with companies funding politicians who serve their interests or align with their political views. For instance, oil and gas companies in the United States tend to fund Republican candidates since the Democrats' views on climate and environment don't serve the companies' goals. Since the 1990 election cycle, more than two-thirds of this sector's contributions to candidates and party committees have gone to the Republicans (Open Secrets, 2024).

Main Strategies of Political Campaign Funding

Strategy	Definition	Example
Direct spending by Non-Governmental Organisations (NGOs)	• Companies can use a network of NGOs to spend an unlimited amount of secret money to back their preferred candidates, rigging the political system in their favour while concealing their involvement. • Companies in most countries are not obliged to disclose their donations under the title of charity.	In countries like India, corporations use Corporate Social Responsibility (CSR) mechanisms to fund NGOs, which can then engage in various activities, including those with political implications, under certain legal frameworks. The Companies Act of 2013 in India mandates corporations to spend a portion of their profits on CSR activities, which can be channelled through NGOs.
Donations to Political Committees and Campaigns	• Donations to cover political committee costs like advertisement, offices, rent… • Donation to political committees doesn't happen in the name of the company but rather in the name of employees and stakeholders. • In most cases, these donations happen through third parties.	• In the 2021 German Federal Elections, the pro-business Free Democrats (FDP) and the environmentalist Greens gained the most from donations (NÖstlinger & Hirsch, 2021).

Hiding Sources of Funding Behind Shell Companies	• Companies use an intermediary entity to transfer funds, and then direct the entity to make a political contribution in their name. • This conceals the true sources of election spending when the contributions are reported by the recipient.	• In 2011, a company called W Spann LLC contributed $1 million to Restore Our Future, a political committee supporting Mitt Romney's presidential candidacy in the US. • W Spann LLC was formed shortly before the donation and dissolved soon after, suggesting it was created solely to make this contribution. The true donor, a friend of Romney and an executive at Bain Capital named Edward Conard, only revealed himself after significant media coverage and complaints from watchdog groups (Ghosh & Wieand, 2022).

Once companies turn into donors and thus share a part in the politician's decision-making, they can affect the views of their receptors regarding peace and war. Having influence over politicians is reflected through the ability to affect their decisions and stances. For instance, if a company with interests in defence contracts funds a politician, it might sway that politician to adopt a more militaristic stance, which could be beneficial for the company's business interests. At the end, companies view political funding as an "investment" whereby they are "buying influence" to use when needed. For instance, on average, House members in the US who voted to authorise $886 billion in military spending in 2024 took four times more money from military contractors than members who voted against the bill. Also, Senators who supported the National Defence Authorisation Act took five times more arms industry cash than the senators who opposed it (Semler, 2023). It is worth mentioning that this act includes provisions for funding war-related issues in Ukraine and the Middle East.

The Revolving Door Phenomenon

When President Obama took office in 2009, he faced the challenge of filling top positions in the federal administration with political appointees (Luechinger & Moser, 2014). Like former Presidents, he also tapped the reservoir of private sector experts. For example, he nominated William J. Lynn III, a former Raytheon (Technology and Defence Company) executive, as Deputy Secretary of Defence (Kirkpatrick, 2009). Lynn's nomination raised concerns over conflict of interest. A senate hearing for his appointment included quotes emphasising on the topic: "The revolving door is an important issue for us to talk about...You went directly from the Pentagon to a defence contractor. You are coming back directly from a defence contractor into the Department of Defence. This is troubling to a lot of people and it's an incestuous business what's going on in terms of the defence contractors and the Pentagon" (Luechinger & Moser, 2014).

The revolving door phenomenon encompasses various scenarios. Initially, it involves business sector professionals being appointed as public officers in areas where they previously worked, enhancing regulatory insights. On the other hand, it also sees public officials entering the private sector in industries they once regulated. The revolving door may also follow a circular pattern: an individual from a specific business sector is appointed public officer for the said sector yet plans to return to private interests once the civic mandate is complete (Yates, 2019).

The literature on political appointees from the private sector focuses on the increase in political control for corporations. Political appointees can directly favour their former employers in regulation, procurement, and merger and acquisition decisions. This can also happen indirectly in strategic planning and preferential access to information and decision-makers. Incentives for such preferential treatment may exist either because appointees expect to rejoin the companies or because they want to return favours (Luechinger & Moser, 2014).

According to data from Brookings Institute, 231 out of 435 members of the House of Representatives in the 114th Congress had previous occupations that fell under the "business or banking" category (Kramer, 2017). The same pattern holds true for the Senate, with 42 out of 100 senators listed under business or banking in the 114th Congress compared to 24 in the 107th. This means that the business and banking sector has significant influence in the Congress's decisions including those related to warfare.

A clear example lies in the appointment of Dick Cheney as Vice President in George W. Bush's administration. Before becoming Vice President, Cheney was the CEO of Halliburton, a major American multinational corporation involved in oil, engineering, and construction, among other services (Rosenbaum, 2004). Cheney's role in advocating for the 2003 Iraq War has been widely discussed and criticised, particularly because Halliburton, through its subsidiary KBR, was awarded substantial contracts in the war's aftermath (Eckholm, 2005). These contracts were for services that included repairing oil fields and handling logistics for the military, which were worth billions of dollars. Critics have argued that Cheney's former ties with Halliburton represented a conflict of interest, especially given the lack of competitive bidding for contracts in Iraq, raising concerns about the influence of prior business affiliations on decisions to go to war.

From Arsenal to Arbiter: The Ascendancy of the Military-Industrial Complex in Decision-Making

The Evolution of the Military Industrial Complex

It seems almost obligatory to begin any discussion of "the Military–Industrial Complex" (MIC) by referencing President Dwight D. Eisenhower's farewell address that made this term public (Bradford, 2009). Dwight Eisenhower, an ex-military Republican President of the USA, in his 1961 Farewell Address, was the first to express concern about the impact of the "conjunction of an immense military establishment and a large arms industry", which, he noted, was "new in American experience" (Dunne & Sköns, 2011). He alerted councils of governments, saying that "we must guard against the acquisition of unwarranted influence, whether sought or unsought, by the military industrial complex (MIC)", adding that "the potential for the disastrous rise of misplaced power exists and will persist" (Eisenhower, 1961).

Later, social scientists developed the concept of military-industrial complex as alliances of vested interests spanning both the state and industry. It consists of a web of mutually beneficial linkages between the government and its defence industry. This framework highlighted the potential for decisions to prioritise the interests of coalition members rather than national security concerns. This coalition was expanded to include not only interests within the military establishment and the arms industry but also within the political organs (Dunne, 1995).

Although most literature links the concept of military industrial complex with President Eisenhower's speech, the concept predates World War II. Brunton (1988) argues that the military industrial complex can be defined as a system of institutions, and after describing the specific institutions comprising the MIC, one can trace their historical development till before World War II. In this way, by defining the MIC as an evolving system of institutions, Brunton identifies specific patterns that can be traced historically.

Brunton's ideas stem mainly from the fact that during World War I, governments began to rely heavily on private companies to produce military equipment (Brunton, 1988). This trend continued during World War II, and by the end of the war, the defence industry had become a significant part of the economy. In this sense, the years after World War II mark not a start but rather a culmination in the process of partially integrating economic and military institutions (Koistinen, 1967).This outsourcing of military functions has blurred the lines between public and private interests, allowing defence contractors to wield significant influence over government decisions.

Moving on, during the Cold War, when the defence was strongly focused on deterrence, a set of specific state-industry relationships were produced that, in turn, generated a beneficial environment for the development and strengthening of the MIC (Dunne & Sköns, 2011). In the Cold War, threats were overemphasised to justify absurdly high levels of military spending. For example, by emphasising the threat from each other, the Soviet Union and the US entered an arms race, which increased the importance of the MIC.

In the US, which has the largest MIC, the generalised and relatively constant fear of the Soviet threat was punctuated by the perception of spectacular and startling Soviet challenges to American nuclear hegemony (Ungar, 1990). These spectacular developments stoked the "Great Fear" and resulted in massive nuclear buildups (Boyer, 1985). The growth of the American arsenal came in three large waves (the Truman, the Eisenhower/Kennedy/McNamara, and the Reagan buildups), each preceded by a specific panic (the Soviet atomic bomb, the Sputnik/Cuban missile crisis, the window of vulnerability, respectively) as an immediate determinant (Ungar, 1990).

Following the end of the Cold War, there was a significant shift in the security landscape, which initially had a profound effect on the military sector. Post-Cold War reductions in military expenditures and changes in military requirements and technology led to considerable changes in the Defence Industrial Base (DIB) and the relations between the DIB, the military, and the legislature (Chapman & Yudken, 1992).

After global military expenditures and arms exports peaked in the mid-1980s, they fell gradually at first with improving East-West relations, then rapidly with the disintegration of the Soviet Union (Dunne & Sköns, 2011). By the beginning of the 2000s, it became evident that the United States and Europe were unlikely to encounter adversaries capable of mounting symmetrical responses. Instead, the rise of informal asymmetric guerrilla-type conflicts highlighted the need for different weapon systems, which, in turn, changed the nature of demand. Additionally, the growth of "homeland security" and the increasing distribution of peacekeeping troops made communications and surveillance technologies more important. Thus, while many of the long-term weapon programmes initiated during the Cold War remained in the 21st century, there has, at the same time, been a clear and important qualitative change in the nature of technology (Dunne & Sköns, 2011).

MIC in the Decision-Making Process

At the centre of any analysis of the Military Industrial Complex lies the presence of a robust Defence Industrial Base, serving as a focal point for vested interests to unite. From an institutional approach perspective, the MIC is composed of conflicting interest groups and institutional linkages where the MIC becomes a self-generating structure (agency), which embodies the interests of various groups in society (Smith, 1977). The strong interests and competition for resources push for more military spending, sometimes exaggerating external threats to justify it.

With the rise of globalisation, the defence sector worked on globalising its industry, which has led to complex interdependencies between governments, corporations, and international actors, further entrenching the influence of the military-industrial complex in decision-making processes. According to the Stockholm International Peace Research Institute (SIPRI), total global military expenditure has risen from US$ 1.14 trillion in 2001 to US$ 1.711 trillion in 2014, a rise of 50 per cent (Amnesty, 2015). This, in turn, gave the MIC an increasingly important economic value for states, thus increasing its ability to affect decisions.

In addition to its economic influence, the military-industrial complex also exerts significant political leverage. Defence contractors often contribute generously to political campaigns and maintain close ties with policymakers, allowing them to sway decisions in their favour. For example, 51 members of the American Congress and their spouses own between $2.3 and $5.8 million worth of stocks in companies that are among the top 30 defence contractors in the world (Shaw & Moore, 2020).

Given that warfare is the arena where the MIC thrives, as the demand for increased production peaks, defence companies strive to wield the greatest influence over decisions about peace and conflict. As discussed above, this influence is obtained through lobbying, political funding, revolving doors, and controlling narratives through the media. A study published in 2017 argued that Russia's MIC's need to obtain new resources was the driver to initiate the war in 2014 (Johannesson, 2017). The study argues that the addition to Russia of the 13.5 million Russian-speaking Ukrainians and the acquisition of Ukraine's huge military-industrial complex along with its huge stockpiles of Soviet-era weapons might potentially have a significant effect in terms of changes in the strategic balance of power in Europe.

Finally, the perceived link between national security and economic prosperity has provided the military-industrial complex with a powerful narrative to justify its influence. Policymakers are often reluctant to challenge defence spending or question the priorities of the defence industry for fear of being seen as weak on national security. This dynamic has perpetuated a cycle of increasing defence budgets and reliance on military solutions to complex geopolitical challenges.

But the problem lies with the divergence of interests between the defence industry and the state. At the end of the road, the MIC, like any other business sector, looks for maximising profit, whereas the state is supposed to look out for the public interest of its people. When the United States invaded Iraq two decades ago, one of the public justifications for the war was that it would help spread democracy throughout the Middle East. The invasion, of course, had the opposite effect: it unleashed a bloody sectarian conflict in Iraq, badly undermining the reputation of democracy in the region and America's credibility in promoting it.

Another clear example is the American war on Afghanistan. According to the Cost of War Project at Brown University (2022), the war in Afghanistan cost U.S. taxpayers $2.3 trillion till 2022 and resulted in the deaths of 2,324 U.S. military personnel, 4,007 U.S. contractors, and 46,319 Afghan civilians. As the American people financed the war through their tax contributions and, tragically, in some instances, their lives, the top five Pentagon contractors experienced a surge in growth through federal contracts during the Afghanistan conflict. Stephen Semler (2021), co-founder of the Security Policy Reform Institute, found that the Congress gave $2.02 trillion to the top five weapons companies, Raytheon, Lockheed Martin, General Dynamics, Boeing, and Northrop Grumman, between 2001 and 2021. And between 2002 and 2020, federal funding for those five weapons increased by many folds (Semler, 2021). Also, a compilation of data from lobbying disclosures archived at Open Secrets shows that those five firms spent over $1.1 billion on lobbying between 2001 and 2021 (Clifton, 2021). Taken as a form of investment in procuring lucrative Pentagon contracts, the top five weapons firms earned $1,813 in Pentagon contracts for every dollar spent on lobbying.

Lobbying was not the only form of influencing policymakers. The weapons firms sent $120 million in campaign contributions to federal candidates between 2002 and 2020, hired former government officials to sit on their boards while simultaneously advising U.S. policymakers to extend the withdrawal timeline from Afghanistan, and bankrolled think tanks that opposed the withdrawal and supported ongoing U.S. military engagement in the Middle East (Clifton, 2021).

References

Amnesty (2015), "Killer facts: The scale of the global arms trade". Amnesty International USA. Retrieved from https://www.amnestyusa.org/updates/killer-facts-the-scale-of-the-global-arms-trade/

Barrios, S., Görg, H., & Strobl, E. (2005), "Foreign direct investment, competition, and industrial development in the host country", *European Economic Review*, 49, pp. 1761-1784.

Bignell, P. (April 19, 2011), "Secret memos expose link between oil firms and invasion of Iraq", *The Independent*. Retrieved from https://www.independent.co.uk/news/uk/politics/secret-memos-expose-link-between-oil-firms-and-invasion-of-iraq-2269610.html

Bonica, A. (2016), "Avenues of influence: On the political expenditures of corporations and their directors and executives", *Business and Politics*, 18(4), pp. 367-394. Cambridge University Press. https://doi.org/S1369525800004034a

Bowen, G. L. (1983), "U.S. Foreign Policy toward Radical Change: Covert Operations in Guatemala, 1950-1954", *Latin American Perspectives*, 10(1), pp. 88-102. Sage Publications, Inc. https://www.jstor.org/stable/2633365

Boyer, P. (1980), "From Activism to Apathy: The American People and Nuclear Weapons, 1963-1980", *Journal of American History*, 70, pp. 821-844.

Bradford, J. C. (Ed.) (2009), *A Companion to American Military History*. Wiley-Blackwell. https://doi.org/10.1002/9781444315066

Brooks, S. G. (2013), "Economic actors' lobbying influence on the prospects for war and peace", *International Organization*, 67(4), pp. 863-888. https://www.jstor.org/stable/43282089

Brown University (2022) ,"Costs of War". Retrieved from https://watson.brown.edu/costsofwar/figures/2021/human-and-budgetary-costs-date-us-war-afghanistan-2001-2022

Brunton, B. G. (1988), "Institutional Origins of the Military-Industrial Complex", *Journal of Economic Issues*, 22(4), pp. 599-606. https://doi.org/10.1080/00213624.1988.11504790

Chapman, G. & Yudken, J. (1992), *Briefing Book on the Military-Industrial Complex*. Washington, DC: Council for a Livable World Education Fund.

Clausewitz, C. von (1968), *On war*.

Clifton, E. (September 3, 2021), "Top defense firms spend $1B on lobbying during Afghan war, see $2T return", *Responsible Statecraft*. https://responsiblestatecraft.org/2021/09/02/top-defense-firms-see-2t-return-on-1b-investment-in-afghan-war/

Curry, S. (2016), "What is the meaning of Brexit?", EMBO Reports, 17(9). https://doi.org/10.15252/embr.201643113

Cui, L., Hu, H. W., Li, S., & Meyer, K. E. (2018), "Corporate political connections in global strategy", *Global Strategy Journal*, 8(3). https://doi.org/10.1002/gsj.1309

Drutman, L. (2015), *The business of America is lobbying: How corporations became politicized and politics became more corporate*. Oxford University Press. Retrieved from https://books.google.com.lb/books/about/The_Business_of_America_is_Lobbying.html?id=f8qqBgAAQBAJ&redir_esc=y

Dunne, J. P. (1995), "The Defence Industrial Base". In K. Hartley & T. Sandler (Eds.), *Handbook in Defense Economics*, pp. 592-623. Elsevier.

Dunne, J. P. &Sköns, E. (March 2011), "The Changing Military Industrial Complex". Research Papers in Economics. https://www.researchgate.net/publication/46450061_The_Military_Industrial_Complex

Eckholm, E. (June 28, 2005), "Democrats step up criticism of Halliburton billing in Iraq", *The New York Times*. https://www.nytimes.com/2005/06/28/politics/democrats-step-up-criticism-of-halliburton-billing-in-iraq.html

Edmans, A. (2021),*Grow the pie: How great companies deliver both purpose and profit–updated and revised.*

Eisenhower, D. D. (1961). President Dwight D. Eisenhower's Farewell Address. National Archives. https://www.archives.gov/milestone-documents/president-dwight-d-eisenhowers-farewell-address

Faccio, M. (2006), "Politically connected firms",*American Economic Review*, 96(1), pp. 369-386. https://doi.org/10.1257/000282806776157704

Ghosh, S. & Wieand, R. (April 20, 2022), "Secret election spending proliferates through shell companies". Campaign Legal Center. https://campaignlegal.org/update/secret-election-spending-proliferates-through-shell-companies

Hertz, N. (2001),*The silent takeover: Global capitalism and the death of democracy*. Free Press. Retrieved from https://books.google.com.lb/books/about/The_Silent_Takeover.html?id=op6fQgAACAAJ&redir_esc=y

Hoynes, W. & Croteau, D. (2006),*The business of media: Corporate media and the public interest*. Pine Forge Press. Retrieved from https://books.google.com.lb/books?id=s1GYiTi2vgAC

Johannesson, J. (2017), "Russia's war with Ukraine is to acquire military industrial capability and human resources",*Journal of International Studies*. Retrieved from https://www.jois.eu/files/4_407_Johannesson.pdf

Kirkpatrick, D. D. (January 22, 2009), "Nominee's vote postponed over concerns on lobbying", *The New York Times*. https://www.nytimes.com/2009/01/23/us/politics/23lobby.html

Koistinen, P. A. C. (1967), "The Industrial-Military Complex" in "Historical Perspective: World War I", *The Business History Review*, 41(4), pp. 378-403. https://www.jstor.org/stable/3112647

Luechinger, S. & Moser, C. (2014) ,"The value of the revolving door: Political appointees and the stock market",*Journal of Public Economics*, 119, pp. 93-107. https://doi.org/10.1016/j.jpubeco.2014.08.001

Mikler, J. (2018), "The political power of global corporations". Wiley. Retrieved from https://www.wiley.com/en-us/The+Political+Power+of+Global+Corporations-p-9780745698458

Nouri, B. (2021), *Elite theory and the 2003 Iraq occupation by the United States: How US corporate elites created Iraq's political system* (1st ed.). Routledge. https://doi.org/10.4324/9781003147558

Nöstlinger, N. & Hirsch, C. (December 7, 2021), "Big money boosts small parties in new German government", *Politico*. https://www.politico.eu/article/germany-election-small-party-big-money-fdp-greens/

OECD (2013), "Money in politics: Sound political competition and trust in government". Retrieved from https://www.oecd.org/gov/ethics/Money-in-politics.pdf

OpenSecrets (2024), "Lobbying data summary". Retrieved from https://www.opensecrets.org/federal-lobbying/summary

OpenSecrets (2024), "Oil & Gas summary". Retrieved from https://www.opensecrets.org/industries/indus?ind=E01

Orts, E. W. (2001), "War and the business corporation". William Davidson Working Paper (No. 427). Retrieved from https://typeset.io/papers/war-and-the-business-corporation-4akfpvyog1

Orts, E. W. (2021), "War and the business corporation", *Vanderbilt Journal of Transnational Law*, 35(2).

Prihandono, I. &Widiati, E. P. (2023) ,"Regulatory capture in energy sector: Evidence from Indonesia", *The Theory and Practice of Legislation*, 11(3), pp. 207–231. https://doi.org/10.1080/20508840.2023.2248837

Reuters (November 3, 2009), "BP, CNPC sign Iraq's 1st big post-invasion oil deal". Retrieved from https://www.reuters.com/article/idUSL3558520/

Rosenbaum, D. E. (September 28, 2004), "A closer look at Cheney and Halliburton", *The New York Times*. https://www.nytimes.com/2004/09/28/us/a-closer-look-at-cheney-and-halliburton.html

Schlesinger, S. & Kinzer, S. (1982),*Bitter fruit: The untold story of the American coup in Guatemala*. Doubleday.

Semler, S. (August 23, 2021) ,"House committee set to boost military budget by $25 billion". Retrieved from https://stephensemler.substack.com/p/house-committee-set-to-boost-military

Semler, S. (August 23, 2021), "The top 5 military contractors ate $2 trillion during the Afghanistan War". Retrieved from https://stephensemler.substack.com/p/the-top-5-military-contractors-ate

Shaw, D. & Moore, D. (January 17, 2020) ,"The Members of Congress Who Profit From War". *The American Prospect*. Retrieved from https://prospect.org/power/the-members-of-congress-who-profit-from-war/

Smith, R. (1977), "Military expenditure and capitalism", *Cambridge Journal of Economics*, 1, pp. 61-76.

Stern, R. N. & Barley, S. R. (1996), "Organizations and social systems: Organization theory's neglected mandate", *Administrative Science Quarterly*, 41(1), pp. 146-162. http://dx.doi.org/10.2307/2393989

Winter, Y. (2014), "The Prince and His Art of War: Machiavelli's Military Populism", *Social Research*, 81(1), pp. 165-191. https://www.jstor.org/stable/26549606

Yates, S. (2019), "The revolving door: Private interest's illegitimate gateway to political influence?" Paper presented at the Canadian Political Science Association Conference, Vancouver, June 4. Retrieved from https://www.cpsa-acsp.ca/documents/conference/2019/686.Yates-Cardin-Trudeau.pdf

Yumatle, C. (2015), "Pluralism". In M. T. Gibbons (Ed.), *The Encyclopedia of Political Thought*, First Edition. John Wiley & Sons, Ltd. Retrieved from https://scholar.harvard.edu/files/cyumatle/files/c.yumatle-pluralism.pdf

6

Tangled Power Game: Tatmadaw and Corporate Influence on Myanmar's Jade Industry

Sampa Kundu

Introduction

C. Wright Mills (1956) theorised about the influence of corporate interests within the political process, particularly in defining national interests, especially in the context of defence production and military expenditure. His analyses were primarily based on US foreign and defence policies. Since World War II, the United States' foreign policy dynamics have increasingly empowered the military-industrial complex. This complex, comprising defence contractors and related industries, wields significant influence by centralising foreign policy decision-making in the executive branch and fostering bureaucracies reliant on perpetuating external threats. Following Mills' insights, elite power theorists contend that the military-industrial complex shapes and refines the notion of "national interest" to maximise profits and secure access to resources. However, they also acknowledge competition among various corporate interest groups in defining this concept.

Influenced by elite power theory, business conflict theorists argue that different capitalist firms, depending on their sector, may adopt varying positions on military expansionism, interventionism, and defence spending. Corporations close to the military-industrial complex exhibit distinct characteristics, notably, a heavy reliance on military production for revenue.

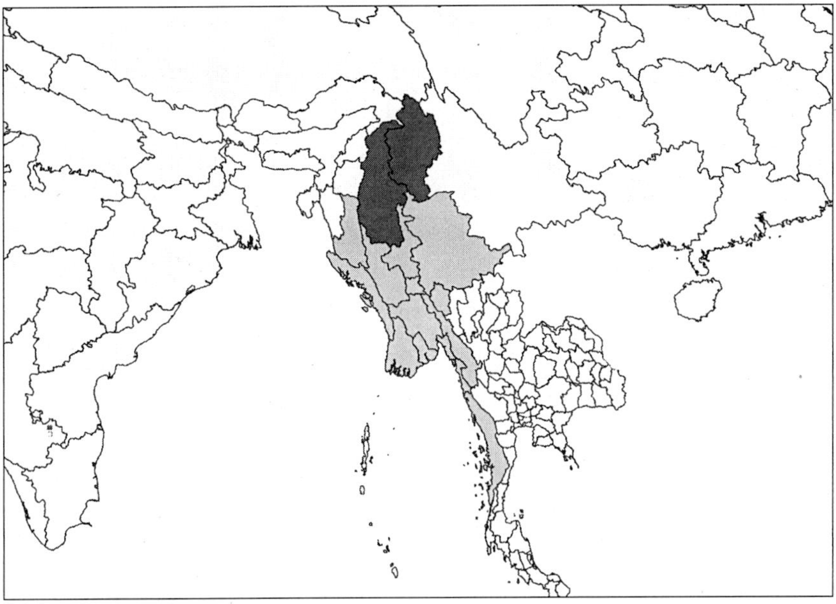

This is a representative map of Myanmar showing Kachin and Sagaing Regions that have the country's most jade mining and production sites (created with mapchart.net)

Lockheed Martin, BAE Systems, Raytheon, General Dynamics, and Northrop Grumman derive significant sales from arms. Unlike firms focused on finance or versatile products, these companies are vested in maintaining and expanding weapons systems, often necessitating sustained military spending. This brings us to the notion of a "permanent war economy" that underscores the role of military spending in stimulating production and demand, akin to military Keynesianism. This approach, preferred by corporate interests, utilises military expenditure as an industrial policy to drive innovation and economic growth, particularly during periods of recession or high unemployment.

Key historical events, such as the 1979 geopolitical shifts in the Middle East and the 9/11 attacks in the USA, provided opportunities for militarisation proponents to advance their agenda. In a nutshell, the influence of corporate interests, particularly those aligned with the military-industrial complex, plays a significant role in shaping national interests, defence policies, and military expenditure. This influence extends beyond mere profit motives, encompassing broader economic and geopolitical considerations (Cox, 2014).

While the concept originated in the context of U.S. foreign policy, comparable dynamics can be observed globally, including in Asia. In some Asian countries, trends of military-industry-corporate nexus have been witnessed, especially where political and economic stability is in question. Also, many Asian countries import arms and weapons from the USA and its allies. Strong arms and weapons nexus can be linked to geopolitical tensions and regional security dynamics in Asia. Arms races, territorial disputes, and military modernisation efforts can be fueled by the interests of weapon contractors seeking markets for their products. This can exacerbate existing tensions and lead to instability in the region. The arms industry can impact economic and industrial policies in Asian countries by influencing government priorities and resource allocation. Defence spending may divert resources away from other sectors, while defence contracts and investments can drive technological innovation and contribute to economic development in specific regions in a positive way.

In Myanmar, the situation is more complicated. In the country, for most of its post-independence time, the military has not only controlled the natural resources but also has had a tight command on resource allocation, political and economic systems, and social structure. Many top-ranking military officials are involved with multiple types of businesses and industries, not only arms and weapons. The semi- precious jade industry of Myanmar is one such instance where one sees huge involvement of the military officials and companies that are affiliated to the Junta. Myanmar is one of the world's largest jade producers. Myanmar illegally exports a significant portion of its jade to China.

Access to the recent data on Myanmar's jade industry is difficult; however, Global Witness, a US-based environment watchdog, has claimed that in 2014-15, Myanmar's jade export was valued at $31 billion, far more than the official statistics of gem trade through Myanmar Gem Emporium in 2013-14 (AA, 2016).The jade industry in Myanmar is highly influenced by the military-industrial complex including alliances and cooperation agreements. Inevitably, the money gained from this lucrative semi-precious stone is mostly bagged by the Tatmadaw and their affiliates, contributing to their growth, helping them attain prosperity and build their empires. Therefore, it is safe to argue that while the dynamics of the military-industrial complex may have originated in the Western context, similar influence patterns can be observed in Asian countries, albeit with some variations. In Myanmar's case, apart from the Junta, the Kachin Independence Organisation (KIO) and similar other ethnic organisations have also profited through taxing the miners in Kachin state, the country's largest jade- producing area. Myanmar stands as an example where military-industry complex has benefitted from unfair resource allocation, in this case, jade production, and impacted the country's economy, politics, and society. The interplay between defence industries, government policies, and regional security dynamics has far-reaching implications for peace, stability, and economic development in the country (Earth Rights International, 2021).

Myanmar: The Crucial Factor of Geography

Myanmar's rich jade deposits are primarily situated in the mountainous regions of the northeast. Notably, jadeite is abundant in Kachin state, while the renowned sources of rubies are mostly found in northern Myanmar's Mogok region. These gems, especially jade and rubies, hold significant cultural and economic value, both in domestic and international consumer markets.

The extraction of these gemstones, however, is fraught with challenges, particularly in conflict-affected areas like Hpakant in Kachin state and Khamti township in the Sagaing region. Ethnic and armed struggles in these regions have further complicated the mining operations, impacting socio-economic issues. Hpakant, in particular, has gained notoriety for its jade mining activities. Despite its global demand, the jade industry has been marred by tragedy, with over 500 reported deaths due to landslides since 2015. Corruption, environmental mismanagement, conflict dynamics, and economic desperation have contributed to this grim situation.

Many Myanmar individuals, driven by the promise of wealth amid economic downturns and rising unemployment, flock to Hpakant, hoping to hunt gemstones. However, their pursuit often comes at significant risk, as landslides constantly threaten their lives. The gemstone mines, while benefitting a select few, fail to uplift the local communities, leading to discontent and resentment among residents. Official records indicate a staggering number of gemstone mines in Hpakant and Khamti, with over 21,000 identified in a 2016 report. Mining operations, often conducted by large companies employing heavy machinery, require permits to be obtained through payments to the mining ministry and local authorities.

However, shadows surround the exact fees paid, with companies citing confidentiality agreements and rampant corruption hindering transparency and accountability (Larkin, 2016).

Control by the Tatmadaw

To continue from the previous section, in Myanmar's jade industry, obtaining concessions is often determined not by transparent standards but by nepotism and bribery. Companies seeking concessions typically approach high-ranking officials, such as the Tatmadaw Northern Commander or state officials, expressing their desire to mine in specific areas. In return for substantial bribes or promises of future profits, these officials ensure that the company receives the concession. The allocation of concessions is not uniform, with more valuable mines requiring closer ties to the Tatmadaw. The most lucrative jade deposits, such as those in Maw Sizar and Kwang San, are typically awarded to companies with strong connections to high-ranking military figures. Meanwhile, concessions for lower-quality deposits are granted to less-connected companies (Human Rights Watch, 2021).

Joint ventures with military-held companies, like Myanmar Economic Holding Limited (MEHL), are often pursued to solidify ties with the Tatmadaw. For years, MEHL, controlled by serving or retired military personnel, has dominated Myanmar's jade business. Its shareholders, including military units and senior officers, some of whom have been implicated in human rights abuses,have profited immensely from dividends. MEHL's extensive portfolio includes mining, telecommunications, textiles, tourism, finance, and construction, with jade mining being one of its most profitable ventures. It has acquired numerous concessions, often invoking emergency powers to seize mines through Section 144 of Myanmar's Criminal Procedure Code. According to reports by Global Witness (2021), in 2018-19, Myanmar Imperial Jade (one of the largest subsidiaries of MEHL) had 362 licences for jade mining, while MEHL's other subsidiaries had another 100 licences.

Crony capitalism is entrenched in Myanmar's jade industry, facilitated by the Tatmadaw's control of key companies and direct involvement in jade businesses. Despite international sanctions and scrutiny, these practices persist, contributing to the exploitation of natural resources and perpetuating socio-economic inequality in the country. MEHL's control over jade mining areas is enforced through violent means, with patrolling soldiers authorised to shoot trespassers on sight under Section 144. This fear of reprisal permeates local communities, leading to widespread displacement and intimidation. Despite MEHL's nominal role as a mining entity, its primary function is to occupy and exploit jade mining lands, often subcontracting the actual mining work to other companies or establishing joint ventures. MEHL serves as the Tatmadaw's de facto agent in the industry, using violence to maintain control while rewarding the military with substantial dividends from jade profits. Top military leaders, such as Senior General Min Aung Hlaing and retired Senior General Than Shwe, further perpetuate crony capitalism in the jade industry. Through their family members and loyalists, they control key jade mining companies, reaping immense personal wealth. Than Shwe's family, for instance, owns several lucrative jade companies, bypassing bidding procedures and disregarding legal and environmental standards (*The Guardian*, 2021).

The intertwining of military and political power with personal enrichment exemplifies the abusive nature of Myanmar's jade industry. While military leaders amass wealth, local communities suffer displacement, poverty, and environmental degradation, perpetuating a cycle of violence and exploitation. Diagram 1 depicts Myanmar Government's shares from the jade industry in the country.

Diagram 1

Source: Global Witness, 2021.

The Corruption Continues

While the Myanmar Mines Law mandates environmental conservation protocols, enforcement could be more lax. In Hpakant, mining licences expired in 2019 and 2020, yet mining activities persist, even under the ruling junta's watch. The area is also subject to control by the Kachin Independence Army (KIA), with companies paying the KIA a percentage of profits from controlled mining sites. The rush to extract resources within a limited timeframe drives companies to exploit the land aggressively, causing environmental degradation and increasing the risk of accidents, such as landslides. The social impact is equally dire, with drug abuse rampant among miners and scavengers, exacerbating public health crises like HIV transmission (Luu, 2022).

Despite the immense revenue potential from jade mining, the benefits rarely trickle down to local communities or the national economy. Much of the profits are siphoned off by corrupt officials, military personnel, and armed non-state groups. Efforts to reform the sector have been stymied by political instability and military rule, leading to continued exploitation and suffering for those living in resource-rich areas.

The former NLD government brought the Gemstone Law 2019 to initiate some reforms in the existing system of corruption and cronyism within the gemstone industry in Myanmar. However, the law could not address some of the persistent challenges that include agglomerating plots next to each other by the big mining corporations to bypass restrictions on large-scale mining at one place. It also allowed Myanmar Gems Enterprise (MGE) to continue as a commercial partner for the mining corporations. In MGE, most of the high-ranking officials are retired Tatmadaw officials. The law even did not prevent mining companies that were previously involved in illegal mining from obtaining new licences for mining. Therefore, the flawed reform process could do little to improve the overall situation in Myanmar's mining industry (Global Witness, 2021).

The decline in jade and gem production, exacerbated by COVID-19 and political turmoil, has further strained the industry. Chinese buyers, exploiting Myanmar's vulnerability, drive down prices, while smuggling routes controlled by militias and government forces contribute to widespread corruption. Myanmar's dependence on China for technology and market access ensures that the gem trade remains skewed in favour of Chinese buyers, perpetuating the cycle of exploitation. There is a growing call for accountability, transparency, and community benefit in the gemstone industry. Efforts to reform the sector, including increased regulation and oversight, are crucial to ensure that Myanmar's natural resources benefit its people rather than enriching a select few.

Response by the International Community

Luxury jewellery companies, including Harry Winston, Tiffany & Co., Cartier, Signet Jewelers, and Boodles, have publicly announced that they will not source gemstones from Myanmar. Advocacy groups like Global Witness (2021a) are raising awareness about the situation and calling for greater accountability from governments and corporations. Sanctions have been imposed on military-affiliated companies, army leaders, and their families involved in the gemstone trade to restrict the flow of revenue to the military regime and hold perpetrators of human rights abuses accountable. The situation in Myanmar demands immediate action from the international community. The gemstone trade is providing revenue to the military regime, which is perpetrating gross human rights abuses. In addition to the measures already taken by the international community, humanitarian aid is urgently needed to support those affected by the political unrest in Myanmar. The United Nations and other international organisations are working hard to provide assistance to those in need, including refugees and internally displaced persons.

The "Burma Unified through Rigorous Military Accountability Act of 2021" or simply, the "Burma Act", is a legislation passed in the United States Congress. The bill aims to hold the military regime accountable for its actions, promote democracy and human rights in Myanmar, and address the ongoing political crisis in the country. Some critical provisions of the Burma Act include:

- Prohibition of Imports: The act proposes prohibiting all imports of Myanmar goods, including gemstones, into the United States. This move is not only symbolic but strategic as it aims to cut off a significant source of revenue for the military regime. It sends a firm message that the United States is firmly committed to restoring democracy in Myanmar and is unwavering in its stance against the coup.

- Sanctions and Accountability: The Burma Act calls for targeted sanctions against individuals and entities responsible for the coup, human rights abuses, and undermining democracy in Myanmar. These sanctions may include asset freezes, travel bans, and other measures to hold perpetrators accountable.
- Support for Civil Society: The act supports civil society organisations, human rights defenders, and pro-democracy activists in Myanmar. This support may include funding for advocacy campaigns, capacity-building workshops, and initiatives to promote human rights, democracy, and good governance.
- Engagement with Regional Partners: The Burma Act encourages diplomatic engagement with regional partners, such as ASEAN, to address the crisis in Myanmar and promote a peaceful resolution. This engagement may involve joint statements, coordinated actions, and support for mediation efforts between the military regime, civilian leaders, and other political actors.
- Refugee Assistance: The act includes provisions for assisting refugees fleeing violence and persecution in Myanmar, particularly in neighbouring countries. This assistance could involve humanitarian aid in the form of food, shelter, medical supplies, resettlement support, and other assistance to refugees and internally displaced persons (IDPs).

In brief, the Burma Act represents a comprehensive approach by the United States to address the political crisis in Myanmar and support the people's aspirations for democracy, human rights, and peace. This comprehensive strategy instils confidence in its potential to bring about significant change (US Department of State, 2021).

Conclusion

The relationship between the corporate, the military, and gemstones in Myanmar is complex and deeply intertwined and is often characterised by corruption, human rights abuses, and illicit activities. Some key aspects of this relationship, as described in the paper, are summarised as follows:

Military Control and Profits: The Myanmar military, also known as the Tatmadaw, holds significant control over the gemstone industry in the country.

State-run conglomerates, such as Myanmar Economic Corp. and Myanmar Economic Holdings Ltd., which have close ties to the military, dominate the jade and gems trade through various subsidiaries. The military benefits financially from the gemstone trade, using the revenues to fund its operations and maintain its grip on power.

Corruption and Nepotism: The gemstone industry in Myanmar is rife with corruption and nepotism. Military officials and their cronies often receive preferential treatment in obtaining mining concessions and licences. Bribery, kickbacks, and under-the-table deals are common practices, allowing military-linked companies and individuals to exploit valuable gemstone resources for their own gain.

Human Rights Abuses: The military's involvement in the gemstone industry has been associated with numerous human rights abuses, including forced labour, land confiscation, environmental degradation, and violence against local communities. Mining operations often result in displacement, exploitation, and marginalisation of indigenous and ethnic minority populations living in gemstone-rich areas.

International Trade and Sanctions: The gemstone trade in Myanmar has international ramifications, as gemstones sourced from the country are exported to global markets, including the United States, China, and Thailand. Concerns about the military's control over the industry and its human rights record have led to calls for sanctions and restrictions on the import of Burmese gemstones by some countries, such as the United States (Yun Po, 2022).

Corporate Complicity: Some multinational corporations and international buyers of Burmese gemstones have been accused of complicity in the military's abuses and exploitation of natural resources. By purchasing gemstones from Myanmar without adequate due diligence and oversight, these companies may be indirectly supporting the military regime and perpetuating human rights violations in the country.

Finally, the jade industry in Myanmar is a complicated network of corporate, military, and gemstone interests that have caused significant harm to the local communities and the environment. The industry has long been plagued by a lack of transparency, accountability, and responsible business practices, which has resulted in unsustainable development and further damage to the already fragile ecosystem. By studying the evolution of the military-industry complex in Myanmar's jade industry, we can gain a better understanding of the impact it has had on the country's society, economy, environment, and politics. This paper focused on the corruption nexus in the industry, the ways in which it has undermined the rule of law and democratic institutions, and the loopholes in domestic and international responses that have allowed this to happen. Additionally, it underscores the role of ethnic organisations, such as the Kachin Independence Organization (KIO), in this matter. Overall, there is a pressing need for greater transparency, accountability, and responsible business practices in the jade industry to ensure sustainable development and prevent further damage to the environment and local communities.

References

AA, "200-ton jade stone found in north Myanmar". Retrieved from https://www.aa.com.tr/en/asia-pacific/200-ton-jade-stone-found-in-north-myanmar/665272. 15.10.2016.

C. Wright Mills, *The Power Elite*, Oxford University Press, 1956.

Chia-Yun Po, "China's Role in Myanmar's Bloody Jade Industry: Poison or Panacea", College of Law, National Taiwan University 2022, *Journal of Academics Stand Against Poverty,* Volume 2, Issue 1, July 2022, pp 35-55.

Earth Rights International (2021), "Corporate Accountability in Burma's Gemstone Industry". Retrieved from https://www.earthrights.org/corporate-accountability-in-burmas-gemstone-industry/

Global Witness (2021), "Jade and Conflict: Myanmar's Vicious Circle". Retrieved from https://www.globalwitness.org/en/campaigns/natural-resource-governance/jade-and-conflict-myanmars-vicious-circle/.

Global Witness (2021a), "Myanmar's Gemstone Trade". Retrieved from https://www.globalwitness.org/en/campaigns/myanmar-gemstone-trade/

Human Rights Watch (2021), "Myanmar: Military-Linked Gem Companies Must Face Sanctions". Retrieved from https://www.hrw.org/news/2021/02/04/myanmar-military-linked-gem-companies-must-face-sanctions

John Sai Luu, "Analysis: Myanmar's gemstone riches bring poverty and environmental destruction", April 25, 2022, at https://news.mongabay.com/2022/04/analysis-myanmars-gemstone-riches-bring-poverty-and-environmental-destruction/

The Guardian (2021), "Myanmar's military and the gem trade: a tangled web". Retrieved from https://www.theguardian.com/world/2021/mar/15/myanmar-military-and-the-gem-trade-a-tangled-web

"The Military-Industrial Complex and US Military Spending After 9/11", Author(s): Ronald W. Cox, Source: *Class, Race and Corporate Power* , 2014, Vol. 2, No. 2 (2014), pp. 1-20. Digital Commons e-ISSN 2690-3458 ISSN 2690-3431

"Transparency's Double-Edged Sword", Col. Sean Larkin, May 11, 2016—*Defense One*. https://www.defenseone.com/ideas/2016/05/transparencys-double-edged-sword/128210/

U.S. Department of State (2021), "U.S. Sanctions Related to Burma". Retrieved from https://www.state.gov/u-s-sanctions-related-to-burma/

Further Readings

"Countering Identity Violence - Sudan" | Rights for Peace. https://www.rightsforpeace.org/copy-of-countering-identity-violence

"Manifesto of the Saharawi people in defense of their natural resources". https://www.pressenza.com/2021/03/manifesto-of-the-saharawi-people-in-defense-of-their-natural-resources/

"PM commits optimal conditions for newly-appointed Russian Ambassador" | VTV. https://english.vtv.vn/news/pm-commits-optimal-conditions-for-newly-appointed-russian-ambassador-20210901103757296.htm

"EU Parliament calls for Lebanon, Afghanistan, UAE & Cuba sanctions" | *Global Sanctions*. https://globalsanctions.co.uk/2021/09/eu-parliament-calls-for-lebanon-afghanistan-uae-cuba-sanctions-2/

7

From Fossil Fuels to Chips Intelligence Gathering in the Era of Big Tech

Shushant Vc Parashar

Introduction

The convergence of technology and geopolitics is reshaping the landscape of intelligence gathering and warfare and heralding a new era, a frontier of unparalleled challenges and opportunities.[1] As nations compete for dominance in data and technology,[2] these resources are becoming catalysts for what some term the 'golden era of intelligence gathering', a term that underscores the potential implications of the current technological advancements on global security and competitiveness while simultaneously revolutionising warfare.[3] This transformative convergence is a force to be reckoned with, and this chapter aims to illuminate its profound implications.

The exponential growth of data, coupled with the widespread adoption of personal devices such as laptops and mobile phones, has revolutionised the practice of intelligence gathering.[4] For instance, the ability to intercept and analyse vast amounts of digital communications has significantly enhanced intelligence agencies' capabilities.[5]During the millennia before the Industrial Revolution, intelligence gathering remained essentially unchanged. However, the widespread use of telecommunication networks and, more recently, computer and mobile communications has led to intelligence gathering determined by encryption and decryption technologies.[6]

The historical parallels between the transformative impact of technologies such as the telegraph and radio in the 19th and 20th centuries and the proliferation of mobile phones, internet technology, and data are noteworthy and serve as a testament to the continuity and progression of our technological advancements. These technological leaps not only facilitated more efficient intelligence-gathering operations but also empowered leaders to monitor and control armies and fleets remotely, thus paving the way for global conflicts on an unprecedented scale.[7] This chapter explores these parallels and their implications for our present and future.

Looking ahead, 21st-century warfare is not just a continuation of the past but a new era defined by the increasing prevalence, magnitude, and sophistication of cyberattacks.[8] This term encompasses a range of digital threats, including hacking, data breaches, and information warfare, that can be launched remotely and with potentially devastating effects. [9]The battlegrounds of future conflicts extend beyond physical territories to encompass the digital realm, where countries compete not only with technology but also for control over technology.[10] The rules, doctrines, and nature of cyberwarfare differ markedly from conventional warfare, necessitating novel approaches to defence and offence.[11] This shift, like warfare, has profound implications for national security, global power dynamics, and the balance of power among nations.[12]

Countries must safeguard their territorial borders, trading routes, data, technology, and critical infrastructure in this new paradigm. The ability to deploy advanced encryption technologies for cyber defence and superior decryption capabilities for cyber offences has emerged as a crucial strategic asset and a key determinant of geopolitical competitiveness.[13]

From Fossil Fuels to Chips

In the contemporary technological race, international dynamics have once again thrust geography, access to land, and control over natural resources into the forefront of numerous geopolitical disputes.[14] This has precipitated a reshuffling of industrial strategies, particularly in sectors crucial to national defence and security. Consequently, certain countries have adopted various intervention strategies, including business, diplomacy, the judiciary, development policies, and military support.

This resurgence of geopolitical competition underscores the enduring significance of territorial control and resource access in shaping global power dynamics. Countries vie for strategic advantages in critical sectors, such as energy production and defence technology, recognising the inherent geopolitical leverage conferred by control over essential resources and territories. [15] However, this intensification of competition has also engendered a countertrend towards increased protectionism and nationalism. With growing geopolitical uncertainties and economic vulnerabilities, some countries have adopted inward-looking policies to safeguard domestic industries, resources, and interests. This retreat from globalisation is evident in measures, such as trade tariffs, investment restrictions, and the repatriation of supply chains.[16]

The current technological race is significantly influenced by the demand for inner transition metals, also known as rare metals, which serve as essential components in various modern technologies. These metals, crucial for the energy transition, information technology, security, and defence sectors, are integral to many products, including computers, mobile phones, hybrid cars, renewable energy systems, medical devices, precision-guided arms, and drones. The rare-earth elements, a group of 17 metals renowned for their unique magnetic, optical, and electronic properties, are essential. [17,18] China, possessing approximately one-third of the global reserves, emerges as the dominant player in the rare metal market. The country's strategic advantage is underscored by its control over these critical elements' production and supply chains, enabling it to exert considerable influence on global technological production.[19]

This dominance has positioned China as the primary exporter of rare metals and facilitated its expansion into technological markets, leveraging its competitive edge in manufacturing and supply chain management. Moreover, China's control over rare metal resources extends beyond its borders, with significant investments in cobalt mines in the Democratic Republic of the Congo and other strategic locations, consolidating its geopolitical influence. The geopolitical implications of China's dominance in the rare metal market are profound, potentially disrupting global supply chains and impacting other countries' defence and communications capacities. This control over critical resources gives China significant leverage in technological production, shaping national security strategies and international power dynamics.[20]

In response to China's hegemony in this domain, other countries, including the United States and various European countries, are endeavouring to diversify their rare metal suppliers and bolster domestic production capabilities.[21] This resurgence of mining nationalism is driven by concerns over supply chain vulnerabilities and the need to secure access to critical resources in an increasingly competitive global landscape. However, this technological race is not without its ethical and environmental implications. The extraction and processing of rare metals, which often involves environmentally damaging practices and human rights concerns, are associated with significant ecological footprints, raising questions about sustainability and responsible resource management. Moreover, the reliance on rare metals for technological advancement poses risks of dependency and geopolitical tensions, potentially compromising efforts towards energy transition and environmental sustainability.[22]

Perspective: Up Goes technology, and Down Goes the World Order

The transition from a bipolar to a multipolar world order has ushered in a new era of geopolitical competition, with the United States and China emerging as primary actors, vying for dominance in various spheres, particularly technology. This rivalry has catalysed a multifaceted struggle for economic, military, and political supremacy, with technology as a critical battleground.[23]

According to reports, China's pursuit of Western technology represents a significant challenge,[24] as it could potentially grant Chinese companies[25] a decisive economic and competitive advantage.[26] Conversely, China perceives American efforts to restrict Chinese access to technology and markets as an assault on its sovereignty and aspirations for global leadership in trade. This trade and technological war between the United States and China has precipitated the formation of distinct technological spheres of influence, as both countries seek to assert the pre-eminence of their respective technological models. This geopolitical rivalry has spurred the consolidation of alliances and partnerships, with countries aligning themselves based on technological dependencies and strategic interests.[27]

While some countries, like Thailand, rely heavily on Chinese technology,[28] others, like Japan, actively pursue partnerships with the United States to mitigate dependency risks.[29,30] However, the interconnected nature of the global technological ecosystem complicates efforts to establish exclusive spheres of influence, as technological interdependence persists despite attempts at decoupling. The configuration of these technological spheres reflects the broader geopolitical struggle for dominance between the United States and China, with the European Union also seeking to carve out its path amidst its inherent limitations and dependencies. While the Chinese model emphasises state-led technological governance, the American model prioritises the role of companies and other non-state actors.[31]

The alliance between Russia and China has emerged as a significant force in this geopolitical landscape. It is characterised by close cooperation in various domains, including technology, energy, and defence.[32] This partnership challenges the traditional Western-centric model of international relations and seeks to promote alternative visions of democracy and digital rights.[33] Furthermore, the coordination among the BRICS countries, spearheaded by Russia and China, underscores efforts to expand their collective influence and define their spheres of dominance. As these countries strive to consolidate their positions in the global technological and geopolitical arenas, their ability to forge alliances and partnerships will shape the contours of international power dynamics in the coming years.[34]

Big Tech and Intelligence Gathering: Disruption of Security

Examining the technological phenomenon known as "Big Tech" and its impact on national security intelligence and decision-making is a pressing topic in contemporary discourse.[35] The ubiquitous nature of data in modern society, as evidenced by its prevalence in various commercial enterprises, underscores its significance in shaping economic activities and security practices.[36]

Big Tech permeates diverse sectors of human activity, from shopping and social interactions to travel logistics, transportation networks, and financial transactions. Its utilisation in national security endeavours has also witnessed a notable surge in recent years, with many highlighting the increasing integration of Big Tech and associated analytics into security frameworks.[37]

Many argue that Big Tech offers immense potential for enhancing national security, promising a safer and more secure nation,[38] thus advocating for the adoption of Big Tech in security practices.[39] However, it is essential to note that adopting such technologies often precedes a thorough understanding of their potential impacts.

The advent of the information age has ushered in an era characterised by the exponential growth of data, forming the foundation for numerous data-driven technologies that significantly impact national security. The proliferation of information in quantity and variety continues unabated, shaping the landscape of contemporary security practices.[40]

Moreover, the contemporary era is characterised by unprecedented levels of digital connectivity. The increasing interconnectivity of systems and infrastructure and our growing reliance on them heralds a transformative paradigm shift. The proliferation of data captured from diverse sources, including humans, machines, and the natural environment, constitutes a significant challenge to existing political and economic models.[41] Technological advancements in data storage and computational capabilities facilitated by technology's widespread digital connectedness and ubiquity are central to the emergence of the substantial data phenomenon. These factors collectively contribute to the exponential growth of data, fuelling the expansion of the extensive data ecosystem.[42] The rapid pace of technological change has fundamentally altered how information is stored, interpreted, analysed, and communicated within society. In this context, the traditional paradigms governing political and economic models face significant disruption.[43] The sheer volume and variety of data challenge established governance, decision-making, and market dynamics frameworks. Moreover, democratising data access and analytics tools introduces new actors and power dynamics into the socio-political landscape, reshaping traditional power structures and hierarchies.[44]

Intelligence activities, primarily funded and conducted by nation-states, are integral to safeguarding national interests and ensuring the safety of citizens. Despite their paramount importance, information about intelligence agencies and their operations is often shrouded in secrecy, leading to a shortage of publicly available data.[45] Intelligence is crucial in modern statecraft, serving as a linchpin for national security efforts during wartime and peacetime.[46] The advent of Big Tech has revolutionised the information landscape, presenting unprecedented opportunities and challenges for intelligence communities worldwide.[47] Data abundance represents a fundamental shift in the availability of information, enabling the capture and storage of vast quantities of previously inaccessible data. This abundance empowers intelligence agencies to create detailed profiles of individuals, locations, and entities, offering insights into previously unrecorded events and behaviours. By leveraging sophisticated analytics, intelligence professionals can extract valuable intelligence from this wealth of data, enhancing their understanding of various threats and risks.[48]

Digital connectivity further amplifies the impact of Big Tech on intelligence processes by facilitating real-time data collection and analysis.[49] The interconnectedness of digital networks enables the rapid dissemination of information, allowing intelligence agencies to monitor unfolding events and respond swiftly to emerging threats.[50] This real-time intelligence-gathering capability enhances situational awareness and improves decision-making in dynamic and evolving security environments. Moreover, the ubiquity of technology underscores the pervasive influence of Big Tech across various emerging technologies. From surveillance systems to social media platforms, Big Tech plays a central role in shaping the capabilities and operations of intelligence agencies. The convergence of information, computation, and commercial power in the digital realm has centralised intelligence resources, enabling more efficient data processing and analysis.[51]

Bending The Rules

The role of Big Tech in shaping contemporary geopolitics cannot be overstated. While traditional military contests between nation-states often dominate discussions of great power competition, major technology companies have emerged as significant geopolitical actors in their own right.[52, 53] Companies such as Alibaba, Amazon, Apple, Google, Meta (Facebook), Microsoft, and Tencent wield resources and influence that rival, and sometimes surpass, those of nation-states.[54] The recent Ukraine conflict has highlighted commercial tech companies' impact on conflict outcomes. For instance, Elon Musk's Starlink satellites played a crucial role during the war, demonstrating how tech companies can make decisions with far-reaching implications beyond the control of states.[55] It is essential to recognise that Big Tech will not replace nation-states but reshape them. [56]The key question revolves around which major powers will successfully leverage new and emerging technologies to enhance their state power.[57] The United States and China are testing two distinct models of military technological progress.[58] The American approach seeks to find common ground between government and commercial innovation, while China's model centralises military and economic power under a single-party state. The success or failure of these models will determine the trajectories of future significant powers and their effectiveness on the battlefield.[59]

Multinational corporations' influence on global powers is similar to that in the Early Modern Period. During the 17th and 18th centuries, European powers sent companies to control trade routes and establish colonies in distant lands. These ventures, often chartered by governments, amassed immense wealth. For instance, the Dutch East India Company was valued at $7.4 trillion, surpassing tech giants like Google, Apple, Meta, Amazon, and Microsoft.[60] However, the landscape today differs markedly. Major tech companies operate with unprecedented autonomy and agility, often outpacing government bureaucracies in technological innovation. Companies like Google and Microsoft are at the forefront of AI development, while SpaceX leads in space exploration with groundbreaking achievements like reusable rocket technology. Moreover, tech giants like Apple, Google, and Amazon have ventured into healthcare, introducing disruptive innovations. The geopolitical significance of tech companies is evident in conflicts such as the war in Ukraine. Companies like Microsoft and Google have played crucial roles in cyber defence and information dissemination, challenging the notion of platform neutrality. Meanwhile, regulatory actions by countries like China and Russia have compelled tech companies to comply with domestic laws or face expulsion.[61]

As tech companies continue to shape geopolitical dynamics, a new model of public-private governance is emerging. Major powers' adaptability to this paradigm shift will be pivotal in determining their future trajectories in great power competition and international relations. Therefore, assessing tech companies as geopolitical actors is crucial for understanding contemporary power dynamics, global stability, and conflicts.

The USA Vs China: Battle of Tech Giants

The ongoing geo-technological tensions between the United States and China are reshaping global dynamics, leading to two fluid techno-spheres of influence. This contrasts with the previous bipolar world, where confrontations primarily occurred within defined spheres of influence. Today's rivalry revolves around contrasting models of capitalism and democracy, with both sides seeking superiority rather than balance.[62] While other centres of power like India and the European Union lack strategic advantages to establish alternative techno-spheres, their interconnections with existing ones complicate efforts to maintain balance.[63]

Traditionally, the United States' international power was associated with capitalism and the defence of democracy.[64] In contrast, China has prioritised technological leadership to bolster its national power, establishing dominance in various high-tech sectors.[65] The competition between these two techno-spheres raises questions about the feasibility of technological decoupling. Attempts to create airtight spheres of influence face challenges due to the interconnectedness of global supply chains and development programmes.

China's geopolitical strategy, including initiatives like the Digital Silk Road, aims to expand its influence globally by investing in infrastructure and securing access to strategic resources.[66] This approach challenges the traditional alliances of the United States, particularly in regions like Europe and Asia. China's technological advancements, particularly in sectors like 5G, have garnered support from numerous countries, amplifying geopolitical tensions. The technological war between the United States and China extends beyond 5G to cutting-edge sectors like artificial intelligence and semiconductors. This competition has accelerated trade and technological decoupling between the two countries.[67] However, recent events, including the COVID-19 pandemic and the war in Ukraine, have underscored the interdependence between countries across various fields, highlighting the need for increased global cooperation to address shared challenges.[68]

Efforts to promote strategic self-sufficiency, particularly in technology, are underway globally, with countries like those in the European Union implementing policies to reduce technological dependencies and enhance cybersecurity.[69] International cooperation is seen as essential in addressing global challenges and initiatives. The COVID-19 pandemic and the outbreak of the war in Ukraine further highlighted the inadequacies and vulnerabilities of many countries, mainly those in the European Union, in terms of strategic autonomy in defence, security, and intelligence gathering. This longstanding issue underscores the urgency for countries to enhance their capabilities and reduce dependencies on external sources.[70]

Conclusion

The pandemic and the conflict in Ukraine have combined to catalyse the strategic pursuits of numerous nations towards achieving autonomy across various domains, including gathering intelligence, industry, technology, security, and defence. Both crises have underscored the vulnerabilities inherent within national infrastructures when confronted with sweeping global disruptions. However, this quest for autonomy is not bereft of attendant risks, as it may engender the adoption of nationalist, protectionist, and competitive policies, occasionally entailing exclusionary tendencies.

Acknowledging the enduring reality of our deeply interconnected and interdependent global landscape is imperative. Consequently, pursuing alliances emerges as an organic response to this paradigm. Such endeavours are poised to stimulate the formation of novel strategic partnerships among governments, driven by shared interests, while concurrently fortifying extant alliances and revisiting antiquated ones. As nations navigate the evolving dynamics of global influence, particularly within the technological sphere, disparities will likely increase. Nonetheless, the imperative of global governance necessitates the identification of common ground to address the myriad challenges confronting humanity effectively.

The prevailing technological and digital governance paradigms, spearheaded principally by China, the United States, and, to a lesser degree, the European Union, confront persistent challenges. A pressing imperative arises to establish inclusive global forums conducive to executive deliberation and discourse. Regionally, ongoing disputes exacerbate such forums' frailty, impeding their functional efficacy. The widening chasm between leading nations compounds the difficulty in fostering international governance and cultivating platforms for deliberative exchange. A palpable risk looms whereby technological advancements may precipitate the formation of insular tech and digital enclaves, thereby imperilling digital rights by propagating technological and digital nationalism.

The clash between divergent regulatory frameworks appears inevitable, not solely between autocratic regimes and democratic systems but also within each model. Geopolitical tensions reverberate across the unaligned global spectrum, where major powers vie for endorsement or acquiescence, leveraging promises to bridge the digital divide. Navigating a world marked by accelerated development of technology poses formidable complexities and monumental challenges. The contemporary technological milieu and its future trajectory stand poised to redefine human activity and fundamentally shape human identity, privacy, consumption patterns, leisure pursuits, occupational landscapes, healthcare modalities, interpersonal dynamics, cultural paradigms, and myriad other facets of societal existence. The spectrum of potential transformations is vast, delimited only by the bounds of human imagination.

In this crucible of technological competition, knowledge and geographic considerations emerge as pivotal nodes within geopolitical contestations. On one axis, the strategic advantage conferred by knowledge along the technological value chain has assumed heightened significance in recent epochs, propelled by aspirations for strategic autonomy and inter-state rivalries. Conversely, geographic factors and natural resource endowments, trailing in the wake of knowledge, serve to universalise the construct of power. Control over territories encompassing continental shelves, mineral reserves, pivotal trade routes, critical infrastructural nodes, or climatic favours confers a competitive edge, irrespective of territorial expanse. Size becomes an ancillary concern; proactive engagement is imperative in technology.

Amidst this scramble for geographic primacy, the geopolitics of fossil fuels persists as a linchpin in international relations. The conflict in Ukraine epitomises this reality, underscoring the vulnerabilities of certain predominantly European nations tethered to fossil fuel dependencies. The ascendance of renewable energies, implicit within the contemporary energy transition, portends a potential upheaval of this status quo. As this transition unfolds, the salience of fossil fuel geopolitics is poised to diminish, compelling producer nations to adapt or face obsolescence. The ensuing terrain of green technology geopolitics promises to be even more fiercely contested than its fossil fuel counterpart.

Against this backdrop, the tripartite engagement of governments, civil society, and the private sector assumes paramount importance, particularly within security and defence. Escalating global geopolitical tensions have precipitated the adoption of securitisation imperatives worldwide, wherein technology assumes a transformative role, especially in curtailing rights and freedoms. Divergent political and social models manifest prominently within this domain, ranging from cybersecurity imperatives to technological surveillance protocols and high-tech military deployments to the propagation of disinformation campaigns. Instances of electoral interference, illicit data exploitation, digital divides, and the crafting of cultural narratives further underscore the pervasive influence of technology within the contemporary security milieu.

The annals of warfare and international security attest to the historical nexus between technological innovation and conflict dynamics, a relationship perpetuated in the contemporary epoch. Conflict scenarios are increasingly characterised by hybrid modalities, wherein the velocity of the technological race mandates a continual appraisal of risks, threats, and opportunities. Against a backdrop of democratic reduction on a global scale, the nexus of power and digital technology warrants judicious channelling.

Big Tech is emerging as the "new frontier" to revolutionise society. This is visible in many aspects, including the management of national security and intelligence gathering, which the rise of Big Tech has disrupted. Emerging sectors like technology evolve daily, and their impact on society is being understood with time. Big Tech has led to the overabundance of data, thereby leading to digital connectivity and an omnipresent technology. Individuals, institutions, and countries have an extensive digital footprint and consume vast data daily. This data consumption has created an infrastructure integral to human society. Technology has become the sun around which the world revolves now. Besides transforming society, Big Tech has captivated the national security and intelligence-gathering market. This growth in technology has led to the creation of critical technologies like Artificial Intelligence (AI) and Quantum Computing. It provides a roadmap to understand the impact of these emerging technologies on the security of a country.

Big Tech has changed global power by making it more centralised. Power is now shifting from the hands of politicians to big tech players. Companies involved in this power shift use data to change the narrative and influence aspects of global political and economic power. Big Tech will continue to alter national security and intelligence gathering and can lead to a "technological arms race" between companies and countries in the future. Companies now hold more leverage over the populace's lives, given their access to vast swathes of personal information. Additionally, they have the power to compute, which only strengthens their position.

Big Tech is changing the very ground rule of intelligence gathering. Previously, intelligence gathering was carried out under a shroud of secrecy. This practice is undergoing tumultuous change as data is now readily available. While the value of information has increased, the need to sift through data and assess the threats that might occur has become more intensive. This has significant implications for the various activities carried out under the garb of intelligence gathering. Now, it is impossible to distinguish who is part of the country and who is not. This now has significant implications for the policymaker as existing compliance, oversight, and accountability mechanisms are not viable. The emergence of critical technology has further muddied the water. The practice of gathering intelligence and the capacity and capability of agencies involved in collecting information is under question. It has further demonstrated that Big Tech has challenged the foundational principles and practices of the intelligence gathering units.

The rise of big tech companies has made national security a topic of national discussion. Rather than being confined to the rooms of governmental agencies, national security has acquired an international flavour. Governments across the world are now being judged by the global audience daily. This now changes how governments perceive other state and non-state actors, and the distinction between those involved in national security and those not involved has been blurred, leading to chaos when interacting with actors to gather intelligence. To overcome the problem, there has been increased collaboration between the public and private sectors, leading to data declassification.

Big Tech is evolving at a phenomenal pace. With the majority of infrastructure being developed by the companies themselves, it has led many to believe that the individual's privacy is at stake. As people post every minute detail about themselves on the internet, it has led to remote and invisible privacy intrusions, targeting and surveillance by emerging actors of known and unknown origins. As data grows, access to it also grows. Now, various aspects of intelligence gathering are available to everyone as the infrastructure around data collection and its use is under regulated. Big Tech has enabled remote tracking, monitoring, and analysis and made surveillance capabilities accessible to many actors, requiring a more robust policy response to protect individuals. Adversaries can now purchase and acquire data to undermine national interests, hindering a country's capability and capacity to achieve its objectives and harming a select few individuals in any shape or form.

Intelligence gathering through big tech can harm the populace in several ways, especially by multiplying disinformation through grey zone tactics. Disinformation has become a form of social control that influences and interferes with ongoing political and civic discourses. Data is being used to target groups for a variety of reasons that may be unethical. Democratic countries like India are seeing a rise in information warfare in the form of social and political interference. This is an important area that requires urgent research and policy consideration.

The rise of Big Tech has profoundly affected the production of intelligence. Knowledge is the collection of skills and information, while intelligence is the application of knowledge. With the overabundance of data, the lines between intelligence and knowledge have blurred. This has led to intelligence gathering becoming a known activity, thereby leading to changes in the organisation's structure in collecting, analysing, and disseminating information. Big Tech has made sure that information stays permanently available in digital format.

The nature of intelligence gathering is changing as Big Tech continues to evolve. Uncertainty is on the rise and can impact the decision-making process of the governments involved. An overabundance of data has significantly impacted the policy maker. As Big Tech continues to evolve, so will the gathering and disseminating of information. Existing ways of collecting, processing, and sharing data are being altered. Big Tech has increased the capacity of those gathering intelligence by giving them access to a vast data dump, connecting the dots in the process and then using it for the required purpose.

Big tech companies have impacted the intelligence-gathering apparatus, and the impact will continue as technology develops by leaps and bounds. Agencies gathering information must transform themselves to use data and other emerging technologies to suit their needs and objectives. As the globe undergoes digitalisation, changes will continue to occur. In many of the changes, there will be the need to work closely with the private sector to assess threats towards national security. Other areas will need more deliberate policy and legislative reform, some of which are being implemented. Big Tech will continue to do intelligence gathering functions in the coming time.

To conclude, the contemporary technological race has engendered multifaceted fronts about resource access and supply, wherein competitive advantage emerges as a pivotal determinant of influence and power, with geography assuming a central role in international dynamics. The confluence of the pandemic and the Ukrainian conflict has precipitated a global surge in governments' pursuit of enhanced strategic autonomy. China's pre-eminence in processing critical resources, notably rare-earth elements indispensable to the technological race, juxtaposed against the substantial reliance of other powers on these reserves, has catalysed geopolitical tensions, intensified competition, and fostered cooperative initiatives among allies and partners. Notably, strategic autonomy transcends technology, concurrently sparking deliberations regarding ethical and environmental considerations vis-à-vis resource access and exploitation.

Technology has become a potent tool for governments worldwide to assume proactive roles in governance paradigms. Democracies, in particular, are grappling with heightened scrutiny and criticism concerning technology's (mis)utilisation, exacerbated by the proliferation of internal and external disinformation campaigns and cybersecurity threats. Conversely, authoritarian regimes leverage technology to consolidate control, survey civilian populations, and infringe upon both human and digital rights.

Governments, civil society entities, and the private sector assume pivotal roles in safeguarding against burgeoning cybersecurity threats and addressing the ethical controversies surrounding technology firms and non-state actors, encompassing illegal data exploitation, surveillance practices, and electoral interference. The escalating contest for digital global governability between divergent models portends heightened geopolitical tensions. The strategic rivalry between the United States and China precipitates global political and trade fragmentation. Both nations promote self-sufficiency, mitigate vulnerabilities, and pursue sectoral decoupling within their technological domains. While avenues for cooperative engagement on shared global challenges endure, the conflict in the technological and digital domains remains fraught with the risk of further escalation. This protracted conflict is poised to entangle additional stakeholders, necessitating a delicate equilibrium amidst the intricate global interconnections, particularly within the technological arena.

Notes

1. Zahid, Fatima Binte (2023), "Digital Domination: How technology is reshaping the geopolitical landscape". Bangladesh Institute of Peace and Security Studies. Accessed from: https://bipss.org.bd/pdf/Digital%20Domination-%20How%20Technology%20is%20Reshaping%20the%20Geopolitical%20Landscape.pdf.
2. Konrad, Kai A. (2024), "Dominance and technology war", *European Journal of Political Economy*, 81. Accessed from: https://doi.org/10.1016/j.ejpoleco.2023.102493.
3. Rajagopalan, Rajeswari Pillai (ed.), "Future warfare and technology: Issues and strategies", *ORF*. Accessed from: https://www.orfonline.org/wp-content/uploads/2022/11/GP-ORF-Future-Warfare-and-Technology-01.pdf.
4. Kallberg, Jan (2018), "Cyber espionage in an era of abundant data". In Warf, Barney. (ed.) *The SAGE Encyclopaedia of The Internet*. Sage.
5. Ünver, H. A. (2018), *Politics of Digital Surveillance, National Security and Privacy*. Centre for Economics and Foreign Policy Studies. Accessed from: http://www.jstor.org/stable/resrep17009.
6. Daalen, OL Van (2023), "The right to encryption: Privacy as preventing unlawful access", *Computer Law & Security Review*, 49. Accessed from: https://www.sciencedirect.com/science/article/pii/S0267364923000146.
7. Rajagopalan, Rajeswari Pillai (ed.), "Future warfare and critical technologies: Evolving tactics and strategies", *ORF*. Accessed from https://www.orfonline.org/public/uploads/posts/pdf/20240212113627.pdf.
8. Hoffman, Frank G. (2007), "Conflict in the 21st century: The rise of hybrid wars". Potomac Institute for Policy Studies. Accessed from: https://www.potomacinstitute.org/images/stories/publications/potomac_hybridwar_0108.pdf.
9. Li, Y. & Liu, Q. (2021), "A comprehensive review study of cyber-attacks and cyber security; Emerging trends and recent developments", *Energy Reports*, 7, pp. 8176–8186. Accessed from: https://doi.org/10.1016/j.egyr.2021.08.126.
10. Litchfield, I. S. (2024), "The Digital Battleground of 21st Century", *Medium*. Accessed from: https://medium.com/@irinalitchfield/the-digital-battleground-of-21st-century-230f07c5985f.

11. Mueller, G. B., Jensen, B., Valeriano, B., Maness, R. C., & Macias, J. M. (2024), "Cyber Operations during the Russo-Ukrainian War", *CSIS*. Accessed from: https://www.csis.org/analysis/cyber-operations-during-russo-ukrainian-war.
12. Lewis, J. A. (2022), "Technology and the shifting balance of power", *CSIS*. Accessed from: https://www.csis.org/analysis/technology-and-shifting-balance-power.
13. Hogeveen, Bart (2023), "The future of cyber warfare in the Indo-Pacific", *ORF*. Accessed from: https://www.orfonline.org/research/the-future-of-cyber-warfare-in-the-indo-pacific.
14. Mehta, Anil & Prakash, Anjal (2023) ,"The geopolitical race for resources: Navigating a path to a successful energy transition", *Forbes*. Accessed from: https://www.forbesindia.com/article/isbinsight/the-geopolitical-race-for-resources-navigating-the-path-to-a-successful-energy-transition/86327/1.
15. Goes, Carlos & Bekkers, Eddy (2023), "The impact of geopolitical conflicts on trade, growth, and innovation". World Trade Organisation.
16. Berndt, C. (2001), *Corporate Germany between globalization and regional place dependence: business restructuring in the Ruhr area*. Springer.
17. Javaid, M., Haleem, A., Singh, R. P., Suman, R., & Gonzalez, E. S. (2022), "Understanding the adoption of Industry 4.0 technologies in improving environmental sustainability", *Sustainable Operations and Computers*, *3*, pp. 203-217.
18. Siengchin, S. (2023), "A review on lightweight materials for defence applications: A present and future developments", *Defence Technology*.
19. Balaram, V. (2019), "Rare earth elements: a review of applications, occurrence, exploration, analysis, recycling, and environmental impact", *Geoscience Frontiers*. 10, pp. 1285–1303.
20. ORF (2022), "China's scramble for Africa's rare earth elements", *ORF*. Accessed from: https://www.orfonline.org/expert-speak/chinas-scramble-for-africas-rare-earth-elements.
21. Hiebert, Kyle (2023), "The fight over critical minerals has just begun". Centre for International Governance Innovation. Accessed from: https://www.cigionline.org/articles/the-fight-over-critical-minerals-has-just-begun/.
22. Dwivedi, Y. K., Hughes, L., Kar, A. K., Baabdullah, A. M., Grover, P., Abbas, R., ... & Wade, M. (2022). "Climate change and COP26: Are digital technologies and information management part of the problem or the solution? An editorial reflection and call to action", *International Journal of Information Management*, *63*, 102456.
23. Cuffley, A. (2024), "Ukraine war ushers in a new bipolar world led by the US and China". Stimson Center. Accessed from: https://www.stimson.org/2023/ukraine-war-ushers-in-a-new-bipolar-world-led-by-the-us-and-china/.

24. Bateman, J. (2022),"US-China technological "decoupling": A strategy and policy framework". Carnegie. Accessed from: https://carnegieendowment.org/research/2022/04/us-china-technological-decoupling-a-strategy-and-policy-framework?lang=en.
25. Ruhlig, Tim (2023), "The sources of China's innovativeness", *DGAP*. Accessed from: https://dgap.org/en/research/publications/sources-chinas-innovativeness.
26. Allen, G. C. (2024),*China's new strategy for waging the microchip tech war*. CSIS. Accessed from: https://www.csis.org/analysis/chinas-new-strategy-waging-microchip-tech-war.
27. Chong, J. I., Hsu, S., Daniels, R., Hargis, S., & Lee, J. (2023), "Finding Firmer Ground: The Role of High Technology in US-China Relations". The Carter Center. Accessed from: https://www.cartercenter.org/resources/pdfs/peace/china/finding-firmer-ground-the-role-of-high-technology-in-u.s.-china-relations.pdf.
28. SKAGGS, R. D., CHUKAEW, N., & STEPHENS, J. (2024), "Characterizing Chinese Influence in Thailand", *Journal of Indo-Pacific Affairs*, 7(1). Accessed from: https://www.airuniversity.af.edu/JIPA/Display/Article/3606690/characterizing-chinese-influence-in-thailand/.
29. Yasuyuki, Todo (2023), "Japan's supply chains at risk: Preparing for a Taiwan contingency". nippon.com. Accessed from: https://www.nippon.com/en/in-depth/d00907/.
30. Aoyama, R. (2023), "Stability and Fragility in Japan-China Relations: China's Pivotal Power and Japan's Strategic Leverage", *China Review, 23*(1), pp. 187–211. Accessed from: https://www.jstor.org/stable/48717993.
31. Wu, X. (2020), "Technology, power, and uncontrolled great power strategic competition between China and the United States", *China International Strategy Review, 2*(1), pp. 99-119.
32. Pant, Himani (2023), "Russia-China relations and a changing world order". Indian Council of World Affairs. Accessed from: https://icwa.in/pdfs/SHPRussiaChinaRelations.pdf.
33. Liu, F. (2023), "Russia's "Turn to the East" Policy: Evolution and Assessment", *Chinese Journal of Slavic Studies*,3 (2). Accessed from: https://www.degruyter.com/document/doi/10.1515/cjss-2023-0020/html?lang=en.
34. Larson, D. W. (2019), "Status competition among Russia, India, and China in clubs: a source of stalemate or innovation in global governance", *Contemporary Politics, 25*(5), pp. 549-566.
35. Khanal, S., Zhang, H., & Taeihagh, A. (2024), "Why and how is the power of Big Tech increasing in the policy process? The case of generative AI", *Policy and Society*. Accessed from: https://academic.oup.com/policyandsociety/advance-article/doi/10.1093/polsoc/puae012/7636223?login=false.

36. Gu, H. (2023), "Data, big tech, and the new concept of sovereignty", *Journal of Chinese Political Science.* Accessed from: https://link.springer.com/article/10.1007/s11366-023-09855-1#citeas.
37. Birch, K. & Bronson, K. (2022), "Big tech", *Science as Culture,* 31(1), pp. 1-14. Accessed from: https://www.tandfonline.com/doi/full/10.1080/09505431.2022.2036118.
38. Kavanagh, Camino (2019), "New tech, new threats, and new governance challenges: an opportunity to craft smarter responses?" Carnegie. Accessed from: https://carnegieendowment.org/research/2019/08/new-tech-new-threats-and-new-governance-challenges-an-opportunity-to-craft-smarter-responses?lang=en.
39. Quach, S., Thaichon, P., Martin, K. D., Weaven, S., & Palmatier, R. W. (2022), "Digital technologies: Tensions in privacy and data", *Journal of the Academy of Marketing Science, 50*(6), pp. 1299-1323.
40. Atske, S. & Atske, S. (April 14, 2024). *Experts say the 'New normal' in 2025 will be far more Tech-Driven, presenting more big challenges.* Pew Research Center. Accessed from: https://www.pewresearch.org/internet/2021/02/18/experts-say-the-new-normal-in-2025-will-be-far-more-tech-driven-presenting-more-big-challenges/.
41. Ciuriák, D. (March 5, 2018), "The Economics of Data: Implications for the Data-driven economy". Centre for International Governance Innovation. Accessed from: https://www.cigionline.org/articles/economics-data-implications-data-driven-economy/.
42. Gill, S. S., Wu, H., Patros, P., Ottaviani, C., Arora, P., Pujol, V. C., ... & Buyya, R. (2024), "Modern computing: Vision and challenges", *Telematics and Informatics Reports,* 100116.
43. Verhoef, P. C., Broekhuizen, T., Bart, Y., Bhattacharya, A., Dong, J. Q., Fabian, N., & Haenlein, M. (2021), "Digital transformation: A multidisciplinary reflection and research agenda", *Journal of Business Research, 122,* pp. 889-901.
44. Hopster, J. (2021), "What are socially disruptive technologies?", *Technology in Society, 67,* 101750.
45. John, Wilson (2023), "Intelligence agencies in India: Need for a public interface". *ORF.* Accessed from: https://www.orfonline.org/research/intelligence-agencies-in-india-need-for-a-public-interface.
46. Rovner, Joshua (2022), "Spies as agents of peace", *Engelsberg Ideas.* Accessed from: https://engelsbergideas.com/essays/spies-as-agents-of-peace/.
47. Kavanagh, Camino (2019), "New tech, new threats, and new governance challenges: an opportunity to craft smarter responses?" Carnegie. Accessed from: https://carnegieendowment.org/research/2019/08/new-tech-new-

threats-and-new-governance-challenges-an-opportunity-to-craft-smarter-responses?lang=en.

48. Sun, N., Ding, M., Jiang, J., Xu, W., Mo, X., Tai, Y., & Zhang, J. (2023), "Cyber threat intelligence mining for proactive cybersecurity defense: a survey and new perspectives", *IEEE Communications Surveys & Tutorials*, 25 (3).
49. Quach, S., Thaichon, P., Martin, K. D., Weaven, S., & Palmatier, R. W. (2022), "Digital technologies: Tensions in privacy and data", *Journal of the Academy of Marketing Science, 50*(6), pp. 1299-1323.
50. Luo, Y. (2022), "A general framework of digitization risks in international business", *Journal of International Business Studies, 53*(2), pp. 344-361.
51. Vial, G. (2021), "Understanding digital transformation: A review and a research agenda", *Managing digital transformation*, pp. 13-66.
52. Tung, R. L., Zander, I., & Fang, T. (2023), "The Tech Cold War, the multipolarization of the world economy, and IB research", *International Business Review*, 102195.
53. Kitchen, K. (2024), "The New Superpowers: How and Why the Tech Industry is Shaping the International System", *National Affairs*. Accessed from: https://nationalaffairs.com/the-new-superpowers-how-and-why-the-tech-industry-is-shaping-the-international-system.
54. Raymond, P. D. (2023), "Re-platformed Planet?: Implications of the Rise and Spread of Chinese Platform Technologies". Center for Strategic and International Studies. Accessed from: http://www.jstor.org/stable/resrep48723.
55. Prakash, A. (February 20, 2024), "How technology companies are shaping the Ukraine conflict", *Scientific American*. Accessed from:https://www.scientificamerican.com/article/how-technology-companies-are-shaping-the-ukraine-conflict/.
56. Walt, S. M. (2021), "Big tech won't remake the global order", *Foreign Policy*. Accessed from: https://foreignpolicy.com/2021/11/08/big-tech-wont-remake-the-global-order/.
57. Wu, X. (2020), "Technology, power, and uncontrolled great power strategic competition between China and the United States", *China International Strategy Review, 2*(1), pp. 99-119.
58. Alfredo, Toro Hardy (2020), "The technological contest between China and the United States",*Global Labour Organisation*. Accessed from: https://www.econstor.eu/bitstream/10419/215885/1/GLO-DP-0521.pdf.
59. Schindler, S., Alami, I., DiCarlo, J., Jepson, N., Rolf, S., Bayırbağ, M. K., … & Zhao, Y. (2023), "The Second Cold War: US-China Competition for Centrality in Infrastructure, Digital, Production, and Finance Networks", *Geopolitics*, pp. 1-38.

60. Salomons, B. (2023), "The Dutch East India Company was richer than Apple, Google, and Facebook combined",*DutchReview*. Accessed from: https://dutchreview.com/culture/history/how-rich-was-the-dutch-east-india-company/.
61. Bremmer, I. (2024), "The Technopolar Moment: How digital powers will reshape the global order", *Foreign Affairs*. Accessed from: https://www.foreignaffairs.com/articles/world/2021-10-19/ian-bremmer-big-tech-global-order.
62. Schindler, S., Alami, I., DiCarlo, J., Jepson, N., Rolf, S., Bayırbağ, M. K., ... & Zhao, Y. (2023), "The Second Cold War: US-China Competition for Centrality in Infrastructure, Digital, Production, and Finance Networks", *Geopolitics*, pp. 1-38.
63. Luo, Y. & Van Assche, A. (2023), "The rise of techno-geopolitical uncertainty: Implications of the United States CHIPS and Science Act", *Journal of International Business Studies*, *54*(8), pp. 1423-1440.
64. IKENBERRY, G. J. (2001), "American power and the empire of capitalist democracy", *Review of International Studies*, *27*, pp. 191–212. Accessed from: http://www.jstor.org/stable/45299510.
65. Goswami, N. (2023), "China prioritizes 3 strategic technologies in its great power competition", *The Diplomat*. Accessed from: https://thediplomat.com/2023/04/china-prioritizes-3-strategic-technologies-in-its-great-power-competition/.
66. Hemmings, J. (2020), "Reconstructing Order: The Geopolitical Risks in China's Digital Silk Road", *Asia Policy*, *15*(1), pp. 5–22. Accessed from: https://www.jstor.org/stable/26891385.
67. Bradford, A. (2023),*Digital Empires*. Oxford University Press.
68. Allam, Z., Bibri, S. E., & Sharpe, S. (2022), "The rising impacts of the COVID-19 pandemic and the Russia–Ukraine war: energy transition, climate justice, global inequality, and supply chain disruption", *Resources*, *11*(11), p. 99. Accessed from: https://doi.org/10.3390/resources11110099.
69. Edler, J., Blind, K., Kroll, H., & Schubert, T. (2023), "Technology sovereignty as an emerging frame for innovation policy. Defining rationales, ends and means", *Research Policy*, *52*(6), 104765.
70. Zandee, Dick; Deen, Bob; Kruijver, Kimberly & Stoetman, Adaja (2020), "European strategic autonomy in security and defence",*Clingendael*. Accessed from: https://www.clingendael.org/sites/default/files/2020-12/Report_European_Strategic_Autonomy_December_2020.pdf.

8

Economic Warfare as a Component of Geoeconomic Strategy in the Global Geopolitical Transformation

Greg Simons

Introduction

There is a great deal of increasing competition and conflict among the political actors in 21st-century international relations, which is driven by the ongoing transformation in the global geopolitical order away from the unipolar Global North (Western-centric) towards the multipolar Global South (non-Western centric) order (Kissinger, 2015; Cooley & Nexon, 2020; Short, 2022). Geopolitics, in its practical sense and application, concerns the management and regulation of power and relationships among different actors and the balance of power (Flint, 2017). It not only involves and invokes grand strategy in the world of power politics in international relations of hegemonic maintenance or expansion by the incumbent power but also the challenging of the hegemonic power or defence of self-interest and autonomy.

To support geopolitical imperatives, geoeconomics can and should play a supportive role, by assisting in the realisation of an actor's power and influence projection and accumulation (Simons, 2024). Therefore, geoeconomics plays a subordinate role to geopolitics. A subset of geoeconomics is economic warfare, which is intended to play a disruptive role in the process of obstructing an opponent's or competitor's realisation of power and self-interest. Economic warfare is a concept and practice that is shrouded in fanciful myth and mystique concerning its presumed power and effectiveness, where the mere invocation of its potential use is intended to intimidate the intended victim. Just how effective is economic warfare and who are the participants using it as a key tool in foreign policy statecraft?

There are a total of five sections in this chapter, which are intended to incrementally reveal the answers to the questions that are posed above. The first section concerns an overview of 21st century international relations, the contemporary trends and processes. In the second section, the definition and application of geopolitics and geoeconomics, as well as the relationship and interaction between these elements is discussed. The third section moves to defining economic warfare as a theoretical concept and a practical and political operationalised practice. The fourth section outlines the method used in this chapter. In the final section, selected literature on economic warfare in the 21st century involving the United States and China is presented, interpreted, and analysed.

21st Century International Relations and the Geopolitical Transformation

In 1991, the Cold War- era bipolar global order of the United States versus the Soviet Union came to an official end with the collapse of the Soviet Union, which ushered in an era of the Western-centric United States unipolar order. It marked the presumption of the so-called end of history as US economic and military power was in an absolute hegemonic state, and Western liberal democracy dominated political ideology, both in strong and uncontested states of global influence and power. However, as the 21st century has progressed and without any form of checks and balances that existed in the Cold War, the US has squandered its hard and soft power assets more and more with increasingly reckless and risky foreign and security policy. Kissinger (2015) noted that various fundamental errors of judgement have been made as the US-led West has created and followed a more messianic and zealous ideological approach to 21st century international relations. The possible result predicted by Kissinger was the decline of US resources of global power and influence and an impetus to other international actors to hedge against risks and threats posed by this ideological turn. It was a trend and process that would threaten the viability of the Global North's hegemony and encourage the Global South's more independent trajectory, which is the Global South's distinction for being a subject or an object in international relations.

At this point in time, there is a good level of consensus on the trend of the Global North's relative hegemonic decline. The split and disagreement are found in the answer to the question as to whether this relative decline is stoppable or not. Brooks and Wohlforth (2016) argue that the decline is reversible given enough political will and a significant change in policy approach. Kissinger (2015) had also warned of the urgent need to change policy to salvage US power and influence. However, Cooley and Nexon (2020) posited that the US needed to plan and manage its relative decline to minimise encountered risks and hazards, because the decline was seemingly irreversible. This stage of international relations creates a geopolitical environment that motivates an increase in competition and conflict among actors as they seek to position themselves in an evolving geopolitical order to maximise their interests that are articulated through foreign and security policy goals.

Geopolitics and Geoeconomics: Definitions and Relations

Even if the substance and intent of great power politics in 21st-century international relations is obscured or obfuscated as concerning the spread of humanitarian and benevolent values, I am concerned with the exercise of raw power in the pursuit of what is defined as being self interest and security by the actor concerned. This is the core of the theory of realism, which defines the world as a dangerous and insecure place, where influence and power are used to defend (and expand) the self-interest and security of states (Dunne, Kurki & Smith, 2007, p. 339; Smith, Hadfield & Dunne, 2008, pp. 396-397; Roselle, Spray,& Shelton, 2020, p. 16). This leads us to the theory of geopolitics and more inclined towards the branch of classical geopolitics that concerns the pursuit and projection of power and influence in international relations.

Flint (2017) defines geopolitics as "the struggle over the control of geographical entities with an international and global dimension, and the use of geographical entities for political advantage" (p. 16). It concerns, in purely pragmatic and practical terms, the regulation of power and influence among different actors over the constraints of time and physical space. Geopolitics is the intellectual conceptual space to systematise and legitimise foreign policy words and actions by actors (Flint, 2017; Simons, 2022). Geopolitics, in terms of its definitions and operationalisation, becomes even more contested when the entire system is in a state of flux owing to the geopolitical transformation away from the hegemony of the unipolar order of the US-led Global North towards the multipolar order of the Global South (Klieman, 2015; Short, 2022; Baykov & Shakleina, 2023). The US is no longer an absolute hegemon given the relative decline of its power and influence, but this does not mean that it is not ready to contest its relative decline. The most hazardous moment for an actor is in the period of transformation of the international order, as to be able to secure their self-interest and strategic autonomy, they need to remain a subject of international relations and not be rendered an object of events.

People tend to gravitate towards the desire for peace, even if this is achieved through competition and/or conflict between states. A means of achieving the desired 'peace' is through the construction of a hegemonic order (Jiang, 2023, p. xxxvii). Hence,periods of relative peace and stability, each associated with a dominant global power that is misunderstood as peace—*Pax Romana*, *Pax Britannica* and *Pax Americana*. But whose peace is this in reality? It is certainly not of those peoples coerced or occupied, which gives context to the current competition and conflict around the construction of a new order. One way to do this is through geoeconomic means to support the geopolitical imperatives.

Geoeconomics is not a singular approach but rather shares several ideas that concern the perception that economic conditions influence, shape, and cause political events. Competition for access to resources that bestow economic advantage can therefore lead to conflict, either in the form of kinetic or non-kinetic warfare (Flint, 2017, pp. 6-7; Vihma, 2018, pp. 47-49). Actors can be drawn from a wide variety of backgrounds in public and private institutions and entities (Csurgai, 2018). The objectives can be manifold within the geoeconomic frame, either to secure the economic resources for oneself and/or to deny another actor access to those economic resources. Either way, it concerns the elements of accumulating power and the active pursuit of self-interest. The creation of alternative (i.e., not controlled by the Global North) global institutional structures, such as BRICS and the Belt Road Initiative, are expressions of geoeconomic hedging to secure self-interest and resources of power from obstructive and disruptive practices of the Global North on the Global South.

Economic Warfare: Definition, Practice, Politics, and Presumptions

There is a great deal more agreement and time spent on academic discussions on the matter of understanding the politics and practice of economic warfare than in defining it in a dry theoretical manner. For the sake of this chapter, "Economic warfare, (is) the use of, or the threat to use, economic means against a country in order to weaken its economy and thereby reduce its political and military power" (Shambaugh, 2023). It is as much about the threat to use economic warfare as in actually immediately using it, which is linked to the cognitive-psychological dimension of its presumed destructive effects on the potential victim.

Economic warfare as a practice is as old as organised human communities and is used in both times of peace and times of war. In times of peace, the intention is to coerce an opponent into a line of thinking or behaviour that they would not otherwise take. It can be used to contain an opponent without resorting to the use of kinetic warfare. However, in times of war, economic warfare intends to weaken and degrade the capability and capacity of an enemy to wage war and can involve the use of kinetic warfare (Bidwell, 1942; Wolfson, 1985; Lowe &Tzanakopoulos, 2012; Clemens, 2013; Spiro, 2023). Economic warfare is very much a political weapon using economic means, which should ideally be linked to the user's geoeconomic strategies that are, in turn, helping to support and realise geopolitical objectives that are imbued in the realism of maximising self-interest and power accumulation in international relations.

Actors that are involved in economic warfare include state and non-state actors, governmental and private entities, and their involvement can be as a subject or as an object of the events. Sanctions can be threatened and used by powerful global state actors as a means of intimidating and coercing state and non-state actors to abide by their dictates, which can seem to be a form of almost random collective punishment. However, this does not mean that this form of economic warfare in peacetime is not anticipated or hedged against by other actors. It can also lead to actions that can cause financial pain to the initiator of the sanctions and those that become obedient objects of the game. The victim and other subjects of international relations will work on creating and maintaining resilience through such strategies as economic diversification and even counter-economic warfare (Wenhong, 2023). Furthermore, economic warfare can bring unpredictable or unanticipated results, depending on the importance attached to the policy or action they are being punished for. When the US placed a then peacetime oil and rubber embargo on Japan for its actions in China, it did not stop the Japanese from concluding that they needed to militarily attack the US to secure their self-interest and power.

There are a few prevailing myths and presumptions concerning the effectiveness of economic warfare. The credibility of economic warfare as a means of influencing the thinking and behaviour of target audiences that benefits the attacker is rooted in trying to establish the façade of belief in the plausibility of the threat being an effective instrument of coercive statecraft and that it is likely to be used. Law makers and practitioners think and behave in a manner that is influenced by what they believe to be true and not necessarily what is physically and objectively true, which directly impacts operational choices and decisions. When miscalculations in operationalising economic warfare are made, especially on a large scale, the results can be catastrophic for the attacking party and the actors that are the objects of the attack. It also may not have the intended and anticipated psychological and physical effects on the victim. The current Ukraine War is an excellent example of this, as Russia,being the most sanctioned country in the world, its economy continues to grow. In contrast, the European Union countries, as the US objects, have devastated and deindustrialised their economies so far.The US does not change its course despite its abject failures in applying economic warfare that has self-inflicted very high economic and political costs (Khudaykulova, Yuanqiong & Khudaykulov, 2022). The US has become increasingly reliant on the use of sanctions, which are specifically used as a means of coercing another actor to do as Washington demands.However, it has an abysmal record of success, and yet, the economic warfare choice of sanctions has not changed or adjusted to its failure to yield intended foreign policy results (Drezner, 2021). A form of tunnel vision is created by a political echo chamber, where the politics of façade demanding the appearance of something being done as a measure of activity rather than a measure of effect takes politicised policy precedence.

Method: Literature Review

The data set to be analysed and interpreted shall be drawn from open-source academic texts. Those texts shall be subjected to discourse analysis that employs the method of conversation analysis, which focuses upon aspects such as orderliness, cohesion, and coherence of the academic texts (Franklin et al., 2011, pp. 61-62). For the purposes of this chapter, a qualitative approach to interpretation and analysis of the selected literature has been adopted. There are several reasons for adopting this approach, which enables the phenomena to be described in context and facilitates the interpretation of processes or meanings using theoretically-based concepts to seek understanding. To achieve this search for meaning, words are used, there is a focus on meanings and the use of cases (Silverman, 2020, pp. 6-7). These tools were applied to a pool of academic journal articles, and details about the gathering of the sample are given below.

Literature shall be drawn from a limited period of time from President Obama's invocation of the geopolitical Asia Pivot (2011) that marked an overt geostrategic intention to contain China's global rise and President Xi's declaration of the geoeconomic Belt Road Initiative (2013) that marked China's intention of a global rise. A search was conducted on Google Scholar using the search terms "economic warfare + United States + China" in the period from the year 2011. This generated about 18,300 results, which were checked manually for key words and, therefore, relevance for the chapter on the first 20 pages of results. A total of 25 articles were gathered for analysis in the following section.

Actors, Actions, and Goals: Us-China Economic Warfare in the 21st Century

As a background and context for the increasing level of competition and conflict between the United States and China, authors have noted this to be driven by strategic competition between the two powers (Buszynski, 2012; Nye, 2015, 2017; Minghao, 2019; Zhang et al., 2019). It is also a political climate and environment that can escalate and is reaching the point where the geopolitical brand of a 'New Cold War' is being invoked by some researchers and observers of the geopolitical and geoeconomic events that are unfolding (Minghao, 2019). China is perceived as closing the gap in national power capability and capacity of the United States, especially in terms of rivalry in the areas of technology and economics, while the US seeks to maintain its global primacy (Beckley, 2011; Clinton, 2011; Brooks & Wohlforth, 2015; Minghao,

2019; Lippert & Perthes, 2020). This is further exacerbated by contradictions in terms of the ideological position of the state and the independence of Chinese foreign policy that clashes with US foreign policy aims (Johnston, 2013; Mead, 2014; Minghao, 2019). The US geostrategic goal is to weaken and contain China, and the Chinese goal is to continue its global rise while hedging and circumventing US moves (Schweller & Pu, 2011; Campbell & Ratner, 2018; Minghao, 2019; Zhang et al., 2019).

The phenomena of sanctions and tariffs are becoming highly routine and standard elements of US foreign policy, which are used to, firstly, intimidate a target country with the threat of use, and secondly, as a means of attempting to devastate the economy of the target. They are intended to create an uneven economic playing and by default, uphold US global primacy. However, there is a miscalculation in the West as to the effectiveness of such mechanisms of economic warfare. Although the US may possess some economic advantages in bargaining and coercion over other members of the international community, it is a country that is experiencing relative hard power decline and economic shocks, and the gap in terms of costs over gains is reduced in the event of China as a power on the rise of attaching greater strategic value that geo-economic situation permits them to absorb the initial costs and if they retaliate, the costs for the US are increased (Layne, 2012; Li, He, Lin, 2018; Kwan, 2020; Sasongko, Bawono & Prabowo, 2021; Bown & Kolb, 2022). There is also the issue of 'collateral' damage to other countries in the global economy, which will react to insulate themselves against US economic warfare and its direct and indirect effects, not to mention the likely corrosive effect on what little remains of US global soft power and reputational brand.

There are various actors involved on each side in the tit-for-tat economic warfare between the US and China, both public and private entities, acting as subjects with their own interests and objectives or objects being manipulated and coerced. Researchers created a concept that tries to make sense (rational logic) of state-business interaction and cooperation, which they have termed 'state platform capitalism'.

> The concentration of global business power within two states, combined with the increasing capacity for these states to leverage and direct platform

> activities for their own geopolitical—economic ends, has catalysed the rise of 'state platform capitalism' [...] Beijing and Washington instrumentalise and mobilise domestic platform firms in pursuit of geopolitical—economic objectives, while platforms become increasingly interdependent with their home state institutions. Competition in the global political economy is increasingly centred on the recruitment of users and nations to these rival state-platform nexuses (national 'stacks') as a means of establishing and exercising extraterritorial economic and political power (Rolf & Schindler, 2023, p. 1255).

Therefore, domestic political and business considerations influence the nature and quality of relations between the state and private enterprise, and especially, in times of tension and conflict. The US and China both have a form of capitalist market economy, although they are far from being identical in nature and outlook. "Sino-capitalism therefore represents an emerging system of global capitalism centred on China that is producing a dynamic mix of mutual dependence, symbiosis, competition, and friction with the still dominant Anglo-American model of capitalism" (McNally, 2012, p. 741). One of the interests that the US Biden administration wanted to protect to ensure continued global primacy is the high-tech sector, and especially, microchip and semiconductor development and production, which is linked to the notion of the current fourth industrial revolution that is being experienced globally, where knowledge and high tech are considered strategic assets for global hegemony.

It has been noted that in the context of the US economic war against China, "US policymakers turned to a legally complex set of export restrictions targeting the semiconductor supply chain in the attempt to safeguard critical infrastructure in the telecommunications sector. The potentially far-reaching tactics included weaponisation of exports by relatively small but highly specialized American software service and equipment providers in order to constrain Huawei" (Bown, 2020). This incentivises China (and other actors) to develop their own high-tech industry and become self-sufficient, which is in the interests of both the state and private business. This is a clear example of the necessity to be a subject of international relations and not a mere object of it, given the various costs and threats to strategic autonomy, the ability to pursue self-interest, and the erosion of national power (together with the corrosive effects on national capabilities and capacities of power and influence projection).

Conclusion

Two related and interlinked questions were posed in the beginning of this chapter—just how effective is economic warfare and who are the participants using it as a key tool in foreign policy statecraft? The intention and the tools of economic warfare that are applied differ, depending on whether the context is in peacetime or in wartime. This chapter is primarily focused on the period of 'cold peace' that is sometimes referred to as being the 'New Cold War'. This is the result of increased global geopolitical tensions that lead to elevated competition and conflict between the Global North (US is the example used in this chapter) and the Global South (China as the example) from the transformation that is taking place. The stakes are high for both sides, which employ geoeconomic measures and countermeasures to support their own geopolitical goals and objectives and to deny their opponent from achieving the same. It is deeply rooted in realism, which concerns the maximising and pursuit of power and self-interest. US self-interest and pursuit of power is focused on attempting to preserve its global hegemonic status and to obstruct China's rise, primarily by means of economic warfare. China's self-interest and pursuit of power is focused upon maintaining its continued global rise and preventing the US from obstructing it, making use of geoeconomic projects, such as the Belt Road Initiative and BRICS, to continue its growth and hedge against US actions. Additionally, China makes use of retaliatory economic warfare to deter the US by increasing the economic and political costs of the latter's economic warfare campaign against China. The seemingly favourite tools of economic warfare used include the traditional obstructive means, such as the use of embargoes, sanctions and/or imposition of tariffs to create an uneven playing field that favours the hegemon and disrupts the challenger.

Although the primary driving force of economic warfare is sourced from the executive and legislative branches of government in the US and China, which is based upon the concerns of geostrategic imperatives rooted in realism, it is not limited to them. Although governments and parliaments are often the public face of the foreign policy words and actions of the tit-for-tat economic warfare, there are also actively involved diverse groups of interests and organisations that seek to cooperate and interact on the basis of collective self-interest or the pursuit of power and influence in the political and/or economic outcome. The various actors, whether state or non-state, may be either subjects of the events (actively driving events) or objects of the events (passively driven by events). Interestingly, although the perception and reputation of the threat of invoking economic warfare can strike fear in the hearts of the intended victims and target, it is far from being an effective (in terms of meeting the stated political goals and objectives) strategy and is rather unpredictable owing to the basic fact that the effects are not unidirectional and can (and will) affect the attacker, too. In spite of this fact and track record, great powers,such as the US, continue to use (and even increase the use and application of) economic warfare. This is seemingly rooted in the informational-cognitive domain of façade politics, where politicians are being seen to be decisive and proactive in addressing a foreign policy issue whose effectiveness is measured in the presence of activity and not the substance of effect.

References

Baykov, A. & Shakleina, T. (2023), *Polycentric world order in the making*. Singapore: Palgrave Macmillan.

Beckley, M. (2011), "China's century? Why America's edge will endure", *International security*, 36(3), pp. 41-78.

Bidwell, P. W. (1942), "Our economic warfare", *Foreign Affairs*, 20(3), pp. 421–437. https://doi.org/10.2307/20029165

Bown, C. P. & Kolb, M. (2022), "Trump's trade war timeline: An up-to-date guide".

Bown, C. P. (2020), "How the United States marched the semiconductor industry into its trade war with China", *East Asian Economic Review*, 24(4), pp. 349-388.

Brooks, S. G. & Wohlforth, W. C. (2015), "The rise and fall of the great powers in the twenty-first century: China's rise and the fate of America's global position", *International Security*, 40(3), pp. 7-53.

Brooks, S.G. & Wohlforth, W.C. (2016), *America abroad: The United States' global role in the 21st century*. New York: Oxford University Press.

Buszynski, L. (2012), "The South China Sea: oil, maritime claims, and US–China strategic rivalry", *The Washington Quarterly*, 35(2), pp. 139-156.

Campbell, K. M. & Ratner, E. (2018), "The China reckoning: how Beijing defied American expectations", *Foreign Affairs*, 97, p. 60.

Clemens, J. (2013), "An analysis of economic warfare", *American Economic Review*, 103(3), pp. 523-527.

Clinton, H. (2011), "America's Pacific century", *Foreign policy*, (189), p. 56.

Cooley, A. & Nexon, D. (2020), *Exit from hegemony: The unravelling of the American global order*. New York: Oxford University Press.

Csurgai, G. (2018), "The increasing importance of geoeconomics in power rivalries in the twenty-first century", *Geopolitics*, 23(1), pp. 38-46. https://doi.org/10.1080/14650045.2017.1359547

Drezner, D. W. (2021), "The United States of sanctions: The use and abuse of economic coercion", *Foreign Aff.*, 100, p. 142.

Dunne, T., Kurki, M. & Smith, S. (2007), *International relations theories: Discipline and diversity*. Oxford: Oxford University Press.

Flint, C. (2017), *Introduction to geopolitics* (3rd ed.). London: Routledge.

Franklin, B., Hamer, M., Hanna, M., Kinsey, M.,& Richardson, J.E. (2011), *Key concepts in journalism studies*. London: Sage.

Jiang, P. (2023), *Geostrategic psychology and the rise of forbearance*. London: Routledge.

Johnston, A. I. (2013), "How new and assertive is China's new assertiveness?", *International Security*, 37(4), pp. 7-48.

Kissinger, H. (2015), *World order*. New York: Penguin Books.

Khudaykulova, M., Yuanqiong, H., & Khudaykulov, A. (2022), "Economic consequences and implications of the Ukraine-Russia war", *International Journal of Management Science and Business Administration*, 8(4), pp. 44-52.

Klieman, A. (Ed.) (2015), *Great powers and geopolitics: International affairs in a rebalancing world*. Cham (Switzerland): Springer.

Kwan, C. H. (2020), "The China–US trade war: Deep-rooted causes, shifting focus and uncertain prospects", *Asian Economic Policy Review*, 15(1), pp. 55-72.

Layne, C. (2012), "This time it's real: the end of unipolarity and the Pax Americana",*International Studies Quarterly*, 56(1), pp. 203-213.

Li, C., He, C., & Lin, C. (2018), "Economic impacts of the possible China–US trade war", *Emerging Markets Finance and Trade*, 54(7), pp. 1557-1577.

Lippert, B. & Perthes, V. (2020), "Strategic rivalry between United States and China: causes, trajectories, and implications for Europe". Politik-SWP-Deutsches.

Lowe, V. & Tzanakopoulos, A. (2012),*Economic warfare*.

McNally, C. A. (2012), "Sino-capitalism: China's reemergence and the international political economy", *World Politics*, 64(4), pp. 741-776.

Mead, W. R. (2014), "The return of geopolitics: The revenge of the revisionist powers", *Foreign Affairs*, 93, p. 69.

Minghao, Z. (2019), "Is a New Cold War inevitable? Chinese perspectives on US–China strategic competition", *The Chinese Journal of International Politics*, 12(3), Autumn, pp. 371–394, https://doi.org/10.1093/cjip/poz010

Nye Jr, J. S. (2017), "Will the liberal order survive: The history of an idea", *Foreign Affairs*, 96, p. 10.

Nye Jr, J. S. (2015), "Is the American century over?", *Political Science Quarterly*, 130(3), pp. 393-400.

Rolf, S. & Schindler, S. (2023), "The US–China rivalry and the emergence of state platform capitalism", *Environment and Planning A: Economy and Space*, 55(5), pp. 1255-1280.

Roselle, L., Spray, S.,& Shelton, J.T. (2020), *Research and writing in international relations* (3rd Ed.). London: Routledge.

Sasongko, B., Bawono, S., & Prabowo, B. H. (2021), "The economic performance of China in trade war: The case study of three global economic crises in 1997–2020". In *Environmental, Social, and Governance Perspectives on Economic Development in Asia*, pp. 1-11.

Schweller, R. L. & Pu, X. (2011), "After unipolarity: China's visions of international order in an era of US decline", *International Security*, 36(1), pp. 41-72.

Shambaugh, G. (Nov. 2, 2023), "Economic warfare". *Encyclopaedia Britannica*, https://www.britannica.com/topic/economic-warfare.

Short, J.R. (2022), *Geopolitics: Making sense of a changing world*. Lanham: Rowman & Littlefield.

Silverman, D. (2020), *Interpreting qualitative data*. London: Sage.

Simons, G. (2024), "BRICS and the geo-economic aspects of engineering a new global order", *TPQ*, 22(4), http://turkishpolicy.com/article/1245/brics-and-the-geo-economic-aspects-of-engineering-a-new-global-order.

Simons, G. (December 2022), "Brzezinski's geostrategic imperatives in a transforming global order", *Geostrategic Pulse*, no. 287, pp. 25-27.

Smith, S., Hadfield, A.,& Dunne, T. (2008), *Foreign policy: Theories, actors, cases*. Oxford: Oxford University Press.

Spiro, D. (2023), *Economic warfare*. Available at SSRN 4445359.

Vihma, A. (2018), "Geoeconomics defined and redefined", *Geopolitics*, 23(1), pp. 47–49. https://doi.org/10.1080/14650045.2017.1379010

Wenhong, X. (2023), "Dedollarization as a direction of Russia's financial policy in current conditions", *Studies on Russian Economic Development*, 34(1), pp. 9-18.

Wolfson, M. (1985), "Notes on economic warfare", *Conflict Management and Peace Science*, 8(2), pp. 1-19.

Zhang, D., Lei, L., Ji, Q., & Kutan, A. M. (2019), "Economic policy uncertainty in the US and China and their impact on the global markets", *Economic Modelling*, 79, pp. 47-56.

9

The Issue of Regulating 'Artificial Intelligence (AI)': Mapping the Division Between the Global South and North on Cyber Security

Simant Shankar Bharti
Saroj Kumar Aryal

Introduction: Understanding Issues of AI Regulation in International Relations

AI governance has become a key issue of governance and a setting agenda in international relations. There are various means to deploy AI in a harmful manner, such as the rise of cross-border data management, misuse, such as deep-fakes against popular leaders and protection under cyber security regulations, pushing for establishing an international institution is the way forward. Veale et al. (2023) argued that AI is silently popularising issues and actors across the world who also have been engaging in global governance regimes and demanding global policy attention in recent times (pp. 255-56). Similarly, Benizri (2023) also raises issues of AI development and deployment when approx. 350 AI experts penned a letter showing serious concern about AI-associated risks, especially on a societal-scale e.g., pandemics and nuclear war. Their further argument also shows that there is a requirement for international AI regulation concerning the 'lack of consensus among key players in both the private and public sectors'.

Before discussing more about AI regulations, we have to also understand the conceptual foundation of AI in international relations. What is AI, and why should we be concerned about it in international relations? AI is frequently used as an umbrella term for the numerous computational techniques in the area of machine intelligence, which include machine learning algorithms, neural networks, deep learning, natural language and speech processing, and computer vision, but are not limited to them. Technology has been a key component of hard power, such as economic and military, in international relations. AI systems are already beginning to produce non-human outputs, invading what was previously thought to be the domain of human cognition and creativity (Garcia, 2023). If we see it from a global perspective, AI evolved optimistically, and the Global South perceived it as a growing and significant challenge to national security (Srivastava, 2023, p. 77). The term 'Artificial Intelligence' is not a modern terminology, and it is frequently known as 'AI'. It originated at the 1956 Dartmouth Conference as a 'creation of machines' and 'capable of emulating intelligent behaviour' for 'task-specific activities' (McCarthy, Minsky, Rochester, & Shannon, 1955; Heng, Tsilionis, Scharff & Wautelet, 2022).

At one time, AI was mainly a computer science-dominated field in real-world applications, the rise of intelligent behaviour in artificial computational systems. On the one hand, AI helped to reduce time and increase efficiency of work, but on the other hand, it also raised issues of privacy and surveillance in changing data geopolitics, e.g., facial recognition data from users and manipulation of information online (Gehl Sampath, 2021). The ethical debate on AI- use brought forward questions about practical applications and also created concern regarding its misuse by radical and extremist hacker groups. The Global North is already concerned with all these issues, and it has adopted AI and digital regulation. For example, supranational organisations like the European Union (EU) have already adopted the General Data Protection Regulation (GDPR) 2018 concerning global digitalisation to protect private life, such as the privacy of personal information. It's 'the world's most stringent privacy and security law' (Bharti & Aryal, 2023, p. 1391). Finally, the EU's parliament also approved the 'Artificial Intelligence Act 2023', which is the world's major regulatory ground rule set to seal and govern the mediatised AI. Thierry Breton, the European Commissioner for Internal Markets, posted on X, "Europe is now a global standard-setter in AI." The President of the European Parliament, Roberta Metsola, referred to this regulation's feature as 'enabling innovation while safeguarding fundamental rights' (European Parliament, 2023; Gilchrist & Iordache, 2024).

Similarly, the US White House also issued a 'Blueprint for an AI Bill of Rights' in October 2022 that focuses on 'the importance of data privacy and protection against algorithmic discrimination'. Meanwhile, China already implemented (on August 15, 2023) its AI regulation regarding the use of generative AI to create text, pictures, audio, video, and other content available to the public within the country (Wang, 2023). Recent developments in AI regulations by all these governments' utilisation of AI maximise benefits and avoid any potential risks. Wang (2023) raised concerns about if these approaches can 'become a global AI government standard'; if not, then there is still a lack of global governance. The digital future of the Global South still has to struggle and lacks access to AI technology, which is only pushing towards being divided and fragmented due to a lack of resources.

Mapping the AI Divide: The Global North Vs the Global South

On one hand, the Global North achieved an AI regulatory framework to achieve benefits and avoid any serious threats, for example, in major advanced economies like the EU and the US. On the other hand, the Global South lacks the effort and capacity to develop intelligent neural networks to replicate human intelligence. In the area of global AI leadership and technological advancement, major powerful countries compete for this supremacy within the global AI governance framework. Other than countries from the Global North, only China is part of this competition (Wang, 2023). Likewise, there is an AI divide, especially centred on algorithmic biases, as well as the digital and infrastructure divide, in the Global South. A proper mapping of the AI divide needs to focus on where the Global North has already adopted AI regulations and where the global-level framework is still missing. Emerging regional powers from the Global South, like Brazil, India, Indonesia, Mexico, and South Africa, are also in this race, but their efforts are still not enthusiastic, and they have to conduct an assessment regarding this divide. The voice of the Global South is required for global governance of AI to provide benefits and to minimise risks.

Gehl Sampath (2021) presents AI's 'exemplified structural inequality' in Global South vs. North: 1) the increasing vulnerability of the user; 2) a disconnect in the data-led industrialisation narrative; 3) the rise of the "political" private sector because the national regulatory framework is viewed as a private sector regulation and historically has viewed this subject; and 4) the opacity of governments and a problem with several national initiatives. Srivastava (2023) links AI to national security with regard to safeguarding integrity, sovereignty, peace, and stability from a Global South perspective. Fundamentally, technology and the advancement of AI are also changing the nature of national defence and security. Machine learning and rapid innovation are constantly evolving, especially in quantum computing, robotics, space-based telecommunications, and military equipment. In this regard, today's security threats blur the traditional distinctions between different domains, such as land, sea, air, cyber, space, and information (Araya, 2022).

Calo (2018) argued that policymakers, investors, scholars, and students need to understand the AI environment and policy debate, especially if it includes: 1) justice and equity; 2) use of force; 3) safety and certification; 4) privacy and power; and 5) taxation and displacement(p. 183). In the Global South, taxonomy is one of the key challenges. Inequality and wealth disparities have already been key phenomena. There is a spread of technological superiority by the West, heading towards another 'new era of algorithmic hegemony and digital neo-colonialism'; there are more asymmetries (Garcia, 2023). There is a requirement for machine neutrality based on socially constructed diplomatic efforts by developing countries. The study of AI and human development called for attention on various aspects, such as 1) fairness, bias, and accountability; 2) surveillance and loss of privacy; 3) job and tax revenue loss through automation; and 4) undermining of democracy and political self-determination (Smith, & Neupane, 2018; Wang, 2023).

There is another divide in terms of education and awareness about AI in the Global South: 1) The main problem is consensual granting of access—users frequently lack sufficient understanding about consent and its implications; 2) a lack of AI framework employs data for bias and abuse; 3) an ethical global framework is lacking, which needs to address the local communities and civil societies by training and education; and 4) personal data is at huge risk, especially in an autonomous regime kind of rule and its matters of human rights (Ahmed, 2023). According to the Open Data Charter (2023), "a superficial attempt to regulate AI that does not consider its specific applications can make it harder for victims of abuse to claim for justice or reparation." Simultaneously, if they are 'ignoring the underlying inequalities' regarding the AI industries, there is a need for a counterbalance. There is economic clout with alternatives and smaller firms, and the market's dominant players stand to gain, thereby sustaining cycles of exploitation and dependency.

Overall, the rapid development and advancement of AI and its supremacy in the Global North create the potential to exacerbate the existing levels of inequality and even social division in the Global South (Depieri & Msipa, 2023). As per the Oxford Insights assessment of 181 countries, there has been the lowest score recorded for the use of AI in public services, especially in the Global South, e.g., sub-Saharan Africa, Latin America, and Central and South Asian countries. There is a lack of preparedness regarding the appropriate operating environment and in support of AI development, which includes a robust technology sector, adequate data infrastructure, and a strategic vision. Moreover, there is a need for attention at the state level towards AI governance and ethics. As per the Oxford report, the top AI-advanced regions are North America (ranked number one) and Western Europe (ranked number two) in the Global North. Worse AI disparities exist in sub-Saharan Africa (Yu, Rosenfeld & Gupta, 2023; Offord Insight, 2024).

AI Benefits and Potentials for Various Sectors in the Global South

Despite the issues of AI regulation and its danger of misuse, it has numerous potentials that can revolutionise industrialisation and development in the Global South in various sectors, such as agriculture, education, healthcare, finance, and governance. AI potential includes a number of computational and machine intelligence technologies, including machine learning algorithms, deep learning, neural networks, natural language processing, and speech processing. All these technological elements have the capacity to shape both economic and military power in international relations (Garcia, 2023). In this regard, India is one of the leading countries in the Global South that is developing new-age AI and the Large Language Model (LLM). India adopted the Digital Public Infrastructure (DPI) strategy, which aims to create and use open data through the deployment of AI. All these initiatives are improving public services and making them more efficient and effective in governmental operations. Guglani & Guglani (2024) explain how "India's strategy involves implementing DPI through open application programmable interfaces (APIs) or stacks, through public-private partnerships and collaborative initiatives that bring together non-profit organisations, the private sector, and governments. With pooling knowledge and resources, this collaborative strategy effectively tackles the digital divide and enhances the innovation ecosystem as the cost of acquiring new customers significantly reduces due to open innovation amongst industry stakeholders. This recognition in the G20 New Delhi Leaders' Declaration emphasises the importance of data in driving progress and innovation across sectors."

Likewise, these kinds of efforts are also needed in other countries in the Global South, especially the least developed countries (LDCs). The gap between the Global North and the Global South can be mitigated only with the transfer of technologies and the focus needed on AI research and development (R&D) locally. Therefore, it is also significant that the benefits of AI need to be shared by the Global North and emerging powers in the Global South, transcending geographical and societal boundaries. Inclusive AI development must be based on a holistic approach that is also responsible, equitable, and aligned with human values. Halim (2024) also explains the potentiality of AI, which can "empower people and those at the grassroots level by providing access to innovative solutions and services. For instance, micro, small, and medium enterprises (MSMEs) can leverage AI for tasks such as automated customer support, inventory management, and personalised marketing, enabling them to operate more efficiently and compete in the digital economy." In the past decade, the Global South has improved in the area of development challenges to adapt AI tools. For example, South Asia has the second largest concentration of the poorest population in the world, but some countries in the region have achieved 99 per cent electrification. However, this study also rejects the argument of scholars in the Global North that there is no such environment for the adaptation of AI deployment (The World Bank, 2024).

The EU has an interest in the food sector, which is mostly dependent on African countries, and the evolution of EU development cooperation with ACP states is an example (Bharti, 2022, pp. 21–22). The Global North supported some agricultural projects based on AI and technology-based tools that brought significant changes in identifying banana diseases, deep learning object detection models, imagery observation systems, building predictive models, and developing clinical decision support tools. These are examples that supported farmers in developing countries, such as Ghana, Zambia, East Africa, Brazil, and India. The current AI practices within the Global South provide opportunities for greater investment. This is also one of the reasons to democratise current AI practices for more inclusive participation of the grassroots farmers' communities that are underrepresented by Western scholars. Grassroots organisations like Masakhane and Gahan NLP are examples of 'developing datasets and machine translation tools to help expand access to low-resource African languages' (Okolo, 2023). The Global South has the potential to use AI to improve crop yield and efficiency by analysing data on weather patterns, soil conditions, and crop health and assisting in precision farming techniques, such as targeted irrigation and pesticide application.

There is a wider adoption of AI-based technology that can help facilitate the rollout of fibre 4G–5G networks in the LDCs, especially in the Global South. Cheap weapons help African markets. Mobile phones are now a viable source of income for many people, thanks to the rise of YouTubers in the Global South, who are educating people about the proper use of AI. All these have future possibilities that include remote diagnosis and crowdsourcing in the healthcare sector (Wall, Saxena & Brown, 2021, p. 971). For example, AI can improve diagnostics, treatment planning, and patient care. Developing countries needed to analyse medical images, such as X-rays and MRIs, to detect abnormalities and assist in diagnosis. The Global South can help in drug discovery and development, personalised medicine, and remote patient monitoring (Gehl Sampath, 2021). The health sector is another crucial opportunity for the Global North to bridge the AI divide and bring profound changes to the government to improve citizen experiences, drive economic prosperity, and enhance public safety and security (Deloitte, 2024). Overall, AI can fill gaps in development benefits in the Global South in 1) healthcare by improving productivity; 2) delivery of government services and information with communication and networking; 3) agriculture; 4) education; and 5) economy and business.

Lack of Data Privacy and Governance Issues in the Global South

Along with AI's benefits and potential, there are several issues connected to data protection and regulations in the Global South. On the one hand, the Global North has already adopted regulations on data privacy and its compliance with liberal democratic adaptation as per fundamental rights. On the other hand, the Global South has a long way to go in order to achieve proper AI governance. There is already an AI divide between the two regions. Before assessing cyber security and raising issues of modern warfare, it is also necessary to trace the lack of data privacy and governance issues. In the current era of misinformation and disinformation, the Global South is significantly affected by 'unique challenges towards building regulatory frameworks for privacy and data protection'. Bhatt & Burman (2024) highlight three major issues: 1) the lack of awareness regarding privacy issues, coupled with the perception of regulatory authorities as pro-government bodies, creates a trust deficit; 2) economic growth in a digital world requires greater data flows across jurisdictions; and 3) even when data protection legislations are in place, data protection authorities (DPAs) face hurdles in enforcement because laws often have extraterritorial implications, while DPAs operate with limited resources and capabilities. Both authors also emphasised the complicated and complex data protection in the Global South. This is not only an issue connected to people's privacy but also raises questions about the lack of data privacy in these regions, which also concerns national security in terms of pitting economic imperatives.

Some of the countries in the Global South have adopted data protection regulations for citizens. For example, the Indian Parliament passed the Digital Personal Data Protection Act, 2023 (Ministry of Electronics and Information Technology, 2023). While the narratives differ across countries in the region, as previously noted, concerns about cyber and national security remain constant. Another observation regarding the Global South is the simultaneous emergence of evolving technological landscapes and political instability, particularly in areas such as Asia, Africa, and Latin America. Additionally, there is a noticeable variation in the stages of legal framework development

(Sherif, 2023). For example, Africa is trying to strengthen its data protection regulations, and 36 out of 54 countries have adopted data protection laws and/or regulations until February 2023 (Sylla, 2023).

Data protection issues are also connected with human rights concerns, and there are some sceptical views of civil society activities towards their governments, e.g., there are narratives about data colonialism in India. The rise of surveillance technologies by nationalist and populist governments is raising threats to digital civil liberties. Surveillance is the implementation of surveillance technologies in the name of national security and public safety in developing countries. China's Social Credit System is one of the most prominent examples of government control over its citizens (Bastion & Mukku, 2020, p. 33). In recent years, the Pegasus spyware has challenged human rights and fundamental freedoms in connection with rights to privacy and freedom of expression. It's not only the issues of the Global South, but firstly, issues that emerged in the EU countries where far-right and populist governments alleged the surveillance of their opposition leaders, advocates, and journalists, which is considered unlawful and unjustified surveillance (Kaldani & Prokopets, 2022). To bridge the lack of data privacy issues and good AI governance, the Global South needs to overcome its complex and multifaceted challenges: 1) an inclusive regulatory awareness among people and the building of trust beyond the colonial sceptical hangover of governments is required; 2) there is a mass increase in the digitalisation of economic management, so the importance of national security is bigger than traditional threats; and 3) central data storage and regulation authorities need to be set up in the Global South.

Assessment of Cyber Security and its Role in Modern Warfare

Considering the facts in the warfare segment, it is important to emphasise how the same policies can be used offensively. Since AI development and data protection are not only associated with personal data privacy and the industrial revolution in the Global South, in the digital age, technology is connected and permeates all aspects of human lives. The emergence of cyberwarfare has been transformed into an armed conflict landscape. There are two important dynamics of cyber threats: 1) cyber security measures for citizen and personal data as well as economic data; 2) cybersecurity measures for safeguarding military operations. Jha (2023) presented five significances of cybersecurity in military operations: 1) disruption of critical infrastructure; 2) espionage and intelligence gathering; 3) propagation of disinformation; 4) weaponisation of malware; and 5) escalation and deterrence challenges. Singh and Jha (2024) indicated concerns that "cyberwarfare has become a strategic means to achieve national interests. Countries with a strong cyber potential are likely to play a larger role in the global order."

In the changing geopolitical context of cyber risks, cyber operations have been recognised as a key component in the conduct of modern warfare, but our understanding of them is limited. Countries in the Global South need to prepare for a comprehensive analysis of cyber operations strategies in the realm of international cyber conflict (Robindimyan, 2024). There is an invisible digital frontline in the modern warfare age, which is a critical component of national defence and corporate security. The government's role has increased to 'protection of critical infrastructure and sensitive information'. Hammons (2024) suggests five recommendations for strengthening cyber defences on the new battlefield: 1) Assume a proactive posture; 2) Implement layered security measures; 3) Educate and train your workforce; 4) Collaborate and share intelligence; and 5) Develop and test incident response plans. The author also presented an example of how the NotPetya malware attack (in 2017) was attributed to state-sponsored actors and damaged business worth billions of dollars (Hammons, 2024). But governments in the Global South are sceptical of each other's cooperation regarding digital information and strategy sharing. This is raising another challenge of trust issues, for tackling the Global South needs a vertical and horizontal level of cooperation that can reduce fear and scepticism.

The role of modern warfare can be seen from the example of Russia's war against Ukraine, where Kyiv's government websites were abruptly unavailable, including those of the parliament, government, foreign ministry, and other state institutions. Russian wipe malware included NotPeya, which caused economic damage and denial-of-service attacks (also known as (DDoS, A DDoS attacks), which were used for online devices to target servers, services, or networks with fake service (Korda & Dapaah, 2023). These are modern examples of changing warfare in the 21st century and have implications for the Global South regarding preparedness and compliance of the national army with cybersecurity adaptation. Another example illustrates this. According to the Microsoft Threat Intelligence Centre (MSTIC), the attackers who gained initial access and exfiltrated material were associated with Iran's Ministry of Intelligence and Security (MOIS) through three distinct groups. The investigation of the digital system traces revealed that 1) the attackers operated outside Iran; 2) the attackers accessed and extracted data using tools from earlier attacks; 3) the data erase code was previously utilised by known attackers; and 4) the ransomware originated from the same digital certificate previously used by Iranian hackers. Cybersecurity is essential, especially for government infrastructure and central data storage units, and governments need to strengthen: 1) security of critical infrastructure; 2) network security; 3) end-user education; 4) end-point security; and 5) website security (Basholli, 2022).

In the era of AI, modern warfare is a rapidly changing landscape, and another aspect is hybrid warfare, which is taking place with the integration of cyber warfare. Cyber operations have become instrumental in accompanying disinformation campaigns and information warfare. In the current conflict between Russia-Ukraine and Israel-Palestine, the Global South has been experiencing the spread of false narratives, manipulation of public opinion, and undermining of trust via social media platforms, fake news websites, and online forums (Jha, 2023). There are four significant concerns about hacking modern warfare: 1) Cyberattacks can come from anywhere; 2) anonymity is used as a defence tactic; 3) deterrence theory is being challenged; and 4) cyber capabilities cannot be measured (Geneva Centre for Security Policy, 2019).

Conclusion

The above discussion indicates that the AI landscape is rapidly changing in the 21st century, bringing forth both pros and cons. Significant differences exist between the Global North and the Global South regarding AI development and deployment. On one hand, the Global North has fourth-generation industrial development, while on the other hand, the Global South remains motionless, struggling to transition from the first generation to the second generation. After the decline of the world order, there is greater danger ahead in this rapidly changing world. The rise of nationalist and populist governments in the Global South poses greater national security risks. Propaganda and disinformation have become the new normal after the new media revolution.

In this critical time of AI, the Global South needs to update its strategic approach in the face of cyber warfare. This includes:

1. ensuring higher security against vulnerable attacks via the internet;
2. strengthening commercial and infrastructure security;
3. encouraging greater responsibility for CSOs and NGOs to participate in awareness campaigns;
4. enhancing military and defence infrastructure and equipment; and
5. recognising the need for the Global North to adapt AI aid, technological support, and cooperation with the Global South in their foreign policy upgrades.

References

Ahmed, N. (September 11, 2023), *A Response from the Global South on the article "Getting Grip on Data and AI"*. Frontiers Policy Labs. https://policylabs.frontiersin.org/content/commentary-response-from-the-global-south-on-the-article-getting-grip-on-data-and-ai.

Araya, D. (2022), "Special Report: Artificial Intelligence for Defence and Security". The Centre for International Governance Innovation (CIGI). https://www.cigionline.org/static/documents/Araya_AI-for-Defence_SpecialReport_Q4fjNfp.pdf.

Basholli, F. (2022), "Cyber warfare, a new aspect of modern warfare", *International Scientific Journal Security & Future*, 5(2), pp. 72-75. https://www.researchgate.net/profile/Fatmir-Basholli/publication/371814918_Cyber_warfare_a_new_aspect_of_modern_warfare/links/6496dc8cb9ed6874a5d4e867/Cyber-warfare-a-new-aspect-of-modern-warfare.pdf.

Bastion, G. D. & Mukku, S. (2020). *Data and the global south: key issues for inclusive digital development*. Washington DC: Heinrich Böll Stiftung. https://us.boell.org/en/2020/10/20/data-and-global-south-key-issues-inclusive-digital-development.

Benizri, I., Evers, A., Mercer, S.T., &Jessani, A.A. (2023), "A comparative perspective on AI regulation", The Lawfare Institute, July 17, https://www.lawfaremedia.org/article/a-comparative-perspective-on-ai-regulation.

Bharti, S. S. (2022), "The EU Development Policy as a Model: an Implication for South Asian Countries", *Humanities and Social Sciences*, 29 (2), pp. 19–28. https://doi.org/10.7862/rz.2022.hss.09.

Bharti, S. S. & Aryal, S. K. (2023), "The right to privacy and an implication of the EU General Data Protection Regulation (GDPR) in Europe: Challenges to the Companies", *Journal of Contemporary European Studies*, 31(4), pp. 1391-1402. https://doi.org/10.1080/14782804.2022.2130193.

Bhatt, C. & Burman, A. (2024), "Data Protection Regulation in the Global South". Carnegie Endowment for International Peace. https://carnegieendowment.org/posts/2024/02/data-protection-regulation-in-the-global-south?lang=en.

Calo, R. (2018), "Artificial Intelligence Policy: A Primer and Roadmap", *University of Bologna Law Review*, 3(2), pp. 180–218. https://doi.org/10.6092/issn.2531-6133/8670.

Deloitte (April 21, 2024), "The Age of With™: The AI Advantage in Defence and Security". Deloitte Canada. https://www2.deloitte.com/ca/en/pages/deloitte-analytics/articles/age-with-ai-advantage-defence-security.html.

Depieri, M. S. & Msipa, S. (October 18, 2023), "Artificial intelligence in the global South: Will AI advancement deepen digital divides and inequalities?" Portulans Institute. https://portulansinstitute.org/artificial-intelligence-in-the-global-south/.

European Parliament (December 09, 2023), "Artificial Intelligence Act: deal on comprehensive rules for trustworthy AI". Press Release of the European Parliament https://www.europarl.europa.eu/news/en/press-room/20231206IPR15699/artificial-intelligence-act-deal-on-comprehensive-rules-for-trustworthy-ai.

Garcia, E. V. (2023), "Artificial Intelligence and International Relations". LinkedIn, November 12. https://www.linkedin.com/pulse/artificial-intelligence-international-relations-eugenio-v-garcia-vmvsc/.

Gehl Sampath, P. (2021), "Governing artificial intelligence in an age of inequality", *Global Policy*, 12, pp. 21-31.https://doi.org/10.1111/1758-5899.12940.

Geneva Centre for Security Policy (2019), "4 ways in which hackers are changing modern warfare". GCSP. https://www.gcsp.ch/global-insights/4-ways-which-hackers-are-changing-modern-warfare.

Gilchrist, K. & Iordache, R. (March 13, 2024), "World's first major act to regulate AI passed by European lawmakers". *CNBC*. https://www.cnbc.com/2024/03/13/european-lawmakers-endorse-worlds-first-major-act-to-regulate-ai.html.

Guglani, A., & Guglani, V. (January 4, 2024), "AI governance outlook: A Global South perspective". Observer Research Foundation: Digital Frontiers. https://www.orfonline.org/expert-speak/ai-governance-outlook-a-global-south-perspective.

Halim, H. A. (January 23, 2024), "AI development for the Global South", *Stratsea*. https://stratsea.com/ai-development-for-the-global-south/.

Hammons, K (March 23, 2024) ,"The Invisible Digital Frontline: Cybersecurity's Role in Modern Warfare". LinkedIn. https://www.linkedin.com/pulse/invisible-digital-frontline-cybersecuritys-role-modern-kelly-hammons-5ikuc/.

Heng, S., Tsilionis, K., Scharff, C., & Wautelet, Y. (2022), "Understanding AI ecosystems in the Global South: The Cases of Senegal and Cambodia",

International Journal of Information Management, 64, 102454. https://doi.org/10.1016/j.ijinfomgt.2021.102454.

Jha, A. (2023),"Cyber Security and Modern Warfare", *South Asia Defence & Strategic Review*, 17(3), p. 38. https://www.defstrat.com/magazine_articles/cyber-security-and-modern-warfare/.

Kaldani, T. &Prokopets, Z. (2022), "Pegasus spyware and its impacts on human rights". Council of Europe. https://edoc.coe.int/en/data-protection/11112-pegasus-spyware-and-its-impact-on-human-rights.html.

Korda, D. R. & Dapaah, E. O. (2023), "The Role of Cyberattacks on Modern Warfare: A Review", *International Journal of Research and Innovation in Applied Science*, 8(7), pp. 286-292. https://doi.org/10.51584/IJRIAS.2023.8733.

McCarthy, J., Minsky, M. L., Rochester, N., & Shannon, C. E. (1955), "A proposal for the Dartmouth summer research project on artificial intelligence", August 31. http://jmc.stanford.edu/articles/dartmouth/dartmouth.pdf.

Ministry of Electronics and Information Technology (2023), Digital Personal Data Protection Act 2023. MeitY, Government of India. Retrieved from https://www.meity.gov.in/writereaddata/files/Digital%20Personal%20Data%20Protection%20Act%202023.pdf.

Offord Insight (April 18, 2024), "Government AI Readiness Index 2023". https://oxfordinsights.com/ai-readiness/ai-readiness-index/.

Okolo, C. T. (November 1, 2023), *AI in the Global South: Opportunities and challenges towards more inclusive governance.* Brookings. https://www.brookings.edu/articles/ai-in-the-global-south-opportunities-and-challenges-towards-more-inclusive-governance/.

Open Data Charter (December 20, 2023), "AI governance for and from the Global South", *Medium.* https://medium.com/opendatacharter/ai-governance-for-and-from-the-global-south-07326645b053.

Robindimyan (March 4, 2024), "Geopolitical Cyber Risk: Cyber Operations in Modern Warfare", *Medium.* https://robindimyan.medium.com/geopolitical-cyber-risk-cyber-operations-in-modern-warfare-db1392ab0df5.

Sherif, S. (November 21, 2023), "Data Protection Laws in the Global South", *Medium.* https://medium.com/illumination/data-protection-laws-in-the-global-south-7d5b636c011b.

Singh, T. K. & Jha, S. K. (2024), "From code to command: Unveiling India's cyberpower strategy", *Comparative Strategy*, pp. 1–14. https://doi.org/10.1080/01495933.2024.2340951.

Smith, M. & Neupane, S. (2018), "Artificial intelligence and human development: toward a research agenda". International Development Research Centre. https://idl-bnc-idrc.dspacedirect.org/bitstream/handle/10625/56949/IDL-56949.pdf.

Srivastava, K. (2023), "Artificial Intelligence and National Security: Perspective on the Global South", *The International Journal of Law in Changing World*, 2 (2) pp. 77-87. https://doi.org/10.54934/ijlcw.v2i2.63.

Sylla, A. (February 24, 2023), "Recent developments in African data protection laws - Outlook for 2023", *Lexology*. https://www.lexology.com/library/detail.aspx?g=baef72ee-10bd-4eb9-a614-a990c236bb45.

The World Bank (April 21, 2024), "Access to electricity (% of population) - South Asia". World Bank Group. https://data.worldbank.org/indicator/EG.ELC.ACCS.ZS?locations=8S.

Veale, M., Matus, K., &Gorwa, R. (2023), "AI and global governance: Modalities, rationales, tensions", *Annual Review of Law and Social Science*, 19, pp. 255-275. https://doi.org/10.1146/annurev-lawsocsci-020223-040749.

Wall, P. J., Saxena, D., & Brown, S. (2021), "Artificial intelligence in the Global South (AI4D): Potential and risks". arXiv preprint, https://doi.org/10.48550/arXiv.2108.10093.

Wang, G. Y. (September 28, 2023) ,"Effective AI governance requires global awareness of local problems". LSE Blogs, https://blogs.lse.ac.uk/medialse/2023/09/28/effective-ai-governance-requires-global-awareness-of-local-problems/#:~:text=An%20effective%20global%20AI%20governance,well%20as%20distinctive%20developmental%20challenges.

Yu, D., Rosenfeld, R., & Gupta, A. (October 6, 2023), "The 'AI divide' between the Global North and Global South", *World Economic Forum*. https://www.weforum.org/agenda/2023/01/davos23-ai-divide-global-north-global-south/.

10

Why Wagner Wins: Deconstructing Mercenary-Governmental Organisations within Russian Foreign Policy

Aaryaman Nijhawan

Introduction

Russia's Wagner group has progressively gone from a shadowy, little known organisation to one of the consistent public bastions of Russian foreign policy initiatives, especially in the African continent's political landscape. The organisation is known for its adaptive capabilities and strong outreach programmes for the often fragile African states, offering comprehensive security architecture in exchange for the state's natural resources.[1] The Wagner model has seen quite consistent success in Africa, with the Wagner group's total worldwide operations covering up to 30 countries including Libya, Syria, Mozambique, Ukraine, Madagascar, and Sudan, among others.[2]

However, it is not the sole Russian PMC operating within Africa. Other prominent corporations, including the RSB Group (or Russian Security Services) and the Sewa Security Group, also operate within the region, providing critical logistical support and military advisors to African nations and undertaking 'counter-terrorism' operations against rebel groups opposing the incumbent regimes.[3] Some, such as the RSB Group, are official partners and providers of security to the United Nations.[4] Oftentimes, such operations are run in-sync with the African states' national armies for better coordination and combined-arms operations. However, at times, these corporations take action to protect their own and Russian interests by undertaking military operations to secure mining and natural resources sites leased to them by the African governments.

Founded by former GRU members, Wagner blossomed to become one of the most prominent asymmetrical warfare weapons to be deployed by Russia. Specialising in grey-zone tactics and plausible deniability, Wagner was a more streamlined, organised and elite 'armed fishermen vessel' deployed by the People's Liberation Army Navy in the disputed South China Sea. Although often working in coordination with local government forces, Wagner troops aren't attached directly under the African states' military commands, thus possessing a completely separate and distinct organisational chain of command. For instance, in the Central African Republic (CAR), Wagner forces have been operating independently of the governmental Central African Armed Forces (FACA) in operations against rebel forces.

The Birth of 'MGO'

In the post-9/11 era, critical divergences in the foreign policy approaches of the United States-led coalition and the Russian Federation became prominent. Highlighted in the famous Munich speech of 2007 by Russian President Vladimir Putin, a resurgent post-Soviet Russia saw itself as being directly or indirectly threatened by Western foreign policy alignments.[5]

However, actively countering Western actions proved to be a completely different ballgame. Contending superior Western influence by a recovering Russia called for asymmetrical, grey-zone tactics.[6] Cyber warfare and the use of proxies were masterminded by Igor Panarin, a renowned ex-KGB political scientist, and political philosopher Alexandr Dugin.[7] Meanwhile, the Chief of the General Staff of the Russian Armed Forces, General Valery Gerasimov, suggested a detailed, exhaustive escalation ladder that involved grey-zone operations, undeclared wars, promotion and suppression of both overt and covert foreign intervention, as well as crisis escalation, management, and reduction. Gerasimov's unique model was highlighted in a report titled 'Main Trends in the Forms and Methods of the Armed Forces' published in January 2013.[8]

Proxy forces as such also include paramilitary organisations (PMCs), which don't currently possess a single universally accepted definition. Dr Tipling, Legislative Liaison Advisor to the United States Air Force, defined PMCs as "corporations of civilian employees who perform on the basis of a contract with the state, military services, escort and support both inside and outside the country."[9]

At the same time, the most extensive and exhaustive definition was provided by Professor A.G. Volevodz who classified PMCs as "non-governmental organizations providing on a contractual basis military and security services to individuals, legal entities and states. In this case, military services are understood as combat operations, strategic planning, information gathering, operational or logistical support, training of military personnel, logistical support."[10]

Dr S.P. Belokonya, Head of the Expert Analytical Department, Main Operational Directorate General Staff of the Russian Armed Forces, focused on the unique agency-client relationship between PMCs and states by opining that such corporations "registered on the territory of the state, in fact, are a kind of state structures and serve as an instrument of foreign policy of this state."[11]

In other words, the international realm bears witness to special transnational corporations whose sole purpose and specialisation is developing a sound and efficient commercial structure within the realm of armed conflicts and military security by simultaneously serving their clients, which primarily happen to be states.[12] In turn, more often than not, such PMCs are directly or indirectly influenced and controlled by states and work for their designated national interests, thereby acting more or less as a medium of furtherance of the latter's foreign policy adjectives. Thus, even with their commercial and autonomous functioning, the "national" origin of a PMC must be kept in mind as their actions follow a pattern of interdependency with statist interests globally.[13]

Such pseudo-commercial, state-controlled organisations can be better referred to as Mercenary-Governmental Organisations or MGOs, which better reflects their ties to national governments, compared to the term "paramilitary organisation", which focuses exclusively on their military character at the expense of portraying a wider, holistic picture of their functioning.

The Russians learnt from the use of private military contractors that were employed, with significant results, by the collective West during the Yugoslav wars as well as in both the Iraq wars of 1991 and 2003.[14] Vital support, logistics, and military training provided by the US government-funded Military Professional Resources Inc. (MPRI) to the Croatian forces proved decisive in their offensives against the Serbs.[15] While direct military support by the MPRI to the Croatians during the offensive is still debated, the significance of MGOs effecting on-ground battlefield changes while providing plausible deniability to major global powers wasn't lost on the Russians.[16]

The emergence of MGOs coincided with rapid globalisation and the rise of privatisation in the post-Cold War political environment. Security-focused corporations were required to protect the private needs of transnational corporations and national interests of states. Some of the famous MGOs, such as Academi (formerly Blackwater),[1] became independent, self-existing megacorporations capable of fielding standalone offensive operations.[18] Currently, there are upwards of 3000 MGOs in the world, with the majority of them registered in the US, the UK and France.[19,20]

Central African Republics: A Case Study

Talk about increasing Russian as well as Chinese engagements with African states is often viewed negatively and with suspicion in the West.[21,22] Oftentimes, European and American governments are prone to classifying states leading towards Russian assistance as being 'misled' or regimes prone to terrorising the local populace and gross violations of human rights.[23] Meanwhile, the Russian argument holds that many of the African states still suffer from neo-colonialist links between the former colonial powers and their African colonies.[24] Such ties are cemented by a common language and established financial and political institutions.[25] A prominent example is the unconventionally strong relations between France and its former Sahel colonies.[26] Till recently, these Sahel African states as well as their subregional organisational structures, such as the ECOWAS, worked in tandem with Western systems.[27] This neo-colonialist dominance is the main reason for continued dependence of so-called 'independent' national African governments, which are nevertheless still held hostage to continuing financial and political links with their former colonial masters.[28]

As such, the main selling point of the Russian government is that through arms supplies and support of 'Mercenary-Governmental Organisations' (MGOs), Moscow offers African leaders an equal-basis partnership based on equality, mutual respect, and trust rather than viewing them from a position of First World dominance.[29]

In general, there has been a proportional relationship between the level of security offered by Russian PMCs to African states in exchange for control over mines and natural resources.[30] The relationship between the Central African Republic (CAR) and Russian PMCs was initiated around 2017 with contracts of security assistance in exchange for joint control over mines.[31] Companies, such as Lobaye Invest SARLU, PMC Sewa Security Group, Midas Resources, Bois Rouge and Diamville, simultaneously went on to secure significant high-level contracts to operate gold and mining locations across the CAR, while providing protection and security for mining workers as well as political leaders.[32] The year 2018 saw the conclusion of further elaborate contracts concerning supply of weapons as well as military support in exchange for mining concessions.

This is further acknowledged by analysing the patterns of Russian MGO operations over the course of the CAR's domestic conflicts. The main opposition force to the state regime was the Coalition for Patriots for Change (CPC), which launched a major offensive just prior to CAR's national elections in December 2020. Wagner suffered loss of access to critical Russian mining regions received as part of the CAR government's contracts. Allying with Wagner and being backed by the United Nations peacekeepers (MINUSCA) allowed the government FACA forces to push back the rebels. However, the biggest third-party beneficiary from this localised clash was the Russian MGOs, especially Wagner, which incidentally focused its military operations in areas possessing significant strategic Russian-run mining sites. Post-battle reports indicate that Wagner became one of the significant actors in the CAR conflict theatre, with a combined strength of approximately 2600 troops.

On the other hand, the United Nations has been concerned with the interoperability of UN peacekeeping personnel deployed in CAR and other private armed groups that have sprung up in the region.[33] In light of consistent human rights violations and violations of humanitarian laws which are, regrettably, a staple in conflict-ridden regions, such blurring of delineating boundaries between state, non-state actors, and MGOs further complicates the fragile situation.[34] Violence against civilians by armed groups as well as political violence perpetrated by the MGOs are an undeniable albeit regrettable by-product of their utilisation, especially since they're freer to pursue 'all means possible' to achieve their stated objectives.[35] Compared to standing national armies, utilising MGOs allows expedient circumvention of international law, which the former might be constrained to follow, and at a fraction of the cost involved.[36]

For instance, the majority of the violence perpetrated was against locals of Fulani ethnicity as well as Muslims since the rebel militias were majorly composed of ethnic Fulani troops with Islam as their religion. Since December 2002, the Armed Conflict Location and Event Data Project (ACLED) has estimated in its report titled "Regional Overview Africa: March 2024" that MGO Wagner's operations constitute 70 per cent of all political violence perpetrated in the region.[37]

Consolidation of political influence and strength also means influence over the lucrative flow of natural resources within the CAR. The diamond industry of the CAR has progressively gone from an independent system of enterprise to being completely dominated by Russian MGOs.[38] People involved in the trade argue that "the majority of independent collectors are financed by the Russians…Today, an independent collector cannot work if he does not work with Wagner."

One defining trend of post-Cold War Russia's relations with the African states is that there is strategic policy formulation towards 'Africa' as a whole with pan-African initiatives and the African Union to tackle common issues like climate change, ivory trade, piracy, illegal mining, poverty, food security, etc.[39] Such an overarching holistic perspective was absent during the Cold War when the USSR enjoyed great, even privileged, relations with some of the individual African governments but less coordination on a strategic level.[40]

Conclusion

The rise in popularity of MGOs or mercenary-governmental organisations as part of foreign policy agendas of states has been due to myriad reasons, two being principal amongst them. First, the end of the Cold War combined with the sweeping capitalist nature of the global economy made MGOs a cheaper, expedient and efficient part of states' foreign policy goals. National interests were defended and extended as part of proxy wars that gained prominence in the post-1990s era. The Syrian example as well as the wars in Iraq highlight the shift in the nature of conflict from conventional battles between standing armies to guerrilla warfare sponsored by global powers sitting continents apart.

Secondly, the effective utilisation of MGOs by the United States and its allies during their campaigns proved insightful for other major powers, such as China and Russia.Moscow, especially, then proceeded to deploy MGOs as effective tools of countering Western hegemonic influence in the African continent. Russian MGOs often enter into a security and defence contract where they provide military advisors, training, equipment, and weapons in exchange for lease of lucrative natural resource and mining locations within the state's territory.

Due to partly the high operational cost of an MGO's activities as well as its work's impact on inducing geopolitical and military shifts in a region's ecosystem, the primary customers are states and large transnational organisations. These MGO-state ties are further amplified by the former acting as foreign policy tools to further the national interests of the sponsor-states. An elite, sophisticated agency-client relationship comes into play with varying levels of interdependency on each other. While states see MGOs as expedient, grey-zone tools of furthering national influence in the international arena, MGOs are for-profit, autonomous organisations working for their own benefit and provided for by their sponsor-state.

In the African theatre, the national governments are more than happy to invite foreign defence partnerships to eliminate rebel groups threatening their regimes, even if it comes at a fraction of the nation's production cost. A relevant case study is the CAR, which has seen extensive defence contracts and partnerships with multiple Russian-based MGOs, the most prominent being the Wagner Group. At times, the MGOs do deviate and focus on securing their interests with the state, even venturing on standalone missions of their own. Another concerning issue is regarding the evident lack of sufficient checks and balances on such organisations since they operate in the grey zone of international great power politics, affording their state-sponsors plausible deniability while extending their influence and national priorities.

The future for MGOs is bright, largely driven by a capitalist, still integrated world economy driven by commercial motivations. An intensifying multipolar world order will only increase the use of proxy forces and indirect confrontational systems by emerging poles to further their scramble of power and influence. However, as witnessed by the brief rebellion by Wagner, MGOs can be a double-edged sword.[41] Effectively wielding them will need a strong sponsor-state with sufficient leverage on its semi-autonomous MGOs to prevent such a black swan event from becoming common practice.

Notes

1. Katz, B., Jones, S. G., Doxsee, C., & Harrington, N. (2020), "Moscow's Mercenary Wars: The Expansion of Russian Private Military Companies". Center for Strategic and International Studies (CSIS).
2. Рождественский, И., Баев, А., &Русяева, П. (2016), Призракивойны: как в Сириипоявиласьроссийскаячастнаяармия. РБК журнал. Сентябрь.
3. International Institute for Strategic Studies (IISS) (2021), "The Armed Conflict Survey 2021: The worldwide review of political, military and humanitarian trends in current conflicts".
4. Веселов, Ю. А. (2021),История и роль ЧВК в современноймировойполитике. Мироваяполитика, (3), 19-40.
5. Putin, V. (2007), "Speech and the following discussion at the Munich conference on security policy". President of Russia, 10(2), 2007.
6. Kharouni, L., Hacquebord, F., Huq, N., Gogolinski, J., Mercês, F., Remorin, A., & Otis, D., "Operation Pawn Storm".
7. Darczewska, J. (2014), "The anatomy of Russian information warfare. The Crimean operation, a case study". OSW OśrodekStudiówWschodnichim. Marka Karpia.
8. МАКАРОВ, Н. (2012), ВыступлениеначальникаГенеральногоштаба ВооруженныхСилРоссийскойФедерации–первогозаместителяминис траобороныРоссийскойФедерациигенералаармии НЕ МАКАРОВА. ВестникАкадемиивоенныхнаук, (2), 16-20.
9. Tipling, D. M. (2006), "The military extraterritorial jurisdiction Act and its implications for private military companies", *Bepress Legal Series*, p. 1393.
10. Волеводз, А. Г. (2009), О международныхинициативах в сфереправово горегулированиядеятельностичастныхвоенных и охранныхкомпаний. Международноеуголовноеправо и международнаяюстиция, (1), 12.
11. БЕЛОКОНЬ, С. П., БЫТЬЕВ, А. В., & СМИРНОВА, Л. А. (2015), Частныевоенныекомпании: мировойисторическийопыт и современныепе рспективыдляРоссии. Военнаямысль, (1), 60-66.

12. Пономарев, В. В. (2019), Частныевоенныекомпании: агентыстратегиинеп рямыхдействий. Азимутнаучныхисследований: экономика и управление, 8(2 (27)), 27-30.
13. Курылев, К. П., Мартыненко, Е. В., Пархитько, Н. П., & Станис, Д. В. (2017). Феноменчастныхвоенныхкомпаний в военно-силовойполитикегосударств в XXI в. Вестникмеждународныхорганизаций: образование, наука, новаяэкономика, 12(4), 130-149.
14. Palmer, J. (2018), "War For Sale: The Case of Blackwater Unaccountable Private Military Companies in Iraq and Afghanistan".
15. Dakovic, M. & Miseljic, B. (2001), "How'OperationStorm'Destabilized the Balkans". Independent Center for Geopolitical Studies, Belgrade, Serbia.
16. Кашников, Б. Н. (2011). Частныевоенныекомпании и теориясправедливыхвойн. Российскийнаучныйжурнал, (1), 83-94.
17. Harden, M. (2017), "Blackwater USA: The Success and Failures of the World's Most Powerful Mercenary Army in the War on Terror", *Pepperdine Policy Review*, 9(1), p. 3.
18. Романчук, С. И. (2013). Частныевоенныекомпаниинаслужбемиротворчест ва. Вестникуниверситета, (8), 222-227.
19. Надтока, Р. В. (2018). Частныевоенныекомпаниикакактивныйпроводникнациональныхинтересовгосударства: угрозаилиновыевозможностидляРосс ии?.Скиф. Вопросыстуденческойнауки, (1 (17)), 206-216.
20. Романчук, С. И. (2013). Частныевоенныекомпаниинаслужбемиротворчест ва. Вестникуниверситета, (8), 222-227.
21. Siegle, J. (2021), "Russia and Africa: Expanding Influence and Instability. Russia's Global Reach: A Security and Statecraft Assessment", pp. 80-90.
22. Beyani, C., & Lilly, D. (2001), "Regulating private military companies. Options for the UK Government". London: International Alert.
23. Ganser, D. (2005), "Fear as a weapon: the effects of psychological warfare on domestic and international politics". *World affairs*, 9, pp. 28-44.
24. Yoroms, G. J. (2014), "The Libyan Question and the Responsibility to Protect: Whither Africa in the 21st Century", *Journal of African Foreign Affairs*, 1(1), pp. 61–82. https://www.jstor.org/stable/26664016
25. Sartre, J. P., Haddour, A., Brewer, S., & McWilliams, T. (2005), *Colonialism and neocolonialism*. Routledge.
26. Taylor, I. (2019), "France à fric: the CFA zone in Africa and neocolonialism", *Third World Quarterly*, 40(6), pp. 1064-1088.
27. The coup in Niger. (2023). Strategic Comments, 29(6), i–iii. https://doi.org/10.1080/13567888.2023.2247717
28. Langan, M. (2017), *Neo-colonialism and the Poverty of'development'in Africa*. Springer.

29. Лукьянов,Ф., Маслов, А. (Hosts) (2022, Фев 20) Возвращение в Африку [Audio Podcast episode]. In *Мировойфакультет.* Россия в глобальнойполитике. https://globalaffairs.ru/articles/africa-podcast/
30. Armed Conflict Location & Event Data Project. (2022). Wagner Group Operations in Africa. Armed Conflict Location & Event Data Project. http://www.jstor.org/stable/resrep42841
31. Rondeaux, C. (2019), "Tracing Wagner's Roots". In *Decoding the Wagner Group: Analyzing the Role of Private Military Security Contractors in Russian Proxy Warfare*, pp. 32–44. New America. http://www.jstor.org/stable/resrep19981.7
32. Searcey, D. (2019), "Gems, Warlords and Mercenaries: Russia's Playbook in Central African Republic",*International New York Times*, NA-NA.
33. Akcinaroglu, S., & Radziszewski, E. (2013), "Private military companies, opportunities, and termination of civil wars in Africa", *Journal of Conflict Resolution*, 57(5), pp. 795-821.
34. Lombard, L. (2016), *State of rebellion: Violence and intervention in the Central African Republic*. Bloomsbury Publishing.
35. Ten Dam, C. (October 2013), "Private Military Contractors: Deplore or Deploy?—Lessons from the 'Blackwater Scandal'in Iraq". In *Forum of EthnoGeoPolitics* (Vol. 1, No. 2, pp. 20-40).
36. БЕЛОКОНЬ, С. П., БЫТЬЕВ, А. В., & СМИРНОВА, Л. А. (2015). Частныевоенныекомпании: мировойисторическийопыт и современныепе рспективыдляРоссии. Военнаямысль, (1), 60-66.
37. https://reliefweb.int/report/central-african-republic/acled-regional-overview-africa-march-2024
38. Reynolds, N. (2019), *Putin's Not-So-Secret Mercenaries: Patronage, Geopolitics, and the Wagner Group* (Vol. 8). Washington, DC: Carnegie Endowment for International Peace.
39. Лукьянов,Ф., Маслов, А. (Hosts) (2022, Фев 20) Возвращение в Африку [Audio Podcast episode]. In *Мировойфакультет.* Россия в глобальнойполитике. https://globalaffairs.ru/articles/africa-podcast/
40. Besenyő, J. (2020), "The Africa Policy of Russia". In *The 21st Century Cold War*, pp. 132-153. Routledge.
41. Schooley, S. E. (2013), "Constitutional ethics and contracting out: The dilemma of public-private partnerships", *Mustang Journal of Business and Ethics*, 5, p. 30.

11

The Nexus Conundrum: Interplay between Military Intelligence and Corporate Forces in Tomorrow's Battles

Antoine Renaux

"At the time of the emergence of the early nation states, the births of most of them were assisted by blood-and-iron warfare. In the same way, during the transition of nation states to globalization, there is no way to avoid collisions between enormous interest blocs. What is different is that the means that we have today to untie the 'Gordian Knot' are not merely swords, and because of this we no longer have to be like our ancestors who invariably saw resolution by armed force as the last court of appeals. Any of the political, economic, or diplomatic means now has sufficient strength to supplant military means. However, mankind has no reason at all to be gratified by this, because what we have done is nothing more than substitute bloodless warfare for bloody warfare as much as possible."

– Liang, Q. & Xiangsui, W. (2015), *Unrestricted Warfare* (p. 241). Echo Point Books & Media, LLC

Introduction

On October 14, 2022, Ukrainian intelligence managed to strike a Russian army training facility in Donetsk, 40 miles behind Russian lines, with the support of Molfar, a national OSINT (Open Source Intelligence) company.[1] Two months prior to this, internet research company Graphika and the Stanford Internet Observatory (SIO) published a report on around 150 fake social media accounts from the US Central Command (CENTCOM) that were deleted by the US company,Meta.[2] These two examples, within two months, highlight opposite approaches taken by private actors toward cyber-intelligence actions.

In the 21st century, the globalisation landscape has modified the face of the battlefield with the rise of social media and advanced technologies like artificial intelligence (AI) and quantum computing. These technological developments blur the lines between peace and war, military and civilian, and private and public sectors.

The privatisation of intelligence represents a lucrative market. According to the article "Contractors and Intelligence: The Private Sector in the Intelligence Community", "some estimates suggest that the total number of contractors supporting the Intelligence Community (IC) could be as high as 70,000, with as much as seventy percent of the intelligence budget spent on the acquisition of private sector goods and services."[3] A decade later, the company Mordor Intelligence estimated the growth of AI and Analytics in Defense Market at a Compound Annual Growth Rate (CAGR) of 13 per cent between 2019 and 2029.[4] Far from being confined to major industries, this technological revolution is also reflected in the number of US defence startups, which,according to the US services company, McKinsey & Company,almost doubled between 2011-17 and 2018-23, from 466 to 849, including 171 sensing, connectivity, and security companies, 140 in biotechnology, 134 in advanced computing and software, 110 in autonomous systems, and 84 in space technologies.[5]

Some companies represent this growing involvement of the private sector in the intelligence field. In June 2013, for example, Edward Snowden's revelations brought to light Booz Allen Hamilton Holding Corporation's role in the NSA's vast PRISM program.[6] The web-consulting, technical support and analysis company works in close cooperation with the US intelligence services. Government contracts account for 98 per cent of the company's revenue, and three-quarters of its 25,000 employees work on classified contracts.

The partnership between the intelligence community and private companies presents significant challenges, particularly in distinguishing military intelligence from strategic intelligence. Military intelligence supports battlefield decisions and operations, while strategic intelligence focuses on long-term threats and geopolitical trends, often operating independently of the military. However, there is an overlap, as seen with CENTCOM's use of fake Facebook accounts in information warfare, blending localised military operations with broader strategic efforts far beyond the framework of declared armed conflicts.

The purpose of this text is to determine the implications of this privatisation of violence for military intelligence. We will explore its extent, challenges, and limitations, as well as its consequences on the major geopolitical trends of the 21st century.

From Private Military Companies (PMCS) to the Rise of Private Digital Sector Companies in Conflicts and Warfare: An Overview of a Phenomenon

The increasing involvement of private companies in intelligence, particularly military intelligence, aligns with two significant trends: the rising use of private military companies in military operations, and the exponential digitisation of human societies along with the development of cyberspace.

The trend of increasing employment of PMCs falls under the concept of "Surrogate Warfare". According to Dr. Andreas Krieg and Jean-Marc Rickli in their book, *Surrogate Warfare: The Transformation of War in the Twenty-First Century*, surrogate warfare is defined as the practice where nation-states outsource the strategic, operational, or tactical burdens of warfare to human or technological substitutes. This can include arming rebel groups, employing contractors, using armed drones, or deploying cyber propaganda. The main goal is to minimise the direct costs and risks of war for the state by leveraging these surrogates.[7]

According to the aforementioned article *Contractors and Intelligence*, US interventions in Iraq and Afghanistan included the involvement of 60 private companies contracted for security and intelligence services. Among the services are "logistical services, technology support, and administrative tasks, in addition to many core mission functions, such as collection management, document and media exploitation, human intelligence and counterintelligence activities, security clearance investigations, overhead imagery collection, linguistic and translation services, interrogation support, targeting functions, and analysis."[8] According to the Department of Defense (DoD), in March 2011, 90,339 contractors were deployed to Afghanistan, compared to around 99,800 armed forces personnel, a ratio of 0.905 to 1, or 48 per cent of deployed personnel. In Iraq, as of March 2011, there were 64,253 contractors compared to 45,660 uniformed personnel in-country, meaning 58 per cent of DOD's workforce.[9] While Blackwater maintains that its personnel were not involved solely in guard or escort missions, various employees have testified to the involvement of contractors in intelligence missions with the CIA or Special Operations Forces (SOF) in Iraq, in particular, "Snatch and Grab" missions, the abduction of civilians suspected of insurgency actions.[10]

Far from remaining an American phenomenon confined to distant counter-insurgency conflicts, the use of PMCs has become globalised and integrated into the game of global powers. In February 2018, American SOF allied with local militias, clashed in Syria with contractors from the Russian group, Wagner, in Deir-ez-Zor.[11] This episode illustrates that the phenomenon of privatisation of violence does not prevent kinetic confrontation between nuclear and conventional military powers, but in a peripheral and indirect context. The actions of PMCs are not confined to the kinetic sphere but seem to integrate the immaterial sphere into the field of conflictuality and business. Indeed, the Russian Wagner group was also involved in the Sahel region in 2023 on information warfare operations against the French presence, actions in which Russian military intelligence (GRU) is also accused of being present, blurring the lines between state entities and PMC actions.[12]

The second trend, the digitisation of human societies and their increasing interconnection, represents a major shift in the strategic framework and international relations. Despite its military origins, the Pentagon's ARPANET program has primarily developed through the actions of private companies and is perceived as a space of freedom outside strict state regulations. However, this private space has been overtaken by warfare, as evidenced by cyber-attack campaigns such as those in Estonia in 2007, Operation Olympic Games against Iran's nuclear project in 2012, and the rising number of information warfare campaigns in both peacetime and wartime.

The privatisation of warfare and intelligence is also taking on a digital dimension, with the development of a "military-digital complex", as Thomas

Gomard, President of the Institut Français des Relations Internationales (IFRI), puts it.[13] General Michael Hayden, former Director of the NSA (1999-2005) and CIA (2006-2009), proposed the creation of a digital "Blackwater" in 2011. He argues, "We have privatized certain defense activities, even in physical space, and now you've got a new domain in which we don't have any paths trampled down in the forest in terms of what it is we expect the government—or will allow the government—to do, and in the past in our history when that has happened, private sector expands to fill the empty space. (...) In those kinds of circumstances you and I may legitimately be expected, or we will have to in order to provide a certain level of Defense, to be more aggressive in how we define defense out there, either on our own or, contracting it out to the private sector."[14]

Since the General's statements, Booz Allen Hamilton has become a textbook example of the increasing privatisation of American intelligence. According to Defense News' Top 100 Defence Companies ranking, Booz Allen is ranked 22nd worldwide. The company ranked above German arms manufacturer Rheinmetall AG and French military aircraft leader Dassault Aviation.[15]

Private Companies Surrogacy: Old Phenomenon, New Causes and Challenges

While the employment of private companies in conflicts is not a recent phenomenon, the British East India Company for imperial control over India being an example, this current public/private partnership is defined by new technology issues, representing not only new opportunities but also challenges.

With the accelerating development of information technologies and digitalisation, the interconnection of societies is creating new vulnerabilities and opportunities for military intelligence, requiring interventions in these environments, often held by the private sector. Examples include Iran's use of commercial satellites for espionage and the planning of ballistic strikes against the US air base at Ain al-Asad Air in Iraq in January 2020, or the terrorist group,Islamic State's (ISIS) use of social networks for recruitment, communication, and Psychological Operations (PSYOPS), making the means of political warfare available to non-state actors.[16/17]

The US services company, McKinsey, highlights various assets from the private sector:[18]

- Advanced Technology Integration from companies at the forefront of developing cutting-edge technologies, such as AI, Cybersecurity, or Unmanned Systems.
- Enhanced Intelligence Capabilities, as the amount of available data is rising, boosting intelligence gathering and processing not only with the development of Big Data Analytics but also the increased numbers of commercial satellites and advanced sensors.
- Increased Efficiency and Innovation, especially a flexible private R&D compared to the government's bureaucracy, as well as cost-effectiveness, as outsourcing might be considered as profitable.
- Flexible and Rapid Deployment, as private entities can bring logistical support or maintenance, allowing armed forces to focus on combat role. Also, private entities can offer specialised skills lacking, notably language and cultural knowledge of a specific region.
- Need for cyber specialists due to the developing role of social media and digital platforms, both offensive and defensive, as well as social media platform expertise to counter or conduct PSYOPS or cyber attacks.

In addition to these economic and technological considerations, Andreas Krieg and Jean-Marc Rickli also discuss the operational necessity of outsourcing:[19]

- Avoidance of public risk aversion to domestic blockade or scandals related to personnel's loss of life and/or failure.
- Plausible deniability, as using surrogates provides a layer of deniability, both at domestic and international levels, allowing states to distance themselves from controversial or covert operations.
- Avoiding legal and ethical restrictions to bypass legal and ethical constraints applied to regular armed forces intelligence services and engage in activities restricted under international law or national regulations.

Despite the several advantages of private sector surrogacy in the new arms race for intelligence capabilities, their growing role raises several ethical and legal concerns:

- Accountability for the contractor can be challenging to determine in the case of domestic and international law violations in conflict areas.
- The employment of private contractors raises the issue of democratic control and political supervision. These fears are particularly pronounced in the U.S., with the employment of former intelligence officers as corporate executives at Meta, TikTok, or Google, including former PSYOPS officers, fuelling fears of the use of these manipulative techniques on the American public.[20]
- The respect for the distinction between the private contractor's support function and the combat functions reserved for the armed forces remains challenging to oversight.
- The phenomenon raises ethical considerations as PMCs' involvement blurs the lines of responsibility and ethical conduct, particularly in areas like surveillance and cyber operations.

These issues can be underlined by the aforementioned example of the CIA's use of Blackwater contractors in Iraq for controversial "Snatch & Grab" operations, demonstrating the inability to strictly separate the support function from the combat function in action and raise the question of responsibility between the commander and the executor.

This blurred distinction between intelligence and private enterprise also raises other issues:

- Security of data held by the private service provider, particularly against cyberattacks or internal leaks: The "Google revolt" from February 2019 highlights the risk of non-cooperation and leaks, with more than 200 Microsoft employees protesting and making public a $480 million contract with the US Army to supply augmented reality headsets.[21]
- Data ownership: Although not a direct defence contractor, the sports application company, STRAVA, made headlines when it published geolocalised user data showing the running routes around secret infrastructures of American and French military intelligence personnel, including those deployed abroad.[22]
- Risk of a conflict of interest between private commercial logic and national security breach: A risk of loss of sovereignty is highlighted in

the case of using foreign solutions in countries where the government has legal obligations to access private company data.[23]

The company can also refuse the partnership, or even condemn it publicly, as in the case of Meta, which is both an ally against Russian or Chinese disinformation and deletes false US CENTCOM or French army accounts used for information warfare (IW). Maj. Geoff Nicholls, Commanding Officer for Digital Operations in the UK's 77th Brigade, has noted that the private sector is instrumental in identifying PSYOPS campaigns targeting NATO. However, responding with white, declared, and official propaganda actions proves ineffective, and attempts to use black propaganda are consistently blocked by digital platforms.[24]

The War of The Future in Ukraine: In Gestation or Stillborn?

The current conflict in Ukraine is seen as a laboratory for involving private digital companies in warfare. Even before hostilities began, the strategic potential of OSINT used by the private sector was evident. The investigation agency, Bellingcat, predicted an imminent attack weeks before February 24. These analyses were cited by US officials, who leveraged private strategic intelligence without exposing clandestine sources. Public disclosure of this intelligence is believed to have delayed the Russian military operation.[25]

Bruno Maçães, former Portugal Secretary of State for European Affairs and consultant at Flint Global, writes about Palantir's algorithmic solutions for artillery strikes on the Ukrainian army: "As we enter the algorithmic age, time is compressed. From the moment the algorithms set to work detecting their targets until these targets are prosecuted - a term of art in the field - no more than two or three minutes elapse." However, faced with the temptation of the miracle weapon, he warns, "How much could the Palantir software achieve in a place like Bakhmut where street warfare has been dominant?"[26]

The current promises of private digital companies for the military intelligence world thus resemble the 1990s revolution in military affairs (RMA). Improved communication and GPS targeting may have impressed the world during Operation Desert Storm, but it soon crashed in the streets of Mogadishu, got lost in the sands of Iraq, and got buried in the mountains of Afghanistan. Today, this RMA 2.0 is illustrated by the unexpected initial success of the Ukrainian army in February 2022 and the counter-offensives of the summer of the same year. However, this "miracle weapon" proved ineffective in the Bakhmut urban battle and the failed summer 2023 counter-offensive. While this public/private partnership in military digital solutions represents an undeniable technological leap in intelligence and targeting, this asset alone cannot be a game-changer, revolutionising the art of war and strategy. On a tactical scale, Palantir's algorithmic solutions were only one factor amongst others in Ukraine's success in February-March 2022, like supporting forces in a defensive position on favourable terrain, against an ill-prepared opponent with deficient logistics. On the other hand, Russian cyberattacks, which were significant in the early days of the offensive with 3,300 Distributed Denial-of-Service (DDoS) attacks against Ukrainian infrastructure, had no major military effects compared with the destruction caused by artillery or aviation.[27] While the contribution of new technologies from the private sector did not affect the outcome of the conflict in Ukraine, we must not be too quick to conclude that they will have an impact on modern warfare and its future development.

Two factors illustrate the upheavals introduced into the military landscape by the contribution of digital solutions from the private sector: a new balance between technology and land deterrence, and the extension of conflict to the civilian and geographical scales.

For Bruno Maçães, quoted above, "One idea I heard in London was that war might increasingly take place as a complex simulation within algorithmic systems. This process could have a certain deterrent power: two adversaries could reach the same conclusion as to the outcome of the conflict, thus avoiding having to trigger a conflict in the physical world."[28] While it is difficult to confirm or deny this prediction, the massive support of digital companies for Kyiv is seen as one of the keys to the latter's unexpected resistance, despite an initial balance of power seemingly greatly to its disadvantage. This factor may, therefore, tend to reinforce a serious conventional deterrent posture.

While the Ukrainian conflict seems to be dispelling the myth of the apocalyptic effects of cyber warfare, the latter is not ceasing in intensity. According to a February 2023 study by the French defence firm, Thales, cyber operations in 2022 shifted from the Ukrainian theatre to the European Union's (EU) countries. In six months, an increase from 9.8 per cent to 46.5 per cent in attacks was witnessed, mainly DDoS, particularly in Scandinavia, the Baltic states, and Poland. This trend illustrates the extension of the domain of warfare on a geographical and civilian scale outside the declared framework of armed conflict.[29] While the EU states may claim direct military non-intervention in this conflict, Russia has the means to retaliate below the spectrum of open warfare. Here, the conflict involves civilian targets, and the means of defence are mainly focused on the private sector of cyber-security companies.

The Privatisation of Military Intelligence: Strategic Revolution or Continuation of the Current Balance?

According to Mordor Intelligence, the Global Intelligence and Analytics Market is set to grow by 13 per cent annually between 2019 and 2029. While the United States is considered the biggest market, Asia is expected to record the fastest growth. Furthermore, the study of leading companies demonstrates the supremacy of the USA, with three companies in the top five—Lockheed Martin, RTX, and Northrop Grumman—followed by the UK's BAE Systems and France's Thales. The lead taken by Anglo-Saxon companies is all the more visible in the top 100 Defense Companies, with Lockheed Martin recording defence sales of $63,334.00 in 2022, i.e., 96 per cent of the company's business, followed by RTX with sales of $39,600.00 or 56 per cent of its business, and Northrop with $32,435.00 or 89 per cent of its business.[30] The UK's BAE Systems is in 7th place, with defence revenues of $25,238.85 or 96 per cent of the company's activities, while France's Thales is only in 16th place, with defence revenues of $9,644.49, accounting for 52 per cent of total revenues.

Behind these figures, it is important to take into account China's weight, despite the Communist Party's opacity surrounding its defence industry. Aviation Industry Corporation of China is in 4th place in the top 100 defense companies, with defence sales of $30,971.31, representing 37 per cent of total business, while China North Industries Group Corporation Limited (Norinco) is in 9th place, with defence sales of $17,963.66, representing 22 per cent of total business.[31]

While American and Chinese companies predominate in this sector in a context of competition and conflict between the world's first and second powers, a number of companies from different types of power also stand out in cybersecurity; Intelligence, Surveillance & Reconnaissance (ISR); Signal Intelligence (SIGINT); Electronic Intelligence (ELINT); and Unmanned Aircraft Vehicles (UAV).

These include the UK's BAE Systems and France's Thales, as well as Israel, unsurprisingly recognised as a technological powerhouse with leading-edge companies in military intelligence applications, such as Elbit Systems (31st) and Israel Aerospace Industries Ltd (37th). South Korea and Singapore, other technological powerhouses, are also represented, with Hanwha (30th), LIG Nex1 (62nd), Korea Aerospace Industries Ltd (59th), and ST Engineering (50th). Finally, Turkey, a regional power with real ambitions, is also represented with Turkish Aerospace Industries (67th, UAV & ISR) and ROKETSAN (86th, UAV & ISR).[32]

This ranking thus seems to reflect a current geopolitical trend, indicating an international order centred on American-Chinese strategic rivalry, coupled with a multipolar order in which Western powers, such as France and the United Kingdom, while maintaining advantages, face competition from Asian technological powers and states with clear political ambitions, such as Turkey.

Beyond the realm of companies and their sales, this issue touches on the state's doctrine for linking private enterprise with military intelligence. While the U.S. focuses on information dominance, the Chinese Communist Party employs the concept of civil-military fusion, supported by the Regulations on National Defense Science and Technology (2011) and the National Intelligence Law (2017), overseen by the Civil-Military Integration Development Commission (2017).[33] This approach integrates the private sector as an extension of the intelligence services under the CCP's authority. In several countries, new technological races and military intelligence revolutions have sparked debates on whether to adopt foreign systems to maintain an advantage, which implies dependence on foreign powers, or to develop these systems independently, as observed in France and India.[34]/[35]

In the context of cyber and information warfare, the American and Russian examples illustrate that the traditional military intelligence framework has been surpassed by a more comprehensive model, transcending geographical boundaries and the civilian-military and peace-war distinctions. While the exact differences between military, strategic, and domestic intelligence vary according to strategic cultures, the growing influence of digital platforms raises concerns about the potential erosion of these distinctions.

Conclusion

The privatisation of intelligence, marked by the growing involvement of private companies in military and strategic operations, represents both an evolution and a challenge for modern warfare. The convergence of advanced technologies and private enterprise has dramatically altered the landscape of intelligence, creating new opportunities and posing significant ethical, legal, and strategic dilemmas.

The cases of Ukrainian intelligence utilising the services of the OSINT company, Molfar, and the deletion of US CENTCOM's fake social media accounts by Meta illustrate the dual nature of private sector involvement in cyberintelligence. These examples underscore the transformative impact of private companies on the intelligence community, highlighting the sector's capacity for innovation and efficiency while also revealing potential vulnerabilities and ethical concerns.

The privatisation trend is underpinned by the lucrative market for intelligence services, with substantial budgets allocated to private contractors. This phenomenon is not confined to the United States; it has global implications, as evidenced by the widespread use of PMCs like the Russian Wagner Group and the increasing digitisation of intelligence operations. The blurring of lines between state and private actions, particularly in cyber warfare and information operations, challenges traditional notions of accountability and sovereignty.

Technological advancements, particularly in AI, big data analytics, and unmanned systems, have enabled private companies to offer sophisticated intelligence capabilities. These developments provide significant strategic advantages, such as enhanced data processing and rapid deployment, but also introduce risks related to data security, ownership, and the potential for conflicts of interest. The integration of private companies into military operations raises questions about democratic oversight and the ethical implications of using private entities for combat and intelligence functions.

The Ukrainian conflict serves as a testing ground for these new dynamics, demonstrating both the potential and the limitations of private sector contributions to military intelligence. While companies like Palantir have provided valuable algorithmic solutions, their effectiveness is context-dependent and does not guarantee decisive outcomes in complex combat scenarios. The role of private companies in cyber operations, exemplified by significant cyberattacks, further illustrates the extended reach of modern warfare into civilian and international domains.

Looking ahead, the growth of the global intelligence market and the strategic rivalry between major powers like the US and China will likely drive further integration of private companies into military intelligence. This trend underscores the need for robust legal frameworks and ethical guidelines to navigate the evolving landscape of privatised intelligence. As technological innovation continues to reshape the intelligence sector, balancing the benefits of private sector involvement with the imperatives of national security and ethical responsibility will remain a critical challenge for policymakers and military strategists.

Notes

1. *A Private Company Is Using Social Media to Track Down Russian Soldiers.* (n.d.). Retrieved June 7, 2024, from https://foreignpolicy.com/2023/03/02/ukraine-russia-war-military-social-media-osint-open-source-intelligence/
2. *Pentagon's secret social media influencing campaign exposed—World Socialist Web Site.* (n.d.). Retrieved June 7, 2024, from https://www.wsws.org/en/articles/2022/09/21/nnzq-s21.html
3. Nicholls, G. (2009), "Contractors and Intelligence: The Private Sector in the Intelligence Community", *International Journal of Intelligence and Counter Intelligence, 22*(4), pp. 586-613. https://doi.org/10.1080/08850600903143106
4. *Artificial Intelligence and Analytics in Defense Market—Forecast, Report & Size.* (n.d.). Retrieved June 7, 2024, from https://www.mordorintelligence.com/industry-reports/artificial-intelligence-and-analytics-in-defense-market
5. *Tech disruptors and the defense innovation future | McKinsey.* (n.d.). Retrieved June 7, 2024, from https://www.mckinsey.com/industries/aerospace-and-defense/our-insights/a-rising-wave-of-tech-disruptors-the-future-of-defense-innovation
6. *Defense Technical Information Center.* (n.d.). Retrieved June 7, 2024, from https://apps.dtic.mil/sti/citations/ADA394533 *"Digital Blackwater": NSA Leak Highlights Key Role of Private Contractors | Common Dreams.* (n.d.). Retrieved June 7, 2024, from https://www.commondreams.org/news/2013/06/11/digital-blackwater-nsa-leak-highlights-key-role-private-contractors

7. Krieg, A., & Rickli, J. M. (2019), *Surrogate Warfare: The Transformation of War in the Twenty-First Century*, pp.1-16. Georgetown University Press. https://books.google.pl/books?id=ZKaODwAAQBAJ
8. Nicholls, G. (2009), "Contractors and Intelligence: The Private Sector in the Intelligence Community",*International Journal of Intelligence and Counter Intelligence, 22*(4), pp. 586-613. https://doi.org/10.1080/08850600903143106
9. Schwartz, M., & Swain, J. (n.d.). *Department of Defense Contractors in Afghanistan and Iraq: Background and Analysis.*
10. *Blackwater Participated in CIA "Snatch and Grab" Raids.* (n.d.). Retrieved June 7, 2024, from https://www.asisonline.org/security-management-magazine/articles/2009/12/blackwater-participated-in-cia-snatch-and-grab-raids/
11. Galeotti, M. (2022), *The Weaponisation of Everything: A Field Guide to the New Way of War*, p. 41. Yale University Press. https://books.google.pl/books?id=sT2MzgEACAAJ
12. *The Threat from Russia's Unconventional Warfare Beyond Ukraine, 2022–24 | Royal United Services Institute.* (n.d.). Retrieved June 7, 2024, from https://www.rusi.org/explore-our-research/publications/special-resources/threat-russias-unconventional-warfare-beyond-ukraine-2022-24
13. *Guerres invisibles, une conversation avec Thomas Gomart | IFRI - Institut français des relations internationales.* (n.d.). Retrieved June 7, 2024, from https://www.ifri.org/fr/publications/publications-ifri/articles-ifri/guerres-invisibles-une-conversation-thomas-gomart
14. *Hayden: "Digital Blackwater" may be necessary for private sector to fight cyber threats | ZDNET.* (n.d.). Retrieved June 7, 2024, from https://www.zdnet.com/article/hayden-digital-blackwater-may-be-necessary-for-private-sector-to-fight-cyber-threats/
15. *Top 100 | Defense News, News about defense programs, business, and technology.* (n.d.). Retrieved June 7, 2024, from https://people.defensenews.com/top-100/
16. "Report: Iran used commercial satellite images to monitor US forces before attack". (n.d.). Retrieved June 7, 2024, from https://www.c4isrnet.com/intel-geoint/2021/03/01/report-iran-used-commercial-satellite-images-to-monitor-us-forces-before-attack/
17. "Modern Political Warfare: Current Practices and Possible Responses" | *RAND.* (n.d.). Retrieved June 7, 2024, from https://www.rand.org/pubs/research_reports/RR1772.html
18. "Tech disruptors and the defense innovation future" | *McKinsey.* (n.d.). Retrieved June 7, 2024, from https://www.mckinsey.com/industries/aerospace-and-defense/our-insights/a-rising-wave-of-tech-disruptors-the-future-of-defense-innovation

19. Krieg, A. & Rickli, J. M. (2019), *Surrogate Warfare: The Transformation of War in the Twenty-First Century*, pp.1-16. Georgetown University Press. https://books.google.pl/books?id=ZKaODwAAQBAJ
20. "The NATO to TikTok Pipeline: Why is TikTok Employing So Many National Security Agents?" (n.d.). Retrieved June 7, 2024, from https://www.mintpressnews.com/nato-tiktok-pipeline-why-tiktok-employing-national-security-agents/280336/
21. "Militarising Big Tech" | Transnational Institute. (n.d.). Retrieved June 7, 2024, from https://www.tni.org/en/article/militarising-big-tech
22. "Militaries Race to Cover their Tracks in Light of Strava Scandal"—AIIA - Australian Institute of International Affairs. (n.d.). Retrieved June 7, 2024, from https://www.internationalaffairs.org.au/australianoutlook/strava-heatmap-exposes-military-bases/
23. Chauvancy, R. (2023), *Les nouveaux visages de la guerre* (pp.91-93). VA éditions. https://books.google.pl/books?id=y4YJ0AEACAAJ
24. *Information Warfare Defining and Analysing—CyCon 2019—YouTube.* (n.d.). Retrieved June 7, 2024, from https://www.youtube.com/watch?v=oEvV8BveDAM
25. Bauer, A. (2023), *Au commencement était la guerre: La globalisation piteuse Vol.1*, pp.401-402. Fayard. https://books.google.pl/books?id=2Gu0EAAAQBAJ
26. "How Palantir Is Shaping the Future of Warfare" | *TIME*. (n.d.). Retrieved June 7, 2024, from https://time.com/6293398/palantir-future-of-warfare-ukraine/
27. Goya, M., & Lopez, J. (2023), *L'ours et le renard: Histoire immédiate de la guerre en Ukraine*, pp. 282-287. Place des éditeurs. https://books.google.pl/books?id=5CG2EAAAQBAJ
28. "How Palantir Is Shaping the Future of Warfare" | *TIME*. (n.d.). Retrieved June 7, 2024, from https://time.com/6293398/palantir-future-of-warfare-ukraine/
29. *De l'Ukraine à l'Europeentière: Un tournant dans la cyberguerre | Thales Group.* (n.d.). Retrieved June 7, 2024, from https://www.thalesgroup.com/fr/monde/securite/press_release/lukraine-leurope-entiere-tournant-cyberguerre
30. *Top 100 | Defense News, News about defense programs, business, and technology.* (n.d.). Retrieved June 7, 2024, from https://people.defensenews.com/top-100/
31. Ibid.
32. Ibid.
33. "At the Nexus of Military-Civil Fusion and Technological Innovation in China"—*The Diplomat*. (n.d.-a). Retrieved June 8, 2024, from https://thediplomat.com/2021/07/at-the-nexus-of-military-civil-fusion-and-technological-innovation-in-china/
34. *Compte rendu de réunion n° 64—Commission de la défensenationale et des forces armées—Session 2022-2023—16e législature—Assemblée nationale.* (n.d.).

Retrieved June 7, 2024, from https://www.assemblee-nationale.fr/dyn/16/comptes-rendus/cion_def/l16cion_def2223064_compte-rendu

35. "India and the geopolitics of technology" | Analysis—*Hindustan Times*. (n.d.). Retrieved June 7, 2024, from https://www.hindustantimes.com/analysis/india-and-the-geopolitics-of-technology/story-dd2DGyVvuhH7XmOfVSpLwL.html

12

Civil-Military Fusion in Artificial Intelligence: Scope and Challenges for India's Future Warfare Capabilities

Niranjan Marjani

Introduction

Artificial Intelligence (AI) is defined as the ability of machines to think, analyse, learn, and decide in a rational way that is analogous to how human beings do (Sharma, 2024). AI is a multidisciplinary science having numerous approaches that are based on the combination of digital data and intelligent algorithms. AI simulates human intelligence processes by machines, particularly by computer systems. In AI, the computer systems emulate human-like cognitive functions, like learning and problem- solving.

AI is rapidly becoming an integral part of various sectors. Defence is one of the sectors that are increasingly employing AI. Countries across the world are now relying on AI to develop cutting-edge technologies that give advantage to their respective armed forces. Major powers like the United States (US), Russia, and China are rapidly developing their respective military capabilities based on AI.

According to a NASSCOM report (2022), India's AI market is expected to grow anywhere between 25per cent and 35per cent by 2027 while the volume of the AI market is expected to be around $17 billion.

India's AI journey started in 2018 when NITI Aayog came out with the National Strategy for Artificial Intelligence (Niti Aayog, 2018). However, this strategy was focused on commercial and private sectors like agriculture, healthcare, education, smart cities and infrastructure, and smart mobility and transportation. It did not include defence. India's foray into AI for defence started in 2019 when the Ministry of Defence created the Defence AI Council (DAIC) and the Defence AI Project Agency (DAIPA). An annual budget of Rs. 1,000 crores (around $120 million) was allocated for AI activities in the defence sector (Ministry of Defence, 2022a).

The rapid expansion in the field of AI is parallel to India's growing quest for indigenisation of defence production. Emphasis on increasing domestic defence production inevitably has to accompany greater involvement of the private sector. It implies that civil-military fusion is necessary for India to modernise its defence sector and accelerate defence production.

This chapter discusses the use of AI in military applications and how civil-military fusion could forward the integration of AI into India's armed forces. Further, this chapter also discusses the challenges that arise from this arrangement from two perspectives. First are the challenges that are peculiar to the use of AI in the military, which arise due to issues with respect to lack of regulation and a possible misuse. Second are the challenges that arise due to the involvement of private entities through the civil-military fusion.

This chapter employs qualitative methodology. It mainly focuses on content analysis of primary and secondary sources. Primary sources include government documents and reports while secondary sources include research papers, journal articles, issue briefs, and articles in popular media.

Application of AI in Military

As discussed previously, India's initiation into AI for defence started in 2019 with the establishment of the DAIC and the DAIPA. The DAIC includes the three service commanders, the defence secretary, the national cybersecurity coordinator, and representatives from the Defence Research and Development Organisation (DRDO), academia, and research, with the defence minister as the chairperson. The task of the DAIC is to convene biannually to deliver guidance to facilitate and execute policy-level modifications, operational framework development or customisation and structural support (Jeevanandam, 2024).

The DAIPA includes Secretary (Defence Production) as the ex- officio president with members selected from academia, industry partners, the services, Defence Public Sector Undertakings, and the DRDO. The task of the DAIPA is to establish and implement benchmarks for AI initiatives' technology development and delivery process and consult user groups regarding the adoption strategy for AI-led AI-enabled systems and processes.

Following are some of the major military applications that have started employing AI technology (Jeevanandam, 2024).

Border Monitoring

This includes integrating cameras, radar feeds, sensors, and other technologies developed by AI, which help in detecting border breaches and improvement in the precision of defence operations.

Unmanned Aerial Vehicles

Drones with AI-based aircraft technology are highly effective in conducting day and night surveillance operations, which include border control and comprehensive surveillance. AI drones are capable of detecting anomalies and engaging in complex operations and can perform search and rescue operations autonomously.

Lethal Autonomous Weapons Systems (LAWS)

This is an autonomous military system that is capable of selecting and engaging targets without human intervention. LAWS can operate on land, in air, on water, underwater, and in space. LAWS contain pre-programmed algorithms and integrated sensors that assist in selecting, identifying, and tracking the targets.

Autonomous Armoured Vehicles and Robotics

These are robotic vehicles that are employed for tasks like bomb disposal, reconnaissance and logistics support. These vehicles can operate in hazardous environments and can handle various missions without putting human soldiers in danger. The autonomous vehicles are also used for transporting injured individuals and for carrying supplies in challenging geographies like mountainous regions and deserts.

Data management

AI's ability to process and manage large amounts of data makes it a crucial application for military purposes. AI can quickly filter through the data and find the most valuable information. AI can also group information from various datasets. AI can analyse and utilise the unutilised or underutilised data that can generate valuable insights for the military, which implies the capability to find connections in large volumes of information that can escape humans' notice. AI can discern patterns by analysing data from various sources. This could help in forecasting possible terror attacks and insurgency activity and could assist in taking proactive measures.

Further, integration of AI into military applications considerably enhances the military's capabilities in the areas of A2AD (anti-access/area denial) and cybersecurity (Bag, 2024). A2AD blends sophisticated technologies and tactical manoeuvres for restricting the adversaries' access to specific areas, thereby reducing their operational effectiveness within defined regions. As regards cybersecurity, AI-driven tools play an important role in detecting and responding to cyber threats, strengthening military networks, and safeguarding critical infrastructure. AI's capacity to analyse large volumes of data in real-time boosts the military's ability to counter cybersecurity threats.

Apart from the above-mentioned applications, AI technology is also used in autonomous weapons and target recognition, surveillance, cybersecurity, combat training and simulation, and robots (Bin Rashid, Karim Kausik, Al Hassan Sunny,and Hassan Bappy, 2023).

India has been nimble-footed in its approach to recognise the importance of incorporating AI for military applications. This is a positive step to keep up with the ever-evolving use of technology in defence and security, as well as to respond to the varying nature of modern-day battlefields. However, the planning and policy formulation needs to be complemented by effective implementation at the operational level. Some of the factors that need to be considered for integrating AI into military applications are (Hooda, 2023):

AI Strategy

Formulation of an AI strategy for military applications would need to be overseen by the Chief of Defence Staff (CDS). The strategy would include scale of application, organisational restructuring, ethical issues, the type of workforce required, and collaboration with private technology companies and academia.

Organisational Structure

To seamlessly integrate AI into the military, certain organisational changes need to be considered. First is establishing a policy section that would be responsible for developing, maturing, and transitioning the AI into operational use. Second is working towards centralisation of data. At present, most of the data is in service silos, and all of it is not machine-readable. The data collected from various sources like sensors, unmanned aerial vehicles, satellites, and ground-based systems should be stored in a centralised repository. Also, it is pertinent to work towards integrating service-specific networks so that the data is available to all the users. Third is establishing an acquisition section that will approve high-cost programmes to ensure that these are in accordance with the policy directions and also meet ethical and technical standards. The acquisition section will prepare procurement policy for AI programmes. It is important that the procurement policy for the AI technology is fast and not as time-consuming as other procurement policies in the military.

Balance between humans and machines

While employing AI in the military, a balance needs to be struck between the human involvement in AI and the autonomy given to the AI technology. There is lack of transparency in several AI applications, which is a cause for concern. At the same time, in the process of establishing accountability, increased human interference could severely restrict the speed and ability of the AI technology to take the best decisions and prove effective. It is, therefore, necessary to have a balance between giving autonomy to AI technology and human oversight.

Apart from these factors, from India's perspective, while employing AI, it is necessary to address the issue of right-sizing the armed forces. It implies that the government needs to take into account the extent to which AI could replace humans in the armed forces (Chinoy, 2023).

The Role of Civil-Military Fusion in AI for Military

Adapting AI technology is not only a necessary step for the Indian armed forces for operational effectiveness; it is also a major step towards military modernisation. One of the most important components of military modernisation is the process of civil-military fusion. The concept of civil-military fusion is an ancient one in which discoveries in the fields of pure sciences like physics and chemistry and innovations in engineering and technology were adapted to warfare (Shankar, 2023). All great nations have gone through the process of civil-military fusion. Civil-military fusion optimises the use of civil and military resources to achieve national objectives (Ghatak, 2023).

The innovations during the Industrial Revolution in Europe strengthened the European armies. Later, the US went through the same process of civil-military fusion during the Second World War. At that time, the entire American industry churned out military equipment that gave the US an edge over Japan and Germany (Shankar, 2021). This process led to the military-industry complex in the US, which is now seamlessly embedded in the US political system. At present, China is following a similar model of civil-military fusion through which it is aspiring to be a great power.

The current industrial revolution, termed as the Fourth Industrial Revolution or Industry 4.0, is characterised by growing automation and use of smart machines. Some of the principal components of Industry 4.0 are Internet of Things (IoT), Industrial Internet of Things (IIoT), Cyber-Physical Systems, smart manufacturing, cloud computing, cognitive computing, and artificial intelligence.

Among the various components of Industry 4.0, AI has emerged as one of the most crucial elements in modern-day warfare. Further, AI technology is finding itself to be a part of civil-military fusion practised by various countries. In light of the security challenges that India is facing, it is imperative to have civil-military fusion to address the emerging security threats in an effective manner, as well as to develop cutting-edge technologies for military applications.

China, a major adversary of India, has been successful in creating its own model of civil-military fusion to suit its needs. China's version of civil-military fusion is called Military-Civil Fusion (MCF). The MCF is formulated by the Chinese Communist Party (CCP) to enable China to develop the most technologically advanced military in the world. A key part of the MCF is elimination of barriers between China's civilian research and commercial sectors and military and defence industrial sectors. Some of the key technologies targeted under the MCF include big data, quantum computing, semiconductors, 5G, and AI.

China had sought to develop the civil-military fusion from 2015 when it issued a white paper that underscored the need for making military and civilian resources more compatible and easily accessible to facilitate development of key technology areas (Xinhua, 2015). In 2015 itself, China designed a 10-year action plan, Made in China 2025 (MIC2025), which identified 10 focus areas of which information technology was one. In this plan, China also acknowledged the need to invite foreign investors to China to invest in the areas of emerging technologies.

China gave a boost to civil-military fusion in the area of artificial intelligence through its 13th National Five Year Plan (2016-2020), which was also known as Internet Plus Plan. Within this plan, China's Ministry of Science and Technology came out with its own plan titled the 13th Five-Year Special Plan for S&T Military-Civil Fusion Development (PRC Ministry of Science and Technology, 2020).

Identifying the importance of emerging technologies in the military, former Chief of Army Staff General M.M. Naravane had called for greater investment in disruptive technologies (Pandit, 2020). General Naravane acknowledged the rapid strides taken by China in developing autonomous surveillance and weapon systems using AI. He also insisted on collaboration with different entities in developing disruptive technologies for the military.

For its part, India has initiated the use of AI in its military applications. AI is being used for surveillance along its borders with China and Pakistan. In 2022, 75 newly-developed AI products and technologies were launched at the first-ever 'AI in Defence' symposium and exhibition (Ministry of Defence, 2022b). While developing the AI technology for the military, the Defence Public Sector Undertakings (DPSUs) have started collaborating with private entities. The government is further planning to harness the private sector's large AI workforce and dual- use products in defence as well as in the digital economy (Levesques, 2024). At present, India's DPSUs are playing a major role in developing AI technology. However, allocation to research and development in the defence budget remains low, which is an impediment in innovation. More partnerships with private sectors would give greater momentum to India in integrating AI in the military. While indigenous production of technologies like AI remains vital for their realistic military incorporation, the government needs to create a conducive environment for their innovation as the majority of technologies grow out of commercial pursuits, which could be transferred to the military because of their dual-use nature (Pant, 2020).

Challenges to The Civil-Military Fusion in AI

As the use of AI grows, there are several challenges that need to be considered, particularly with reference to the involvement of the private sector in the military domain. AI is emblematic of the constantly changing and evolving nature of warfare. The warfare in the contemporary era has come to include several components, such as hybrid warfare, grey zone warfare, and asymmetric warfare, apart from the conventional warfare that involves direct kinetic actions by the armed forces of two or more countries against each other.

Information warfare forms an integral part of the modern- day war. It implies that disinformation, fake news, and deep fakes are among the major threats that form part of contemporary warfare.

Some concerns that are specific to the use of AI include whether AI is transparent in decision making, whether AI systems are impartial, whether there are necessary mechanisms in place to protect privacy, and whether there are sufficient human resources that are competent in AI (Marwala, 2023).

There are certain challenges to the civil-military fusion in India. These include limited interaction between the wings of the armed forces, lack of awareness among the civilian entities about the functioning of their military counterparts, lack of mutual trust, an overarching bureaucracy, and lack of inter-sectoral interaction between the civilian, research, industrial, commercial, military, and defence sectors (Ghatak, 2023).

Further, the dual-use nature of AI facilitates higher and easy accessibility of AI-based tools to non-state actors that can control the flow of information as also the spread of misinformation/disinformation, hate speech, and radicalisation (Sharma, 2022). Besides, the private sector with its technological advantage could gain control over the data, which could lead to possible weaponisation.

The employment of AI for military purposes is a necessity mandated by the emerging nature of the modern-day battlefield. To achieve modernisation, speedy involvement of the private sector is also imperative. However, it is important for the government to balance between the need to modernise the armed forces and the participation of the private sector and to address the risks associated with the use of AI, which range from ethical and regulatory considerations to control and prevention of misuse by private entities as well as non-state actors.

Conclusion

The role of disruptive technologies is increasingly determining the nature of warfare. For any nation to seamlessly adapt to future warfare, integrating technologies like AI into its military applications is imperative. India has been responsive to these technological advancements and has initiated an upgrade of its military technologies by focusing on AI. For India, inclusion of AI for military applications is not just a technological upgrade but also a structural recalibration. On the structural front, insistence on domestic defence manufacturing has been an important step for India. To build upon this, it is necessary that India works towards greater involvement of the private sector, implying strengthening of civil-military fusion. While the DPSUs have been taking the lead in developing emerging technologies, issues like delayed and limited funding for research and development often have an adverse impact on the functioning of these units. The private sector, with its cutting-edge technologies, adequate funding, and nimble-footed approach to the developments in the technological field, would contribute to rapid development of AI in partnership with the government. The dual-use nature of the technology developed by the private sector further offers it greater opportunity to partner with the government. While issues like regulation, control, and possible misuse of AI remain a concern in case of military applications, persistent security threats from adversaries necessitate that the government must find the right balance in prioritising technological upgrade for the military and sort out the issues of control and misuse through partnerships with the private sector. Civil-military fusion, in general, is important to boost the efficiency of defence manufacturing. The emergence of AI further calls for expediting this process to boost innovation and to equip India's military with cutting-edge technology in AI.

References

Bag, S. (January 30, 2024), "Guardians of tomorrow: How AI shapes the future of the armed forces". Retrieved June 13, 2024, from Observer Research Foundation website: https://www.orfonline.org/research/guardians-of-tomorrow-how-ai-shapes-the-future-of-the-armed-forces

Bin Rashid, A., Karim Kausik, A., Al Hassan Sunny, A., & Hassan Bappy, M. (2023), "Artificial Intelligence in the Military: An Overview of the Capabilities, Applications, and Challenges", *International Journal of Intelligent Systems*, *2023*, pp. 1–31. https://doi.org/10.1155/2023/8676366

Chinoy, S. R. (December 31, 2023), "Civil-military fusion for Atmanirbhar Bharat". Retrieved June 13, 2024, from Observer Research Foundation website: https://www.orfonline.org/expert-speak/civil-military-fusion-for-atmanirbhar-bharat

Ghatak, Lt. Col. S. (2023), "Civil Military Fusion for National Security", *Journal of the United Service Institution of India*, *CLIII*(632).

Hooda, Lt. Gen. D. S. (February 16, 2023), "Implementing Artificial Intelligence in the Indian Military". Retrieved June 17, 2024, from Delhi Policy Group website: https://www.delhipolicygroup.org/publication/policy-briefs/implementing-artificial-intelligence-in-the-indian-military.html

Jeevanandam, Dr. N. (January 15, 2024), "Impact of AI in the Indian Army". Retrieved June 13, 2024, from INDIAai website: https://indiaai.gov.in/article/impact-of-ai-in-the-indian-army

Levesques, A. (January 18, 2024), "Early steps in India's use of AI for defence". Retrieved June 18, 2024, from International Institute for Strategic Studies website: https://www.iiss.org/en/online-analysis/online-analysis/2024/01/early-steps-in-indias-use-of-ai-for-defence/

Marwala, T. (2023, July 24). Militarization of AI Has Severe Implications for Global Security and Warfare. Retrieved June 19, 2024, from United Nations University website: https://unu.edu/article/militarization-ai-has-severe-implications-global-security-and-warfare

Ministry of Defence (March 28, 2022a), "TASK FORCE FOR IMPLEMENTATION OF AI". Retrieved June 16, 2024, from *Press Information Bureau* website: https://pib.gov.in/PressReleaseIframePage.aspx?PRID=1810442

Ministry of Defence (July 11, 2022b), "Raksha Mantri launches 75 Artificial Intelligence products/technologies during first-ever "AI in Defence" symposium & exhibition in New Delhi; Terms AI as a revolutionary step in the development of humanity". Retrieved June 18, 2024, from *Press Information Bureau* website: https://pib.gov.in/PressReleasePage.aspx?PRID=1840740

NASSCOM (2022), *AI Powered Tech Services: A Roadmap for Future Ready Firms.* Retrieved from https://www.nasscom.in/knowledge-center/publications/ai-powered-tech-services-roadmap-future-ready-firms

Niti Aayog (2018),*National Strategy for Artificial Intelligence.*

Pandit, R. (August 25, 2020), "Indian armed forces need to invest in disruptive technologies: Gen Naravane", *The Times of India.* Retrieved from https://timesofindia.indiatimes.com/india/indian-armed-forces-need-to-invest-in-disruptive-technologies-gen-naravane/articleshow/77744148.cms

Pant, H. V. (August 31, 2020), "Disruptive technologies in the Indian military matrix". Retrieved June 18, 2024, from Observer Research Foundation website: https://www.orfonline.org/expert-speak/disruptive-technologies-in-the-indian-military-matrix-72494

PRC Ministry of Science and Technology (June 24, 2020), "The "13th Five-Year" Special Plan for S&T Military-Civil Fusion Development". Retrieved June 18, 2024, from Center for Security and Emerging Technology website: https://cset.georgetown.edu/publication/the-13th-five-year-special-plan-for-st-military-civil-fusion-development/

Shankar, Lt. Gen. P. R. (November 19, 2021), "Civil Military Fusion: An Indian Necessity". Retrieved June 17, 2024, from MyIndMakers website: https://www.myind.net/Home/viewArticle/civil-military-fusion-an-indian-necessity

Shankar, Lt. Gen. P. R. (May 13, 2023), "Civil Military Fusion: A Model for India". Retrieved June 13, 2024, from The Jaipur Dialogues website: https://www.thejaipurdialogues.com/strategic-and-military/civil-military-fusion-a-model-for-india/#google_vignette

Sharma, S. (2022), *AI and National Security: Major Power Perspectives and Challenges.* Manohar Parrikar Institute for Defence Studies and Analyses.

Sharma, V. (April 11, 2024), "Artificial Intelligence: Definition, Evolution, Working, Importance, Tools". Retrieved June 13, 2024, from Y20 India website: https://y20india.in/artificial-intelligence/

Xinhua (May 26, 2015), Full Text: China's Military Strategy- China.org.cn. Retrieved June 18, 2024, from China.org.cn website: http://www.china.org.cn/china/2015-05/26/content_35661433_5.htm

13

An Analysis of Russia's Counter-Terrorism Efforts in The Sahel: The Case of Burkina Faso and Mali (2015-2023)

John Mwangi Githigaro

Introduction

This study principally appraises Russia's counter-terrorism efforts in the Sahel region with a focus on Burkina Faso and Mali and their effectiveness The study contributes to emerging discourses on renewed Russian foreign policy interests in the African continent.

The study problematises the security dynamics within the Sahel region by identifying different security actors and their interests. The study examines Russia's counter-terrorism efforts with a case study approach. The rationale for the two case studies is largely geographical but also partly around the emerging security dynamics in this region. Studies focused on Russia's security engagement in the region have been marginal. There is, however, a multiplicity of other scholarly perspectives that have focused predominantly on France, the United States, and the European Union. Shifting dynamics and military coups in both countries, including the withdrawal of European intervention in Mali, presents opportunities to explore how recent actors, such as Russia, are intervening in an increasingly multipolar world. Moreover, Burkina Faso and Mali are almost at the bottom of the global Fragile States Index. In 2020, Burkina Faso and Mali were ranked 182nd and 184th respectively by the United Nations Human Development Index (HDI).[1] These two countries fit the contextualisation of poor and fragile countries and can be said to be in a state of negative sovereignty.

This study acknowledges that what constitutes terrorism continues to be debated in the scholarship. Perspectives range from the mobilisation of political violence through insurgencies and guerrilla warfare to its transnational and ideological effect in a wider sense. There is, however, general consensus about what constitutes counter-terrorism, which is the focus of this paper. Counter-terrorism refers to a broad range of policy practices that include strategies, activities, and initiatives to address terrorism threats. Counter-terrorism as a policy field has now come to be associated with discourse around 'Preventing and Countering Violent Extremism' (P/CVE). The P/CVE landscape, however, is not uniform and remains blurry in accessing its implications. On one hand, P/CVE is considered to be replete with uncertainties around the purpose of interventions and expected outcomes. On the other hand, it is a field laden with competition and influence by multiple actors involved. The multiplicity of actors in the P/CVE landscape in contexts such as Mali and indeed in the entire Sahel provides a worthy area of engagement to unravel how different actors are projecting their space, authority, and power.[2]

The Sahel region has generally been framed as an arc of insecurity, particularly in the war on terror. Terrorism, a notable security challenge in the region, is a cross- cutting regional threat and has been linked to the presence of weak and fragile states in the region. Current debates in the Sahel have therefore focused on violent extremist threats and the reconfiguration of armed groups that cut across local conflicts, regional alliances, and global terror groups, such as the Al-Qaeda and Daesh.[3]

The aftermath of the Arab Spring and the revolutions that occurred in parts of the Middle East and North Africa further created conditions that had an impact in the Sahel. The collapse of the regimes in Egypt and Tunisia, a weakened Libya and Yemen, and the waning authority of the central governments in Syria and Iraq most notably led to the rise of the Islamic State (Daesh). Its cells began to appear in several parts of Asia and Africa. In

Burkina Faso, for instance, some terrorist organisations swore their allegiance to Daesh.[4]

Whereas discourses such as failed and fragile states have been contested in the literature, they enable a contextualisation of threats, particularly from western-centric perspectives. Taken from a western-centric perspective, the use of the term 'fragile state' denotes the lack of a central authority in a country to guarantee safety and order and hence, the rise of criminal and/ or non- state actors within a territory. This is then termed as 'ungoverned space', which, in turn, leads to internal conflicts with implications for international security. In other words, states in the Sahel, including our case studies Mali and Burkina Faso, have been characterised as states experiencing negative sovereignty and hence, the prescription for state stabilisation initiatives. These stabilisation initiatives are focused on reconstruction of state security capacities and the entrenching western- oriented governance arrangements.[5] The Sahel has, since the 2000s, been conceptualised by multiple actors, such as states, international organisations, and the media, as a security threat. Each of the actors has stakes and interests in how they perceive the nature of threats in the region.[6] These state stabilisation interventions, however, need to take into account local contexts, political economy, and national perspectives. [7] Securitising initiatives should, therefore, pay attention to the intersection between poverty, security, and development within the Sahel region.[8]

Counter-insurgency and counter-terrorism cooperation (COIN-CT) has become a significant element of cooperation between African nations and key global actors following the September 11, 2001, attacks in the United States (hereafter 9/11). Whereas, primarily, western countries have been engaged in the COIN-CT domain, there is a growing influence of non- western states in this domain. The Russian Federation is one such actor engaged in this sphere. Counter-terrorism is a growing agenda for Russia's Africa policy, with multiple military and technical cooperation agreements being signed with the African continent. It was at the first Russia-Africa Summit in 2019 in Sochi that President Putin observed that, among others, terrorism and extremism were hindering Africa's development trajectory. In this summit, President Putin emphasised the value of building contacts between Russian and African law enforcement agencies and special services to counter terrorist groups operating in the African continent. He referenced the Sahel-Sahara Zone, the Lake Chad Basin, and the Horn of Africa.[9]

Furthermore, at the second Africa-Russia Summit held in July 2023 in St. Petersburg, there was a call to strengthen security cooperation in addressing multiple security threats. Russia, in this summit, called for enhanced bilateral cooperation and UN and regional arrangements, such as the African Union, to counter threats like terrorism, extremism, and violent extremism. This summit also called for terrorism prevention initiatives, such as ensuring favourable social and economic conditions and opportunities for education and self-expression. This summit further reiterated the value of adequate, sustainable, and predictable funding for counter-terrorism interventions in Africa. It further underscored, in this pursuit, respect for principles and norms, such as the relevant United Nations Security Council Resolutions, including the provisions of the UN Global Counter-Terrorism Strategy.[10]

This study is, however, focused on appraising Russia's counter-terrorism interventions in the Sahel. It undertakes two case studies to unravel Russian counter- terrorism agenda in the Sahel region. The study's principal puzzle with a case of Burkina Faso and Mali situates how Russia's engagement in this domain is proceeding, particularly with the withdrawal or scaling down of prior predominant counter-terrorism actors in the Sahel, such as the French. The study's novelty lies in part with an evolving counter-terrorism agenda that has been unfolding with African nations more predominantly since 2015. Failed western counter-terrorism interventions in Africa, including anti- western and anti- French sentiments particularly in the Sahel, has offered Russia an opportunity to engage in Africa. Russia has signed inter-governmental agreements centred on military and defence cooperation with all the member countries of the G5 Sahel. These include arm supplies and military training.[11]

The study is structured as follows: following a short methodology note, the study's first part situates the security actors in the Sahel, then presents backgrounds of Mali and Burkina Faso, followed by Russia's counter-terrorism engagements in the two case studies. The last part concludes with an appraisal and policy implications.

Methodology Note

This study adopted desktop-based research with a focus on document analysis to respond to the study questions. A comparative case study approach was applied. These included the review of academic journals, books, periodicals, speeches, conference outcome documents, mainstream media, communiques, and social media discourses. These materials were analysed thematically to respond to the study questions.

Generally, the issue of terrorism in the Sahel region is viewed through the lens of the securitisation theory. Lack of resources drives African states into the dilemma of getting attention from international donors and great powers. The most common answer is to connect local challenges to regional and global problems and then turn them into challenges for the donors themselves.[12] Since 2012, the Sahel area has been relatively successfully positioned by regional states as a possible shelter for terrorist groups and transnational crime[13]. However, the securitisation theory generally tends to ignore why some issues are getting more attention and some are getting less.[14]

Thus, we combine the securitisation theory with the elements of the international regimes theory. Cooperation between the Sahel countries and the great powers is developing due to a set of norms and expectations that are agreed on at the international level and that are streamlining the behaviour of states.[15] Particularly, an international counter-terrorism regime has emerged since 2001 and there are structured efforts in different regions across the globe. This international regime is much more developed than some other global frameworks (on migration or AIDS), which makes it more useful for states to be involved in actions in the counter-terrorism issue area. So, when terrorism got into the securitisation process in the Sahel, acertain amount of expectations and supply rules was in place for security providers (like France).[16] When those expectations and rules were not met by these providers, the Sahel countries opted for alternatives that were able to meet international counter-terrorism regime standards and to address security concerns.

Security Actors in the Sahel

There exists a multiplicity of security actors within the Sahel who play varied roles either in the enhancement of security and or in the promotion of insecurity in the Sahel region.

International actors

Post September 11, 2001, which marked the rise of the so- called 'Global War on Terror', there have been a host of international actors intervening to build peace in the region. The more active interveners within the region and in the context of different conflict dynamics within the region include the United States, France, and the European Union, with Russia as the most recent actor in the Sahel. Whereas these geopolitical actors have sometimes competing visions of security management in the region, there is a sufficient level of convergence around enhancing border management and states' capacities.[17] Security sector reforms top the foreign policy agendas of international actors. These partners in the context of donor support have to contend with low institutional and administrative capacities to absorb funding by Sahelian states, including corruption and mismanagement.[18]

Jihadi insurgent groups

Within the Sahel Region and, in particular, with the two case studies chosen for this study, Burkina Faso and Mali, there exists a multiplicity of jihadi groups. These groups have managed to exploit local grievances and, in particular, their framing of marginalisation from states at different levels, such as economics, religion, and ethnic reasons. Moreover, they have also taken over state- linked functions in areas they control through the provision of public goods, such as health, security, and education.[19]

These terrorist groups include the Al-Qaeda in the Islamic Maghreb, the Islamic State in the Greater Sahara formed in Mali in 2015, and the Ansarul Islam, which operates in both Mali and Burkina Faso. These groups have, therefore, been securitised by France, the US and the EU as presenting threats to regional and international security. Their responses have varied, including counter-terrorism operations, capacity development for militaries, and related state stabilisation initiatives, even as they secure their strategic interests they considered at risk due to rising insurgencies in the region.[20]

Similarly, outside of the Sahel's context, other social movement groups, such as the Al-Shabaab in Eastern Africa, have continued to wage their insurgencies on the basis of perceived grievances blamed on the state and, by extension, external geopolitical actors. Furthermore, such actors have continued to build on their legitimacy with local populations by providing state-linked functions in the context of fragile states. They continue to offer humanitarian aid, security, and judicial functions, in return taxing these populations and expecting allegiance to the group.

The plethora of these armed groups in the two case studies are considered by some commentators in the Sahel to be in competition for status, territorial control, and resources.[21] The table below illustrates that terrorism threats have been on an upward trajectory, as captured by terrorism deaths.

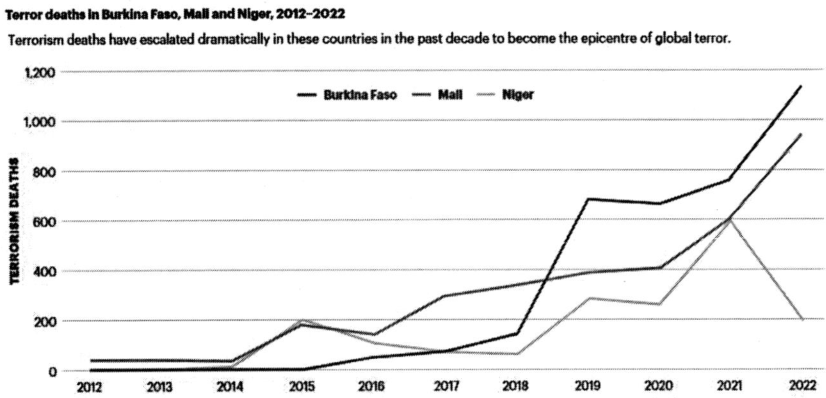

Source: Global Terrorism Index (GTI), 2023, p. 66.

Regional mechanisms

Within the Sahel, the African Union, and the sub-regional organisation, the Economic Community of West African States (ECOWAS), have been part of conflict management. They have, however, in certain instances, been relegated to the periphery by extra regional actors. Africa regional organisations' responses have been impacted by inadequate funding, external interference, and sovereignty concerns by member states.[22]

The Case of Mali

In order to understand the current stabilisation efforts, including counter-terrorism in Mali, it is imperative to discuss the context and the range of actors that have destabilised the country and indeed, the Sahel region. In January 2012, Tuareg rebels, in alliance with jihadist armed groups, captured the northern territories of Mali. In March 2012, a component of the Malian army staged a coup, arguing that the state had been unable to handle the ensuing crisis. In January 2013, the French government, under President Francois Hollande, ordered the launch of Operation Serval. This military intervention was justified on the threats that a destabilised Mali posed to the West Africa neighbourhood and indeed, to Europe. Operation Serval was intended, among other objectives, to restore the territorial integrity of the state and was later transformed into Operation Barkhane. This operation securitised the Sahel states as battlegrounds for transnational terrorist forces within the context of 'ungoverned spaces' and therefore, aided in Sahelian state formation and nation- building. The French later passed on the mantle of stabilisation to the United Nations, the African Union, and other partners. Since 2013, there has therefore been a series of regional and international interventions aimed at stabilising Mali, and indeed, the Sahel,and preventing and countering violent extremism.[23]

Mali has become a site of external interventionism by external actors often with competing geopolitical interests. The securitisation of the region has led to a host of responses from France, the United States, the European Union, and the UN, as was with the case of the Multidimensional Integrated Stabilization Mission in Mali (MINUSMA).[24] These interventions have been critiqued as being disjointed and uncoordinated with a series of failures identified. Security sector reforms, for example, fail to account for incoherent military structures, gaps in professionalism, and entrenched corruption within the structures generally.[25] These interventions have largely followed liberal interventionism with prescribed ideas about how to order political authority and monopoly of violence. Following this logic, interventions, including military engagements, are focused on enhancing state sovereignty.[26] The range of interventions may include counter-terrorism, migration control, and political stabilisation, some of which may not be properly coordinated, leading to failures that may require counter-interventions. These interventions acquire different lexicons depending on the different actors. For the French, these could be termed 'interventions' while for other actors, such as the United States, these may be termed 'security cooperation'.

Two coups in August 2020 and May 2021 further changed the political dynamic in and around Mali. In June 2021, French President Emmanuel Macron announced the end of Operation Barkhane.[27]

Russia's Counter-terrorism Engagements in Mali

Russia, through her varied foreign policy engagements including the Russia-Africa summit, has continued to call for security cooperation in addressing the threats of terrorism, extremism, and violent extremism. This cooperation is notable for support in such areas as information exchange and sharing of best practices for countering threats and challenges. These include capacity development for law enforcement officials, support in countering transnational organised crimes, and foreign terrorist fighters including countering terrorism financing. Moreover, Russia has noted the valuable role of the African Union as the regional architecture in ensuring peace and stability in the continent, which, in turn, enables the realisation of Agenda 2063, the African Union's continental blueprint.[28]

Military and Technical cooperation

Russia, in 2019, signed a new military cooperation agreement with the then Malian government. This cooperation included military and political cooperation, as well as collaboration in counter-terrorism work.[29] Some of the immediate outcomes included the supply of several defence equipment including attack helicopters, weapons, and ammunitions. Prior to this new agreement, Russia has a long history of military cooperation with Mali, having signed a cooperation agreement in 1994. This cooperation came in the context of the then growing resentment of the French military presence in Mali and other parts of the Sahel. The French military interventions prior to its withdrawal in Mali were interpreted on the premise of neo- colonial objectives, particularly on France's raw materials interests. The warming up of countries towards Russia can be partly explained by the fact that Russia has no colonial ties and has minimal specific conditions for the host countries unlike other western partners.

Private Military Diplomacy

Following the military coup of August 2020, the Malian military interim government forged a partnership with the private security actor, the Wagner group. With roots in Russia, the group was contracted to offer military training, close protection, and more fundamentally, support with counter-terrorism operations in Mali. Prior to this agreement, the Wagner group has since 2017 been engaged in the continent, including in the Sudan and the Central African Republic (CAR).[30] Wagner was founded in 2014, with its operations commencing in 2014 during the conflict in Eastern Ukraine.[31]

The entry of the Wagner group came shortly after France announced the withdrawal of its counter-terrorism units. The activities of the group on the African continent have elicited competing perspectives as to its motives and interests. It has been termed in some quarters as a quasi- state agent of Russia's foreign policy on the continent. As a private military actor in comparison with similar PMCS, it offers a variety of services, including intelligence collection, reconnaissance, and protection work. Wagner's more visible engagements have been in Syria and Ukraine.[32]

In late 2021, the Wagner group arrived in Mali and embarked on a series of counter-terrorism initiatives. Subsequently, it was engaged in counter-terrorism operations with the Malian forces, including combat with JNIM and ISIS militants. There is yet to be considerable success in the counter-terrorism efforts in a fragile security situation, with multiple claims of human rights violations in their operations.[33] Wagner's operation in Mali is interpreted from the broader lens of a geopolitical context with the West. Wagner has, therefore, presented itself as an alternative to western partners in the counter-terrorism domain. However, a section of scholars commenting on Russia-Africa relations contend that Wagner and Russia's influence on the African continent has been largely motivated by the need to counter international isolation efforts by the West. This has particularly been so since 2022 with Russia's operations in Ukraine.[34] The demise of the key leaders of the Wagner group, including Yevgeny Prigozhinfollowing a plane crash in late August 2023, makes it uncertain how its operations will proceed in the near future.[35] Prior to an attempted mutiny by the group in June 2023, analysts contended that it had been a critical actor in Russia's recent projection of power and influence in multiple African countries including Mali.

The Case of Burkina Faso

Since 2019, Burkina Faso has experienced more extensive jihadist attacks than other country in the Sahel. The border region of Liptako-Gourma, which separates Mali from Burkina Faso and Niger, has been home to several social movements groups including the Movement for the Oneness and Jihad in West Africa and the Ansar Ul Islam. Similar to the Malian case study, a combination of poverty, inequality, and multiple violent extremist groups has served to complicate further the security situation. The deteriorating security situation has, in the last couple of years, contributed to internal displacement. Given the complexity of the security situation, defence budgets shot up even as external actors, most predominantly France, have engaged in a range of security interventions. Previous policies under the G5 Sahel group have been focused on cooperation to address the complex security situation in the Sahel Belt. The French, in particular, had been concerned by terrorism threats, even though some analysts have contended that the strategic intention of France in the military interventions in this region have been to tame migration emanating towards Europe. Migrants from this region often move to the Libyan Coast and onto the Mediterranean Sea and head to Europe.[36]

Between 1990- 2014, Burkina Faso had minimal terrorism incidents with only three situations recorded. Terrorism incidents, however, escalated after 2015 for several reasons. One was the fall of the Compaore regime through a revolution after a 27-year grip on power in 2014 and subsequently, a failed military coup. Compaore's resignation also halted a series of agreements and informal ties that he had built with regional jihadist organisations. Moreover, Burkina Faso's close proximity to Mali and the presence of multiple terrorist groups with cross- border reach served to destabilise the country further.[37] Instability in Burkina Faso has further been complicated by a series of coups in 2022. Two coups were witnessed in 2022, with the recent coup of October 2022 being blamed on the previous junta's failures to counter terrorism threats. According to the 2023 Global Terrorism Index, Burkina Faso is ranked second. The current context of political instability and ecological degradation further complicates the counter-terrorism responses. Whereas state counter-terrorism efforts are required, there also needs to be careful balance to avoid heavy securitisation that can lead to terrorist groups' recruitment. Security commentators portend that heavy-handedness, especially by state officials, can create conditions for further recruitment.[38]

Counter-terrorism Appraisal in Burkina Faso

Burkina Faso and Russia have a nascent relationship in the counter-terrorism domain. One of the earliest cooperation agreements dates back to a 2018 intergovernmental agreement to share experiences in the field of peacekeeping and counter-terrorism.[39]

Prospects for Military and Technical Cooperation in Burkina Faso

There are signals that with the emerging dynamics in the Sahel, such as France's withdrawal of its troops, Russia offers security support including in counter-terrorism. This evolving partnership can be read from a series of diplomatic engagements between Russia and Burkina Faso. On August 31, 2023, the Burkinabe military leader welcomed a Russian delegation led by Deputy Defence Minister, Yunus-Bek Yevkurov. In this meeting, there were discussions on future military cooperation. These discussions included Russia training Burkinabe soldiers and pilots. This meeting was a follow- up of the previous discussions that were held during the second Russia- Africa summit at St. Petersburg in July 2023, where Burkina Faso sought Russia's cooperation in fighting jihadist groups in the country. There are likely projections that private actors, such as the Wagner group, who already have a presence in neighbouring Mali since 2021 could be deployed there. Private military actors could therefore be relied upon for counter-terrorism efforts in Burkina Faso.[40]

Appraisal and Conclusion

Within the study period, the threats of terrorism have continued to escalate in Mali and Burkina Faso. In the last decade, there has been a measure of hard kinetic counter-terrorism measures with the support of international actors, such as Russia. Russia's engagement in the counter-terrorism domain has included a mix of interventions, including capacity building for the military, equipment, and engagement in private military diplomacy. Burkina Faso, Mali, and, by extension, Niger, have continued to be the epicentre of Sahelian terrorism. This is based on a combination of factors that include political instability and the growth of ISIS- affiliates in the region. [41] Both countries' case studies demonstrate that gaps in state capacities have meant that terrorist groups will continue to exploit the region. This study speaks to a growing foreign policy agenda for Russia in counter-terrorism. This is predicated on several factors. One is Russia's acknowledgment that international terrorism is a national security threat and which has seen the shift from a regional focus, such as the North Caucasus to engagements in countering glocalised terrorism. Additionally, it is also involved as part of a geopolitical competition at the global and regional levels. Moreover, Moscow is determined to counter political and diplomatic isolation efforts by the West, and counter-terrorism is an opportunity to demonstrate that it shares security concerns such as those of the West. This can be interpreted as boosting Russia's profile globally by its engagement with regional and global actors in this domain. Furthermore, Moscow has been keen to advance its own counter-terrorism narrative within the international counterterrorism regime. In this regard, Russia was a critical actor in the development of the UN Global Counter-terrorism Strategy and has been keen to influence the UN counter-terrorism architecture. Moscow is further motivated to be in the counter-terrorism field in Africa for pursuits of its interests, which includes arms sales and military technical assistance. Moscow, in this regard, is a potential partner in the COIN- CT agenda for Africa and can leverage on its counter-terrorism successes in the Central African Republic and Syria.[42]

Some commentators have pointed to several weaknesses around Moscow's COIN- CT model in Africa, which have relevance to the current case studies. One is that Russia is yet to create or join an international CT coalition and works within bilateral defence and military technical agreements and neglects the institutionalisation of CT cooperation. This becomes challenging, particularly in the contexts of regime changes, which has implications for long- term counter-terrorism cooperation. Secondly, there has been very minimal cooperation between Russia, the African Union, and regional communities. This would be critical given the cross-border nature of terrorism threats. Thirdly, there has been an undervaluing of soft power interventions. Russia's support to developmental projects remains limited and would be central to addressing the socio-economic causes of terrorism. Despite these aforementioned weaknesses, there are opportunities for Moscow to expand its influence on the continent through provision of security. Joint COIN-CT exercises and military and technical cooperation are areas that Russia has competence in and which African countries require.[43] The Concept of the Foreign Policy of the Russian Federation of March 2023 speaks to supporting interested African states through security assistance and deepening African cooperation on a bilateral and multi-lateral basis, including working with the African Union.[44]

As a long- term strategy for counter-terrorism, it is imperative for states in the Sahel, including Mali and Burkina Faso, in partnership with foreign interveners, to take into account the grievances of diverse communities. This would include putting in place institutional mechanisms that would address the social-political and cultural contexts of the conflicts in this region.[45]

Notes

1. Morten Bøås & Francesco Strazzari (2020), "Governance, Fragility and Insurgency in the Sahel: A Hybrid Political Order in the Making", *The International Spectator*, 55:4, pp. 1-17, DOI: 10.1080/03932729.2020.1835324
2. Edoardo Baldaro & Silvia D'Amato (2023), "Transnational counterterrorism assemblages: the case of preventing and countering violent extremism in Mali", *Territory, Politics, Governance* https://Doi.Org/10.1080/21622671.2023.2268651
3. Morten Bøås & Francesco Strazzari (2020), "Governance, Fragility and Insurgency in the Sahel: A Hybrid Political Order in the Making", *The International Spectator*, 55:4, pp. 1-17, DOI: 10.1080/03932729.2020.1835324
4. Issaev et al., (2022),*The Global Terrorist Threat in the Sahel and the Origins of Terrorism in Burkina Faso*
5. Baldaro, Edoardo (2021), "Rashomon in the Sahel: Conflict dynamics of security regionalism", *Security Dialogue* 52 (3), pp. 266-283.
6. Stambøl, Eva Magdalena, and Tobias Berger (2023), "Transnationally entangled (in) securities: The UAE, Turkey, and the Saharan political economy of danger", *Security Dialogue* 54(5), pp. 493-514.
7. Morten Bøås & Francesco Strazzari (2020), "Governance, Fragility and Insurgency in the Sahel: A Hybrid Political Order in the Making", *The International Spectator*, 55(4),pp. 1-17, DOI: 10.1080/03932729.2020.1835324
8. Stephen Osaherumwen Idahosa, Denis Andreevich Degterev & Solomon Ijeweimen Ikhidero (2021),"Securitisation initiatives and the lingering security challengesin Sub-Saharan Sahel region: An appraisal",*African Security Review*, 30(3),pp. 338-367, DOI:10.1080/10246029.2021.1970597
9. Sergey, V. Kostelyanets (2021), "Russia's Counterterrorism and Counterinsurgency Strategy in Africa" in *Terrorism in Africa: New Trends and Frontiers*. Moscow Institute for African Studies; University of Haifa, pp, 154-166.
10. Cf. Declaration of the Second Russia–Africa Summit available at http://en.kremlin.ru/supplement/5972 (accessed 28/08/23).
11. Leonid M.,Issaev Alisa, R. Shishkina, Yakov B. Liokumovich (2023), "Russian Policy of Securitization in Africa: Features of Perception", *Vestnik RUDN. International Relations*. 23(2), pp. 322-338.

12. Fisher, Jonathan and David M. Anderson (2015), "Authoritarianism and the securitization of development in Africa", *International Affairs* 91(1), pp. 131-151.
13. Sour, Lotfi (2015), "The Strategy of Securitization in African Sahel: Regional Arrangements and Transnational Security Challenges", *International Journal of Political Science* 1(2), pp. 6-18.
14. Williams, Paul D. (2008), "Regional arrangements and transnational security challenges: the African Union and the limits of securitization theory", *African security* 1(1), pp. 2-23.
15. Stephan Haggard and Beth A. Simmons (1987), "Theories of international regimes", *International Organization,* 41(3), pp. 491–517.
16. Whitaker, Beth Elise (2010), "Compliance among weak states: Africa and the counter-terrorism regime", *Review of International Studies* 36(3), pp. 639-662.
17. Ibid. Baldaroet al.
18. Morten Bøås & Francesco Strazzari (2020), "Governance, Fragility and Insurgency in the Sahel: A Hybrid Political Order in the Making", *The International Spectator*, 55(4), pp.1-17, DOI: 10.1080/03932729.2020.1835324
19. Ibid. Baldaroet al.
20. Stephen Osaherumwen Idahosa, Denis Andreevich Degterev & Solomon IjeweimenIkhidero (2021), "Securitisation initiatives and the lingering security challenges in Sub-Saharan Sahel region: An appraisal", *African Security Review*, 30(3), pp. 338-367, DOI:10.1080/10246029.2021.1970597
21. Morten Bøås & Francesco Strazzari (2020), "Governance, Fragility and Insurgency in the Sahel: A Hybrid Political Order in the Making", *The International Spectator*, 55(4), pp. 1-17, DOI: 10.1080/03932729.2020.1835324
22. Martin Welz (2022), "The African Union, France, and Conflict Management in Mali: Preferences, Actions, and Narrations", *Journal of Intervention and Statebuilding*, 16(3), pp. 287-305, DOI: 10.1080/17502977.2022.2045147
23. Charbonneau, B. (2021), "Counter-insurgency governance in the Sahel", *International Affairs*, 97(6), pp. 1805-1823.
24. Ibid.
25. Niagalé Bagayoko (2022), "Explaining the failure of internationally-supported defence and security reforms in Sahelian states", *Conflict, Security & Development*, 22(3), pp. 243-269, DOI: 10.1080/14678802.2022.2097776
26. Bernardo Venturi & Nana Toure (2020), "The Great Illusion: Security Sector Reform in the Sahel", *The International Spectator*, 55(4), pp. 54-68, DOI: 10.1080/03932729.2020.1835326
27. Charbonneau, B. (2021), "Counter-insurgency governance in the Sahel", *International Affairs*, 97(6), pp. 1805-1823.
28. Declaration of the Second Russia–Africa Summit, available at http://en.kremlin.ru/supplement/5972 (accessed 28/08/23).

29. Elena Pokalova (2023), "The Wagner Group in Africa: Russia's Quasi-State Agent of Influence", *Studies in Conflict & Terrorism*, DOI: 10.1080/1057610X.2023.2231642
30. Adela, G. (2023), "A Force for the Right Purpose? Rethinking Western COIN Interventions in Africa's Sahel", *Journal of Military and Strategic Studies, 22*(3).
31. Theo N. (2023), "Russian Para-Military Operations in Africa: The Wagner Group as a De Facto Foreign PolicyInstrument", *South Africa Journal of Military Affairs*, 51(1), pp. 1-23 DOI: 10.5787/51-1-1403
32. Elena Pokalova (2023), "The Wagner Group in Africa: Russia's Quasi-State Agent of Influence", *Studies in Conflict & Terrorism*, DOI: 10.1080/1057610X.2023.2231642
33. Ibid.
34. Theo Neethling (2023), "Russian Para-Military Operations in Africa: The Wagner Group as a De Facto Foreign PolicyInstrument",*South Africa Journal of Military Affairs,* 51(1), pp. 1-23, DOI: 10.5787/51-1-1403
35. Kimberly Marten (2023), "Whither Wagner? The Consequences of Prigozhin's Mutiny and Demise", *Survival,* 65(5), pp.45-64, DOI: 10.1080/00396338.2023.2261245
36. G. M. Sidorovaa &. A. Zherlitsyna (2023), "Migration Processes in Africa and the Problem of Security On the Occasion of the Second Russia–Africa Summit", Vestnik Rossiiskoi Akademii Nauk, 93(2), pp. 141–149.
37. Issaev, L. M., Korotayev, A. V., &Bobarykina, D. A. (2022), "The global terrorist threat in the Sahel and the origins of terrorism in Burkina Faso",*Vestnik RUDN. International Relations,* 22(2), pp. 411—421. https://doi.org/10.22363/2313-0660-2022-22-2-411-42
38. Institute for Economics & Peace. "Global Terrorism Index 2023: Measuring the Impact of Terrorism", Sydney, March 2023. Available from: http://visionofhumanity.org/resources (accessed November 27, 2023).
39. https://en.sputniknews.africa/20230811/burkina-faso-defense-minister-to-visit-russia-next-week-1061257230.html (accessed November 21, 2023).
40. https://www.counterterrorismgroup.com/post/burkina-faso-says-leader-discussed-possible-military-cooperation-with-russian-delegation (accessed November 21, 2023)
41. Institute for Economics & Peace. "Global Terrorism Index 2023: Measuring the Impact of Terrorism", Sydney, March 2023. Available from: http://visionofhumanity.org/resources (accessed November 27, 2023).
42. Sergey, V. Kostelyanets (2021), "Russia's Counterterrorism and Counterinsurgency Strategy in Africa" in *Terrorism in Africa: New Trends and Frontiers*. Moscow Institute for African Studies; University of Haifa, pp. 154-166.

43. Ibid.
44. The Concept of the Foreign Policy of the Russian Federation March 2023.
45. Dauda Abubakar. (2023).*The Role of Foreign Actors in African Security* in H. Solomon and J. Cocodia (eds.), African Security in the Anthropocene, The Anthropocene: Politik—Economics—Society—Science 36, https://doi.org/10.1007/978-3-031-25151-1_9 Chapter 9

14

Political Ethics and the Politicisation of Intelligence Services in Modern Statecraft

David Shakarishvili

Introduction

Political ethics, the moral principles governing political behaviour and decision-making, are foundational to the legitimacy and functionality of democratic governance. In modern statecraft, the ethical landscape becomes increasingly complex, particularly when considering the role of intelligence services. Intelligence agencies are tasked with providing accurate and unbiased information critical for national security and informed policymaking (Thomas, 2016). However, the politicisation of these services—where intelligence is manipulated to serve specific political objectives—poses a significant threat to the integrity of democratic institutions and the ethical standards they are meant to uphold (Miller, Regan, & Walsh, 2021). Justice, protection of state interests, and narrative of ethical values are the components that distinguish intelligence services from criminal organisations, even though intelligence activities are completely illegal. The interplay between political ethics and the politicisation of intelligence services is a critical area of concern in modern statecraft. Upholding ethical standards within intelligence operations is essential for the integrity of democratic governance and the effective functioning of state institutions (Bellaby, 2014).

Any branch of science can be involved in intelligence activities; however, only social science can develop such an academic construct that will make intelligence services politically decentralised, providing the latter with optimal alternatives for achieving goals based on the chain reaction principle. In the historical context, it is impossible to develop scientific frameworks and determine when states began to recognise ethical adepts in intelligence activities. The sources include information on the development of armed conflicts, military decisions, and campaigns outside borders, as well as the challenges faced by commanders and monarchs(Leary, 2014). In some developing countries, a clear sign of equality is seen between the state interest and the interests of the ruling political parties, which is a deadly disease for the power structures (and therefore, for the national security system)—the intelligence service must fulfil the public order.

Theoretical Frameworks

Scientific Narratives on Intelligence Politicisation

Politicisation can be defined as the shaping of analysis to match current policy or politics. Politicisation of intelligence happens when intelligence analysis is inclined, either intentionally or unintentionally, to generate the desired outcomes for policymakers (Drylie, 2024).

There are several perspectives on the relationship between intelligence and state security. A particular group of experts believes that erroneous state security systems had a critical part in the emergence of intelligence—intelligence and all the illicit activities linked with it are the outcome of state security flaws (George, 2020). The second group of experts feels that intelligence is derived from a military perspective (Drylie, 2024) (Wagner, 2015). It has such an impact on the state security system that its creation and specificity are proportional to the degree of intelligence.

According to British scientist Barry Buzan (1983), state security is closely linked to the corporate resources of private organisations operating in the state. The blurred view of this union obscures the security intelligence of post-Soviet countries. Other sciences associate state security with the state's defensive capability, social consensus, environmental protection, and equitable development within the country's regions and other territorial-administrative units (Leuprecht & McNorton , 2021). At its core, the goal is to reduce poverty by ensuring internal and external stability. Simply expressed, this direction is a collection of complex tactics whose successful implementation contributes to the country's role in the region and on a global scale (Uthoff, 2021).

One of the most debated hypotheses on the politicisation of intelligence is confirmation bias and groupthink. Confirmation bias is the tendency to seek out, analyse, and retain information that supports one's pre-existing opinions (Janis, 1982). In the context of intelligence, analysts or decision-makers may use information that supports their favoured policies or outcomes while disregarding or downplaying evidence to the contrary (Feldman, 2023). Groupthink is a related notion in which a cohesive group of decision-makers promotes consensus over critical thinking (Schafer & Crichlow, 2010). Irving Janis, who coined the phrase, defined it as a way of thinking in which the need for consensus trumps the motivation to consider other courses of action. In intelligence agencies, groupthink can lead to homogeneity of thought that matches with political goals, suppressing competing opinions and critical assessment.

Another theory holds that intelligence agencies may participate in policy advocacy, consciously altering intelligence to support policies. This might occur because of internal pressures, career incentives, or alignment with leadership preferences. Intelligence personnel may intentionally or unconsciously adapt their analyses to reflect their bosses' political agendas, with the hope of positively influencing policy results (Mandelbaum, 2022). This phenomenon was prominently investigated by Robert Jervis in his research of intelligence failures (Jervis, 2005). According to Jervis, the alignment of intelligence assessments and policy preferences is frequently driven by implicit pressures rather than formal commands (Jervis, 2005). Analysts may predict what their superiors want to hear and tailor their reports accordingly, resulting in a subtle but considerable level of politicisation.

Institutional pressures and bureaucratic politics play an important part in the politicisation of intelligence (Wagner, 2015). Intelligence agencies operate inside broader bureaucratic organisations and face a variety of internal and external challenges, including budgetary constraints, inter-agency rivalries, and the desire for institutional survival (Fingar, 2011).

Graham Allison's model of bureaucratic politics, given in his seminal work "Essence of Decision", demonstrates how decisions within government agencies are frequently the outcome of power conflicts between various individuals rather than a coherent, rational process (Allison, 1999). In the context of intelligence, this means that agencies may prioritise organisational interests over objective analysis, aligning their intelligence products with prevalent political currents to gain funding and influence (Allison, 1999).

Leadership and the broader political context play critical roles in the politicisation of intelligence. Leaders with significant control over intelligence organisations can alter intelligence creation and dissemination (Feldman, 2023). Political leaders may selectively exploit intelligence to support their policies, frequently forcing agencies to follow their objectives. Michael Desch's theory of civil-military interactions sheds light on how political leaders might affect intelligence organisations (Desch, 2001). According to Desch (2001), the balance of power between civilian authorities and military or intelligence professionals influences the impartiality of intelligence. When civilian leaders have power, they may pressure or persuade intelligence organisations to issue positive evaluations. In contrast, when intelligence organisations have more autonomy, they can withstand political pressure and produce more balanced analyses (Absher, Desch, & Popadiuk, 2011).

The theories of confirmation bias, groupthink, policy advocacy, bureaucratic politics, and leadership influence all contribute to a comprehensive understanding of how and why intelligence gets politicised. Each theory emphasises a different component of the process, ranging from cognitive biases and institutional dynamics to the influence of political leadership and circumstances.

Today, intelligence is undergoing transformation and commercialisation, in particular, government agencies are actively trying to transfer intelligence tools from the state to the private sector. There are legal and political reasons for this: first, international law can curtail the powers of the state to the extent that it is powerless in relation to the private sector, and second, in the business environment of all countries, regulations are specific.

Accountability and the Standard for Reducing Politicisation

Accountability in intelligence agencies is critical for a variety of reasons. For starters, it guarantees that these agencies operate within legal boundaries, limiting abuses of power (Leary, 2014). Unchecked intelligence activities can result in civil rights violations, such as unauthorised surveillance, arbitrary detentions, and invasions of privacy. Accountability increases public trust. Citizens are more likely to support and collaborate with intelligence agencies if they perceive their acts are transparent and accountable (Leuprecht & McNorton , 2021). Accountability helps to uphold democratic norms. In democratic nations, all government bodies, including intelligence agencies, must be accountable to elected officials and, by extension, the public (Wagner, 2015).

Despite these methods, ensuring accountability in intelligence services presents numerous obstacles. Secrecy, while necessary for effective intelligence operations, frequently stifles transparency and public criticism. Balancing confidentiality with monitoring is a tough task (Johnson, 2017). Furthermore, the complexity and technological nature of intelligence work can make effective oversight challenging, necessitating knowledge and skills (Gaskarth, 2020). Political dynamics can have an impact on accountability as well. Governments may be hesitant to audit intelligence organisations rigorously, particularly when national security concerns are strong. This can result in a lack of fair scrutiny and possible abuses of authority (Mandelbaum, 2022).

Accountability in the intelligence community is critical for protecting civil rights, maintaining public trust, and adhering to democratic ideals (Bakir, 2018). While numerous systems exist to ensure monitoring, issues including secrecy, technical complexity, and political influence must be addressed. Building accountability mechanisms and cultivating a culture of transparency inside intelligence organisations are critical steps toward striking a balance between national security and individual rights (Chapman, 2004). Effective oversight not only strengthens the legitimacy of intelligence activities but also promotes democracy's core ideals.

International Experience

Review of the United States Economic Espionage Act of 1996

The Economic Espionage Act was passed in 1996 in the United States of America. Due to the novelty of the act, it is a model of how to draft a state document that maintains a clear balance between state intervention in commercial activities and state regulation. Due to the novelty, modernity, and unprecedented nature of the act, several dozens of economists, legal experts, and public administration specialists worked on it, and the necessity of its adoption on the agenda was determined, on the one hand, by several high-profile cases, and on the other hand, by the new intelligence reality—states actively began to integrate intelligence functions into the private sector. Intelligence bias is the product of logical, legal "loopholes"—while international law can limit state power (particularly in sensitive areas such as intelligence and counterintelligence), it cannot interfere with a country's internal and external corporate activities (Roper, 2013).

At the close of the 20th century, because of American corporations' hard experience, a new legal term—trade secrets—emerged, previously unknown in American statute. The Act is well defined in terms of what it means; nevertheless, as firms' capabilities increase, it becomes more difficult to define and increasingly vital. For example, in the process of global digitisation, businesses gain a new direction, digital intellectual property. Today, the Economic Espionage Act protects the latter not as part of general intellectual property but as a set component.

There is no precedent for the act in developing countries' legal systems, particularly in the post-Soviet space. For example, the complex articles gathered in the Economic Espionage Act are broken down into elements in Georgia's legal documents. This can be explained by the fact that business regulation and corporate security regulation are distinct disciplines, hence each country's legal systems are built differently. Fundamental indicators determine state defensive materials against economic and corporate espionage, such as whether the country is a "night watchman" or a social function bearer, whether the economy is centrally regulated or reliant on market prices, and so on (Buzan, 1983). Why should post-Soviet countries, particularly Georgia, control this field? This is primarily because Russia, the formal successor to the Soviet Union, operates multiple private intelligence agencies and undertakes informational, propaganda, and cyberattacks on targets of interest.

The Federal Bureau of Investigation of the United States of America provides a scientific definition of a trade secret, which is any firm technique or method that is not widely recognised outside of the company (Nasheri, 2004). Information regarding trade secrets provides a corporation with an economic advantage over its competitors and is frequently the result of research and development. Trade secrets in different countries may change based on the circumstances of the jurisdictions, but they share three characteristics: they are not made public, are designed to give business benefits, and are actively protected (Roper, 2013).

The sub-chapter on economic espionage consists of two articles and five sub-articles that supplement the first article, as well as a chapter on trade secret violation. They collect and describe the strategies used to steal economic secrets and undermine the country's economic stability. What is the major distinction between "economic espionage" and "stealing trade secrets"? First and foremost, it should be noted that the act is separated into two legal sections: one dealing with secrets obtained outside of the United States, and the other with domestic theft (Allison, 1999). The preceding two sub-chapters are also based on these principles: economic espionage limits the intelligence actions of a foreign government and the mutual intelligence of American firms.

State and Civil Surveillance on Intelligence Services in Lithuania

Parliamentary monitoring of intelligence activities is critical for maintaining a balance between national security and civil freedoms in democratic democracies. In Lithuania, this oversight is primarily carried out by the Seimas,* which has a substantial responsibility in monitoring and regulating the country's intelligence institutions (Šalčius & Bilius, 2023).

Several laws govern Lithuania's intelligence efforts, including the Intelligence Law, the Seimas Organization Law, and the Classified Information Protection Law. The Law on Intelligence, passed in 2000, establishes the structure, tasks, and limitations of Lithuania's intelligence services, which include the State Security Department and the Second Department of Operational Services under the Ministry of National Defense (Greičiūtė & Paurienė, 2023). These statutes establish the legal framework for parliamentary supervision by specifying the scope of intelligence activities and the Seimas' obligations for monitoring them (Lefebvre, 2012).

The principal instrument for legislative supervision of intelligence in Lithuania is the intelligence services' regular reporting to the Seimas.

* The Lithuanian Parliament

The VSD and AOTD must produce annual reports on their actions, which include details on the operational environment, important risks to national security, and the effectiveness of counterintelligence measures. The NSDC reviews these reports and has the authority to request additional information, summon intelligence personnel to hearings, and make legislative amendments as needed In addition to annual reports, the Seimas can conduct ad hoc investigations of specific intelligence activity. This authority is especially crucial when there are concerns about possible abuses of power or violations of citizens' rights. The Seimas can call intelligence officers to testify in committees, request access to classified information, and launch investigations into the legality of certain actions. These inquiries aim to ensure that intelligence activities are carried out in accordance with the law, and that any misbehaviour is treated correctly.

The efficiency of parliamentary supervision of intelligence activities in Lithuania can be measured in a variety of ways. One measure is the Seimas' ability to hold intelligence agencies accountable for their conduct. In recent years, the Seimas has proved its commitment to oversight by investigating contentious intelligence operations and advocating legislative changes to strengthen the legal framework that governs intelligence activities (Šalčius & Bilius, 2023). Another indicator of effectiveness is the public's faith in intelligence services and the oversight process. Public trust in the VSD and AOTD is generally strong, reflecting the notion that both agencies follow the law and are subject to rigorous monitoring by the Seimas. However, continuous efforts are required to maintain and improve this confidence (Bellaby, 2014).

Non-Governmental Surveillance on Intelligence Sector

One of the most important functions of civil society in this environment is to lobby for legal reforms and the safeguarding of civil freedoms. Lithuanian non-governmental organisations have been instrumental in advocating for stricter data privacy regulations, safeguards against mass surveillance, and increased transparency in intelligence service operations (Chapman, 2004). By participating in public consultations, presenting reports to international human rights groups, and engaging with the media, these organisations ensure that intelligence services' operations are scrutinised and debated (Leuprecht & McNorton, 2021).

The most effective approach is through public reporting and awareness initiatives. NGOs release frequent assessments on the state of intelligence supervision in Lithuania, stressing issues such as a lack of openness, potential overreach in surveillance activities, and the need for stronger legal frameworks (Caparini, 2014). These reports are frequently based on data obtained through freedom of information requests, interviews with experts, and collaboration with international organisations. By publicising their results to the public and policymakers, NGOs contribute to a more educated and engaged citizenry capable of holding intelligence services accountable (Svenonius, Björklund, & Waszkiewi, 2014).

Despite these limitations, Lithuanian civil society and non-governmental organisations have made substantial contributions to intelligence service supervision. Their activities have raised public awareness of monitoring tactics and sparked debates about the balance of security and privacy (GAILIŪTĖ, 2016). For example, non-governmental organisations have affected debates about the use of mass surveillance technology and helped shape Lithuania's data protection regulations. NGOs have also helped in the creation of a stronger legislative framework for intelligence monitoring. By challenging problematic activities in court and pressing for legal reforms, they have helped to develop protection against intelligence agencies' abuses of power (Wagner, 2015). Furthermore, the reports and publications generated by these organisations serve as useful tools for journalists and educators.

Civil society and non-governmental organisations play an important role in the surveillance of intelligence services in Lithuania, helping to defend democratic values and human rights. These groups contribute to ensuring that intelligence activities are done in accordance with the law and civil liberties through legal advocacy, public reporting, and policymaker engagement. Despite major limitations, such as limited access to information and resources, their influence on intelligence oversight has been significant. Going forward, the sustained involvement of civil society and non-governmental organisations will be critical in maintaining the balance between national security and individual rights in Lithuania.

Conclusion

Intelligence activity lasts as long as the universe does. Political parties, regardless of democratic principles, will always seek to expand their power. The two above-mentioned concepts are like the laws of physics, and societies will have to manoeuvre so that the power is clearly identified and, most importantly, limited in time.

The experiences of the USA and Lithuania show that reduced politicisation of intelligence is critical to sustaining the integrity, efficacy, and impartiality of intelligence services. When intelligence agencies are influenced by political objectives, their capacity to give reliable, unbiased information is jeopardised, which can lead to poor decision-making, a loss of public trust, and potential abuses of power. To overcome this issue, numerous techniques can be implemented to ensure that intelligence services operate independently and are free of political influence.

Building and maintaining a culture of professionalism and integrity inside intelligence services is critical for preventing politicisation. This includes supporting merit-based hiring and promotions, in which decisions are made based on qualifications and performance rather than political affiliation. Training programmes emphasising ethical norms, the significance of impartiality, and the important function of intelligence in ensuring national security can help to reinforce this culture. Furthermore, creating a climate in which intelligence professionals feel empowered to speak truth to power without fear of retaliation is critical. Whistleblower protections should be tightened to promote the disclosure of any attempts to politicise intelligence activity.

Finally, studying worldwide best practices and collaborating with global intelligence networks can assist in avoiding politicisation. Intelligence agencies can improve their operational standards and lessen their vulnerability to political influence by participating in communications with other countries and implementing effective tactics from around the world. International cooperation also allows for the benchmarking of practices and regulations, which promotes a culture of professionalism and impartiality across boundaries.

Finally, reducing the politicisation of intelligence necessitates a holistic approach that includes legal reforms, cultural shifts, increased transparency, nonpartisan leadership, and international collaboration. By following these measures, governments can ensure that intelligence services work with the independence, integrity, and efficacy required to safeguard national security and democratic principles.

References

Absher , K. M., Desch , M. C., & Popadiuk , R. (2011), *Privileged and Confidential: The Secret History of the President's Intelligence Advisory Board.* Kentucky: The University Press of Kentucky.

Aldrich, R. (2009), *Secret Intelligence.* Washington: Routledge.

Allison, G. (1999), *Essence of Decision: Explaining the Cuban Missile Crisis.* New York: Pearson P T R.

Bakir, V. (2018), *Intelligence Elites and Public Accountability: Relationships of Influence with Civil Society.* Washington: Routledge.

Bellaby, R. (2014), *The Ethics of Intelligence: A new framework.* Sheffield: Routledge.

Buzan, B. (1983), *People, states, and fear: The national security problem in international relations.* North Carolina : University of North Carolina Press.

Caparini, M. (2014), "Comparing the Democratization of Intelligence Governance in East Central Europe and the Balkan", *Intelligence and National Security,* pp. 498-522 .

Chapman, B. (2004), *Researching National Security and Intelligence Policy.* London: CQ Press.

Desch, M. C. (2001), *Civilian Control of the Military: The Changing Security Environment.* Baltimore: Johns Hopkins University Press.

Drylie, J. (July 13, 2024), *Intelligence Studies: Politicisation of Intelligence.* Retrieved from https://usnwc.libguides.com/, https://usnwc.libguides.com/c.php?g=494120&p=3381573

Feldman, P. (2023), *Stampede Theory: Human Nature, Technology, and Runaway Social Realities.* London: Elsevier .

Fingar, T. (2011), *Reducing Uncertainty: Intelligence Analysis and National Security.* Stanford: Stanford Security Studies.

GAILIŪTĖ, D. (2016), *National intelligence authorities and surveillance in the EU: Fundamental rights safeguards and remedies* . Vilnius: EU Agency for Fundamental Rights.

Gaskarth, J. (2020), *Secrets and Spies: UK Intelligence Accountability after Iraq and Snowden.* Washington: Brookings Institution Press.

George, R. Z. (2020), *Intelligence in the National Security Enterprise: An Introduction.* Georgetown: Georgetown University Press.

Greičiūtė, E. & Paurienė, G. (2023),"Historical relationship between operational activities and criminal intelligence: the case of Lithuania",*Visuomenės saugumas ir viešoji tvarka* , pp. 18-28.

Janis, I. L. (1982), *Groupthink: Psychological Studies of Policy Decisions and Fiascoe.* Boston: Cengage Learning.

Jervis, R. (2005), *American Foreign Policy in a New Era* . Routledge: New York.

Johnson, L. K. (2017), *Spy Watching: Intelligence Accountability in the United States.* Oxford: Oxford University Press.

Leary, W. M. (2014), *The Central Intelligence Agency: History and Documents.* Alabama: University Alabama Press.

Lefebvre, S. (2012), "Lithuania, the CIA, and Intelligence Reform",*International Journal of Intelligence and Counterintelligence*, pp. 571-594.

Leuprecht, C. & McNorton, H. (2021),*Intelligence as Democratic Statecraft: Accountability and Governance of Civil-Intelligence Relations Across the Five Eyes Security Community—The United States, United Kingdom, Canada, Australia, and New Zealand.* Oxford: OUP Oxford.

Mandelbaum, M. (2022), *The Four Ages of American Foreign Policy: Weak Power, Great Power, Superpower, Hyperpower.* Oxford: Oxford University Press.

Miller, S., Regan, M., & Walsh, P. F. (2021), *National Security Intelligence and Ethics (Studies in Intelligence).* New York: Routledge.

Nasheri, H. (2004), *Economic Espionage and Industrial Spying.* Cambirdge: Cambridge University Press.

Roper, C. (2013), *Trade Secret Theft, Industrial Espionage, and the China Threat* . New York: CRC Press.

Šalčius, M. & Bilius, M. (2023), "Control of Criminal Intelligence: An Evaluation of the Lithuanian Situation in Light of International Practice", *Baltic Journal of Law & Politics*, pp. 1-23.

Schafer , M. & Crichlow, S. (2010), *Groupthink Versus High-Quality Decision Making in International Relations.* New York: Columbia University Press.

Svenonius, O., Björklund, F., & Waszkiewi, P. (2014), "Surveillance, lustration and the open society", *Histories of State Surveillance in Europe and Beyond*, Routledge.

Thomas, G. (2016), *Secret Wars: One Hundred Years of British Intelligence Inside MI5 and MI6.* London: Thomas Dunne Books.

Uthoff, C. S. (2021), *Cyber Intelligence: Actors, Policies, Practices.* New York: Lynne Rienner Publishers, Inc.

Wagner, S. B. (2015), *Statecraft by Stealth: Secret Intelligence and British Rule in Palestine.* Cornell: Cornell University Press.

15

Increasing Role of Private Military and Security Companies (PMSCs) and Impacts on Future Warfare

Anuradha Oinam and Monojit Das

Introduction

With the resurfacing and the increasing role of Private Military and Security Companies (PMSCs) lately, countries prefer to employ them as a tool in waging modern warfare. Since warfare is transforming, its character in terms of weapons used and actors involved is also changing. Hence, PMSCs do not fight or are employed in covert operations anymore rather taking an active role in today's warfare. In addition, states perceive them as capable and efficient while performing their assigned tasks by host countries. A case in point is the use of PMSCs and their tireless involvement in the ongoing Russia-Ukraine war. Black Water, name now changed to Xe/Academi, and Wagner group are a few PMSCs owned by the U.S.A. and Russia. Examples are not limited here; there are private forces from Georgia, Chenchen, and Syria that took part in the Russia-Ukraine war (Oinam, 2022). Instead of the West- based PMSCs, China began using Private Security Companies (PSCs), whose numbers are multiplying rapidly, to gain its political, economic, and military goals. Although China officially refused to recognise Private Military Companies (PMCs), its PSCs are now employed in Central Asia, Africa, and East Asia, etc.

In the contemporary globalised world, PMSCs, irrespective of their tasks, seem to develop a close nexus between states and global affairs, wherein they play a vital role. Earlier, they disguised themselves and were involved covertly as a shadow force until the Falluja incident in Iraq in 2003, where four contractors were killed. The incident opened a new page in the global community, highlighting the increasing use of contractors by many states. Since then, PMSCs began fighting along with the state security apparatus or as a vanguard in any conflict or war without any hesitation. In 21st century warfare, PMSCs are actively taking part, fighting at the frontline in a full-fledged war. An example could be the Wagner group, representing Russia on one side, and volunteers from across the world representing Ukraine on the other side, fighting along with their respective regular soldiers in the ongoing Russia-Ukraine war.

In this context, it is indisputable that states seem spineless without the support of PMSCs, especially while waging war or hiring for security purposes abroad. Thus, PMSCs have become a part and parcel of today's warfare, and surely, future wars will be fought by them. Nevertheless, the ambiguous and complex nature of PMSCs often questions their feasibility as their regulation is outside the national and international legal lacunae. Therefore, there has been a constant debate and discussion within the ecology of scholars, policy makers, and war strategists with regards to the implementation of PMSCs as well as implications generated by them. To explicate more, the follow- up sections will explore PMSCs, their narratives, and roles in future war.

PMSCs: Evolving Roles and Functions

It is a general fact that PMSCs are profit-oriented, non-state entities that behave and function like a military man to achieve the host states' military or security purposes in any war or conflict. They are largely from the military veteran community with enormous experiences and trained especially in fighting wars, which are skilled and know war fighting tactics. Even though their involvement can be traced back since time immemorial, they became prominent since the post-Cold War period, especially resurfacing in the early 1990s, filling the security void left by the great powers. Those newly independent states, who used to depend on the former USSR and the USA, scouted for security in the global market. Because of this reason, the industry got enlarged in the international market where one can buy security as a commodity. Hence, PMSCs flourished and is now one of the most in-demand military and security industries owned and run by powerful contractors.

PMSCs are a conglomeration of two entities: Private Security Companies (PSCs) and Private Military Companies (PMCs). PSCs perform security-related tasks and PMCs, the military-related tasks. Scholars like Peter W. Singer (2002) categorise PMSCs into three kinds: Military Provider Firms, ii) Military Consulting Firms, and iii) Military Support Firms, as shown in Figure 15.1.

Figure 15.1: Singer's 'Tip of the Spear', explaining different categories of PMSCs

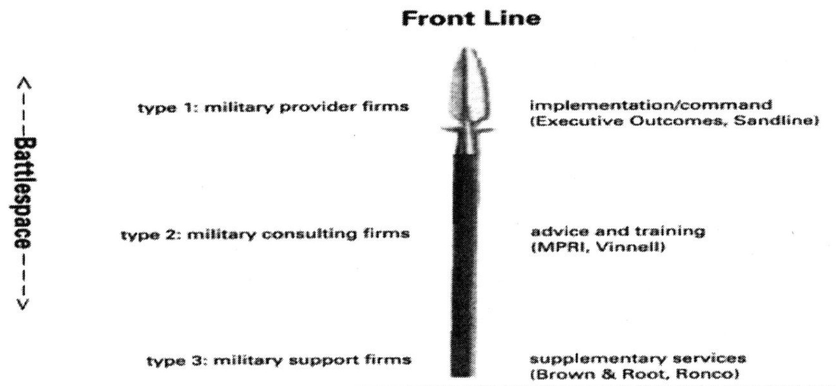

Source: https://www.jstor.org/stable/pdf/3092094.pdf

Figure 15.1 shows the illustration of a spear to explain Singer's classification of PMSCs. In his model, 'tip of the spear', the 'upper part' illustrates the military provider firms—deploy or follow command; the 'middle part' represents the military consulting firms—advice or training; and 'the lower part' signifies military support firms—supplementary roles of providing services (Singer, 2002). Besides Singer's classification, PMSCs perform myriad functions according to the tasks assigned to them by the contractors. Figure 15.2 and Table 15.1 show more roles performed by PMSCs in different states.

Figure 15.2: Roles Performed by PMSCs

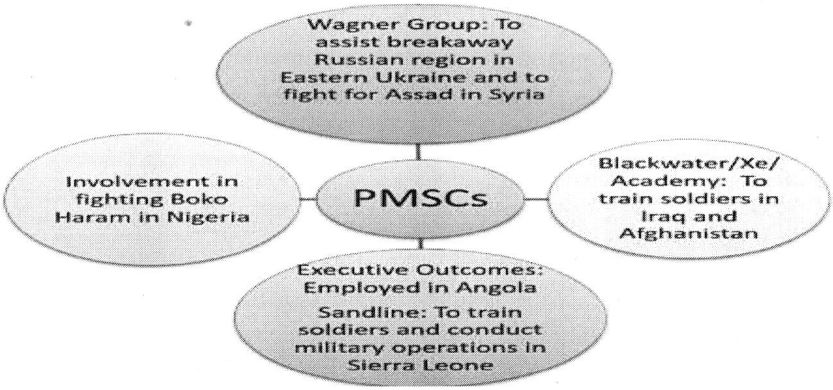

Source: "Private Military and Security Companies' (PMSCs) Trend in Contemporary Global Conflicts", *CLAWS Issue Brief*, June 14, 2022.

Table 15.1: PMSCs' Multiple Functions

	Private Military and Security Companies			
	(----------------------- Leave of Force ---------------------------)			
Type of Company	**Military Support Firm**	**Military Consulting Firm**	**Private Security Company**	**Private Military Company**
Primary Role	Sustainment	Force Generation Intelligence Mission Command	Defence and Protection	Offense
Activities	Transportation Engineering Medical Support Procurement Personnel Services	Intelligence Subject Knowledge Management Training Support	• Facility Security • Physical Security • Personnel Protection • Convoy Security • Refugee Protection	• Combat • Combat Support • Close Air Support • Fire Support
Notable Examples	Kellogg Brown & Root (KBR)	Military Professional Resources Incorporated (MPRI) Dyncorp	Blackwater Xe Ac ademi	Executive Outcomes

Source: Anuradha Oinam, 2022.

From the above illustrations, it is important to note the significance of PMSCs both as combatant and non-combatant actors in many countries and their myriad functions, viz., logistics, intelligence, training, and war fighting. Hence, more states are inclined to depend on PMSCs because of their efficiency to achieve their goals without fail. Table 15.2 shows PMSCs being deployed by the USA and Russia in different countries for different tasks. The table elucidates the effectiveness of PMSCs in executing their multiple roles, depending on the needs of the respective countries.

Table 15.2: Use of PMSCs by the USA and Russia in different Countries

U.S.A's PMSCs		Tasks
PMSCs	**State Used PMSCs**	
Blackwater XE Academi	Liberia	Armed Operational
Blackwater XE Academi	Iraq and Afghanistan	Armed Operational Support Logistical Support Military Training Security Management
Military Professional Resources Inc	Croatia Bosnia Equation Guinea and Colombia	Military Training Intelligence Surveillance
Russia's PMSC's		
PMSC's	State Used PMSCs	
Wagner Group	Syria, Nigeria, Libya, Mozambique, Guinea, Sudan, Chad, Mah, Burundi, Comoros, Madagascar, Botswana, Congo, Bunmdix	All types of Tasks depending on the need of the state
Wagner Group	Venezuela	Military Training, Intelligence, Surveillance and Logistical Support
Wagner Group	Ukraine	Military & Security purpose Logistics and Intelligence Surveillance

Source: Annotated by Authors.

China, like the US and Russia, engages with the industry. The Dragon has been deploying PSCs for various purposes, as is clearly exemplified in Figure 15.3. Thus, states are now heavily dependent on PMSCs to accomplish their interests and goals.

Figure 15.3: Export of Chinese Weapons or PSCs or Both to Other Countries

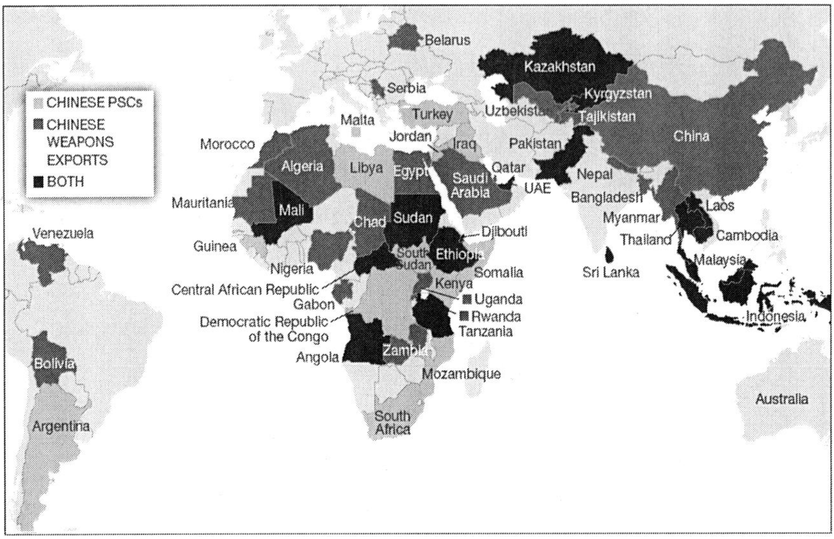

Source: https://www.rand.org/content/dam/rand/pubs/tools/TLA2000/TLA2045-1/RAND_TLA2045-1.pdf

Defining Wars and How Do Future Wars Look Like

War has traditionally been viewed as an organised conflict between nations or significant groups, usually involving extensive military campaigns and clear, strategic objectives, such as territorial acquisition or political control. Conflicts like the World Wars or the Cold War era's proxy wars defined the conventional terms involving large-scale troop movements and confrontations between regular armies. However, the evolution of geopolitical dynamics and technology has led to a more nuanced understanding of warfare. In the present context, war is increasingly seen as a multifaceted phenomenon that extends beyond traditional battlefield engagements with asymmetric warfare, cyber operations, and even economic and psychological strategies including targeting civilian populations. This broader perspective reflects how modern conflicts often involve both state and non-state actors, each employing diverse tactics ranging from guerrilla operations to sophisticated cyberattacks (Smith, 2006; Hoffman, 2007).

The contemporary landscape of conflict highlights the integration of unconventional methods and hybrid strategies. Hybrid warfare, for example, combines traditional military actions with cyber operations, misinformation campaigns, and economic pressures to achieve strategic goals without resorting to full-scale war. Countries like Russia have employed such strategies in Ukraine and elsewhere, using a blend of conventional and non-traditional tactics to create confusion and undermine their adversaries without engaging in open, large-scale conflict (Galeotti, 2016). This expansion in the scope of what constitutes war reflects the increasing complexity and interconnectedness of global interactions, where economic sanctions, information warfare, and covert operations are just as significant as military engagements. As a result, modern definitions of war encompass a broader spectrum of activities that challenge the conventional distinctions between peace and conflict (Mumford, 2013). That is why, PMSCs fit in modern warfare.

How Future Wars Might Evolve

The landscape of warfare is set to undergo significant transformations, driven primarily by advances in technology and shifts in geopolitical power structures. Future conflicts are expected to heavily rely on modern technologies including Artificial Intelligence (AI), sophisticated cyber capabilities, and autonomous systems. These technologies will reshape military operations, enabling new forms of engagement and strategies. Autonomous drones could revolutionise surveillance and combat roles by operating without direct human intervention, reducing risks to personnel and changing the dynamics of military tactics. AI systems could be pivotal in analysing vast datasets to predict enemy actions, optimise logistical support, and manage real-time battlefield decisions, providing a decisive edge through enhanced speed and operational efficiency (Bendett, 2019).

Cyberspace is anticipated to become a crucial battleground where different actors participate in digital warfare to disrupt critical infrastructure, financial systems, and communications networks. In future conflicts, cyberattacks might target power grids, banking systems, or public information networks, aiming to create chaos and weaken adversaries from within. The interplay between traditional military actions and these digital confrontations will form a complex, multi-domain conflict environment where dominance in the technological and informational spheres is as vital as physical control over territories. Additionally, the militarisation of space could emerge as a new frontier, with nations deploying and defending satellites crucial for global communications, navigation, and surveillance (Burgess, 2018).

In this evolving context, the motivations for commercialising combat and combat support services will play a critical role in shaping conflict dynamics. Non-Western states, particularly those with limited indigenous military capacity, often turn to private companies to bolster their defence capabilities. This trend is driven by the necessity to strengthen the countries' military power, especially those in sparsely populated regions like the Arabian Gulf. For example, countries such as Qatar and the UAE, which struggle to recruit sufficient personnel from their small populations, rely heavily on PMCs to staff their extensive security sectors (McFate, 2019). Another instance is the UAE's contract with Reflex Responses LLC that illustrates its explicit aim to procure manpower and capabilities that the Emirati Armed Forces could not produce all alone (Mazetti & Hager, 2011).

States contract out services to PMCs due to the capability gap. These companies offer specialised skills and expertise, particularly in counterinsurgency operations where client states lack experience. Examples include the UAE's involvement in Yemen and Nigeria's fight against Boko Haram,where both have seen the employment of contractors with combat; the Colombian fight against FARC rebels; the South African bush warfare (Singer, 2008)etc.. This approach allows states to acquire instantly needed capabilities without long term investment and development of indigenous forces. Additionally, PMCs provide force multipliers that enhance the effectiveness of local military operations by offering training, planning, and direct combat support.

Moreover, the use of PMCs offers states a degree of deniability and discretion in their military engagements. The use of private actors by Russia in Ukraine and Libya exemplifies this strategy, enabling Moscow to support proxy forces while maintaining plausible deniability and mitigating political repercussions (Galeotti, 2016). In Syria, contractors have allowed the Kremlin to obscure the true cost of its involvement, with official casualty figures significantly underreporting the actual number of Russian contractors killed (Marten, 2019).

In non-liberal states, PMCs can also serve as tools for expanding patrimonial networks, enriching elites, and ensuring regime security. This is evident in countries like Angola and Nigeria, where military elites own PMCs that receive lucrative contracts, fostering extensive networks of corruption and patronage (Avant, 2005). For example, senior Nigerian Navy officials have redirected funds meant for naval capabilities to support their own private maritime security enterprises, effectively commercialising national security for personal gain (Isima, 2004).

Thus, the commercialisation of military services will likely continue to influence the evolution of future wars. By enabling states to rapidly acquire sophisticated military capabilities and maintain operational flexibility, PMCs are set to become increasingly integral to modern warfare. This reliance on the private military sector highlights the ongoing transformation of global conflict dynamics, where financial power can be directly translated into military might through market mechanisms.

Use of Latest Technology and Weapons in Wars

In the growing landscape of 21st century conflict, the character of war has dramatically transformed from conventional war fighting to complex, multi-faceted engagements involving a variety of new actors. This shift is driven largely by technological innovations that have redefined both the means and the methods of warfare. Unlike past conflicts dominated by armies and conventional weaponry, modern wars often feature a fusion of state forces, insurgents, and PMSCs operating with advanced technologies. For instance, in the Russia-Ukraine war, PMSCs like the Wagner Group have been pivotal in integrating sophisticated weapon systems and cyber tools into their operations, blurring the lines between conventional military engagements and asymmetric warfare (McFate, 2019). The advent of cyber warfare capabilities, AI-driven decision-making tools, and advanced unmanned aerial vehicles (UAVs) allow these actors to execute highly precise and impactful operations remotely. This not only reduces the risk to human operatives but also enhances strategic efficiency and effectiveness on the battlefield (Singer, 2008).

One striking example of this technological integration is the usage of Pegasus spyware by various actors to conduct surveillance and gather intelligence. Developed by the Israeli company, NSO Group, Pegasus allows for deep infiltration into target devices, providing access to vast amounts of data without physical proximity. This capability has transformed intelligence operations, enabling actors to gather critical information and conduct espionage without traditional on-ground resources (Marczak et al., 2016). Similarly, the proliferation of UAV technology has revolutionised both surveillance and strike capabilities in conflict zones. Companies like General Atomics, known for their MQ-9 Reaper drones, provide platforms that offer real-time aerial reconnaissance and precision strike options, drastically altering the tactical landscape. These drones can loiter for extended periods, gather intelligence, and deliver precise ordnance, thus minimising collateral damage and maximising operational effectiveness (Singer, 2010)

Chinese state-owned corporations, such as China Aerospace Science and Technology Corporation (CASC) and China Electronics Technology Group Corporation (CETC), are also at the forefront of this transformation. They are heavily investing in and deploying advanced UAVs, cyber warfare tools, and artificial intelligence systems. For example, CASC's development of the Wing Loong series of drones has provided both China and its international clients with robust aerial capabilities, from intelligence gathering to targeted strikes. These drones have been exported to various conflict zones, where they have played critical roles in local power dynamics. Moreover, CETC's advancements in cyber capabilities and electronic warfare have equipped Chinese forces with tools to disrupt, degrade, and deceive adversaries' systems, underscoring the increasing role of cyber operations in modern warfare (Tian & Su, 2020; Kania, 2020).

In reality, countries cannot negate PMSCs' importance as they become the backbone in modern warfare. Figure 15.4 shows the privatisation of conflicts due to involvement of private actors.

Figure 15.4: Participation of PMSCs in Global Wars

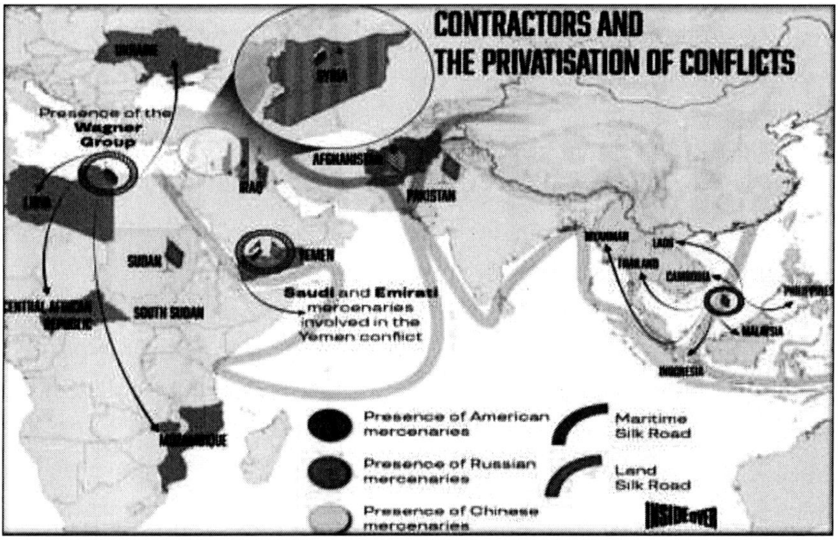

Source: Lorenzo Vita, "The Dark World of Private Military Contractors", 2020, available at https://www.insideover.com/war/the-dark-world-of-private-military-contractors.html

The adaptability of PMSCs to rapidly integrate and leverage such advanced technologies gives them a substantial edge over traditional military forces, which often face bureaucratic delays and rigid procurement processes. This agility is not only operationally advantageous but also strategically crucial as it allows PMSCs to offer specialised services tailored to the dynamic demands of contemporary conflict environments. As these private entities continue to harness and deploy emerging technologies like AI for predictive analytics and autonomous operations, their role in the global security landscape will likely expand. This growth challenges traditional military paradigms and necessitates a rethinking of how national and international security frameworks address the rising influence of technologically equipped non-state actors. Thus, the future war is poised to be increasingly shaped by those who can most effectively integrate and innovate with the latest technological advancements (Avant, 2005).

Concerned Issues and Challenges

Undoubtedly, PMSCs have become the pertinent actors in modern times due to their booming business model and wide global scope. They are powerful and heavily equipped multinational corporations that discount the sentiment of patriotism in their operational behaviour. Nevertheless, the world community finds PMSCs a tough lacuna on account of understanding their characteristics and the nature of war fighting due to their legality issues in addition to moral and ethical questions that remain the key concerns.

PMSCs are ambiguous in nature as there is no legal mechanism to regulate them. They do not come under the straight jacket of the International Humanitarian Law (IHL). No law is binding on them to punish them when they commit a human rights violation. Though some scholars project them as the new incarnation of mercenaries, PMSCs are different from mercenaries in academia and international security studies. The oldest documents, such as the Magna Carta (1215), international conventions such as the UN Charter and its related resolutions, Article 47 (Additional Protocol 1), the International Convention against the Recruitment, Use, Financing and Training of Mercenaries (1989) etc., mention mercenaries but not PMSCs. Hence, PMSCs are vague and intricate in nature, especially while operating in battlegrounds. Besides, there is absence of legitimate checks and balances and thus, PMSCs continue to be a challenge. There were multiple cases where PMSCs misused their power and authority, such as the Abu Ghraib incident of April 28, 2004; the Nisour Square incident of September 16, 2007; and heinous crimes committed in Afghanistan prior to August 2021. Such incidents reflect PMSCs' notoriety and contentious behaviour due to lack of legal mechanisms to regulate them under the national and international legal frameworks.

In addition, PMSCs do not have any emotional connection with the people for whom they are fighting. Hence, there is lack of patriotism while waging wars. They do not fight under any flag, wear uniforms, or follow any moral code of conduct and laws of war, which resulted in the frequent misuse of their power and often,perpetuation of heinous crimes. Therefore, there are ethical and moral questions on PMSCs' code of conduct, and this further problematises in the ethos of the regular soldiers. Therefore, the legalisation of PMSCs under the International Humanitarian Law (IHL) is an urgent task to be undertaken by states in the days to come. Otherwise, the situation may backfire, generating disastrous consequences for mankind.

As their goal is profit-oriented, the contractors, who seem to be warmongers, are likely to employ a greater number of PMSCs, thus encouraging war instead of stopping it. The ongoing Russia-Ukraine war is a clear example of the same. Last but not the least, with the emergence of PMSCs and their profit motives, security can be sold and bought in the market that can result in the commodification of war (Williams, 2014). This commodification of security challenges states' monopoly of power. The states used to be the sole authority of inflicting violence; however, this power is now being transferred in the hands of the private actors. The commodification of war might pose a threat to the world order as these private actors incline towards having more wars to achieve their financial gains. They sustain their business model by intensifying wars across the globe.

Way Ahead

With the evolving trend of warfare, there is a possibility that PMSCs are going to play a crucial role in future warfare. Hence, researchers, policy makers, and war strategists must study PMSCs and their involvement more cautiously. As conflicts are becoming more defined, states, including the great powers, are going to increasingly depend on PMSCs as a tool to shape their foreign policy as they provide plausible deniability. In addition, more states will hire PMSCs to use in false flag operations (already exploited both by Russia and Ukraine in the ongoing war) to change the narrative or manipulate the story on the ground. Hence, PMSCs are here to stay.

Privatising war is another significant trend in future warfare due to the involvement of private actors. This will change the character of warfare in a perilous manner. Another trend is the privatisation of Jihad by PMSCs such as 'Malhama Tactical' that connect terrorist organisations globally. Since they use modern technologies, PMSCs like Malhama Tactical pose a severe global security threat.

Given the complexities of international relations due to the changing character of warfare, the role of private forces will increase, attributed to the evolution of a new warfare. Hence, it is high time for all states to come forward to bring PMSCs under the legal framework and regulate them with legal mechanisms. Without it, the privatisation of war will spread like wildfire, also make the market economy boom, and the industry that is vested in conflict will flourish.

As an implication, PMSCs might pose a negative threat as they could become extremely powerful, and the world may not be able to control their misconduct and misbehaviour to civilians, especially women. Since, PMSCs are increasingly getting involved as proxy groups because of their plausible deniability, they are not going to vanish; instead, they will undoubtedly play a critical role in future warfare. Hence, this is the right time to regulate them under IHL for a safer world.

References

Anuradha Oinam (2022), "Increasing Trend of Private Military and Security Companies (PMSCs) in Contemporary Global Conflicts", available at https://www.claws.in/publication/increasing-trend-of-private-military-and-security-companies-pmscs-in-contemporary-global-conflicts

Avant, D. D. (2005), *The market for force: The consequences of privatizing security.* Cambridge University Press.

Bendett, S. (2019), "Russia's AI Quest is State-Driven—Even More than China's. Can It Work?" Defense One. Retrieved from (https://www.defenseone.com/ideas/2019/11/russias-ai-quest-state-driven-even-more-chinas-can-it-work/161519/)

Sayler, K. (2021), *Defense Primer: U.S. policy on lethal autonomous weapon systems.* Congressional Research Service.

Galeotti, M. (2016), "Hybrid, ambiguous, and non-linear? How new is Russia's 'new way of war'?", *Small Wars & Insurgencies*, 27(2), pp. 282-301.

Hoffman, F. G. (2007),"Conflict in the 21st century: The rise of hybrid wars". Potomac Institute for Policy Studies.

Isima, J. (2004), "*Demilitarisation, non-state actors and public security in Africa: A preliminary survey of the literature*", *Journal of Security Sector Management*, 2(4). Retrieved from https://ciaotest.cc.columbia.edu/olj/jssm/jssm_2_4/jssm_2_4_isi01.pdf

Kania, E. B. (2020), "*The implications of artificial intelligence for international security*" (Brookings Institution). Retrieved from https://www.brookings.edu/wp-content/uploads/2020/04/FP_20200427_ai_weapons_kania_v2.pdf

Marczak, B., Scott-Railton, J., McKune, S., Abdul Razzak, B., & Deibert, R. (2016), "The Million Dollar Dissident: NSO Group's iPhone Zero-Days used against a UAE Human Rights Defender". The Citizen Lab. Retrieved from (https://

citizenlab.ca/2016/08/million-dollar-dissident-iphone-zero-day-nso-group-uae/)

Marten, K. (2019), "Russia's use of semi-state security forces: The case of the Wagner Group", *Post-Soviet Affairs*, 35(3), pp. 181-204.

Mazetti, M. & Hager, E. (2011), "Secret Desert Force Set Up by Blackwater's Founder", *The New York Times*. Retrieved from https://www.nytimes.com/2011/05/15/world/middleeast/15prince.html

McFate, S. (2019), *The new rules of war: Victory in the age of durable disorder*.

Mumford, A. (2013), *Proxy Warfare*. Polity Press.

Singer, P.W. (2002), "Corporate Warrior: The Rise of the Privatized Military Industry and Its Ramifications for International Security", *International Security*, Vol. 26, No. 3. Winter 2001-2002. Available at https://www.jstor.org/stable/pdf/3092094.pdf

Singer, P. W. (2008), C*orporate warriors: The rise of the privatized military industry*. Cornell University Press.

Singer, P. W. (2010), *Wired for War: The Robotics Revolution and Conflict in the 21st Century*. Penguin Press.

Smith, R. (2006), *The utility of force: The art of war in the modern world*. Penguin UK.

Tian, N. & Su, F. (2020), "*Estimating the arms sales of Chinese companies*". SIPRI Insights on Peace and Security. Retrieved from https://www.sipri.org/sites/default/files/2020-01/sipriinsight2002_1.pdf

Williams, Dodeye U. (2014), "The Commodification of War: Political, Legal and Moral Issues", *Mediterranean Journal of Social Science*, Vol 5, No. 7, 2014. Available at https://www.mcser.org/journal/index.php/mjss/article/view/5231

Conclusion: The Future of Warfare—Corporate Dominance or Military Leadership?

The intersection of corporate intelligence and military strategy is reshaping the future of warfare, with profound implications for global security, economic dominance, and geopolitical stability. Throughout *Corporate Military Intelligence*, we have examined how corporations influence intelligence gathering, cybersecurity, military operations, and economic warfare, raising fundamental questions about the evolving balance of power between state actors and private enterprises. The findings across this volume indicate that future warfare will no longer be defined solely by military strength but will be equally, if not more, driven by corporate intelligence, technological innovation, and economic influence.

Key Takeaways: The Emerging Trends in Corporate-Military Intelligence

1. The Merging of Corporate and Military Intelligence Capabilities

Traditional state-controlled intelligence operations are increasingly dependent on private corporations for cybersecurity, surveillance, and data analysis. As seen in Chapter 1, naval intelligence principles are now applied in corporate intelligence strategies, while Chapters 3 and 15 demonstrate how private military security companies (PMSCs) are filling operational gaps in modern warfare. This shift signals a broader trend—states are no longer the sole arbiters of military intelligence, and private actors are now deeply embedded in global security frameworks.

2. Economic Warfare and Intelligence as Strategic Tools

Economic warfare is no longer a secondary tool in statecraft—it is now a primary weapon of influence. Chapters 2, 6, and 8 show how corporations are being used as instruments of geopolitical power, whether through controlling critical supply chains, leveraging financial sanctions, or influencing global trade policies. This suggests that future conflicts will be fought not just on the battlefield but also in boardrooms and stock markets. The ability to control economic intelligence will determine a nation's strategic advantage.

3. **The Role of Private Military and Cybersecurity Firms in Future Conflicts**
Mercenary groups such as Wagner, analysed in Chapter 10, reveal a new trend—corporate-backed paramilitary organisations can operate beyond the legal and ethical constraints of state-controlled militaries. Similarly, Chapter 12 highlights the increasing reliance on AI-driven intelligence and cyber warfare, where private firms often have technological capabilities that outmatch those of governments. This growing dependency raises critical security risks, as private entities might prioritise profit over national security imperatives.

4. **The Intelligence Arms Race: The Battle for AI and Cyber Dominance**
AI-driven intelligence, as explored in Chapters 7 and 9, is becoming the primary battlefield for geopolitical competition. The Global North dominates AI development, while the Global South faces challenges in cybersecurity and AI governance. The increasing privatisation of AI research creates a fragmented intelligence landscape, where corporate control over data and algorithms can influence military decision-making and even disrupt democratic processes.

5. **Ethical and Political Challenges in the Privatisation of Intelligence**
As discussed in Chapters 13 and 14, intelligence agencies are increasingly vulnerable to political manipulation and corporate lobbying. The lines between state control and private sector influence are blurring, raising serious concerns about transparency, accountability, and ethical governance. The politicisation of intelligence services can lead to biased threat assessments, misinformation, and misuse of intelligence for corporate or political gains.

Strategic Recommendations for Nations: Preparing for the Next Phase of Warfare

Given these evolving dynamics, states must rethink their approach to intelligence, security, and economic warfare. Future conflicts will be won by those who can integrate corporate intelligence into national security strategies while maintaining state control over critical information. Below are key strategic recommendations for countries based on their geopolitical positioning:

1. **Investing in Homegrown Startups: Enhancing National Technological Sovereignty**

To reduce reliance on foreign corporations for intelligence and cybersecurity, nations must:

- increase funding for domestic AI and cybersecurity startups to prevent dependence on external tech firms that may have conflicting geopolitical interests;
- create national intelligence incubators that bring together government agencies, private sector leaders, and academic institutions to develop indigenous intelligence technologies; and
- ensure data sovereignty by establishing strict regulations on how private firms handle sensitive national security information.

Example: The U.S. and China have already implemented this approach, investing billions in homegrown AI firms to ensure control over their intelligence capabilities. Other countries must follow suit to remain competitive in the intelligence landscape.

2. **Offensive Investment in Foreign Startups: Gaining Strategic Insights in Global Competition**

While building homegrown intelligence capabilities is crucial, nations should also invest in foreign startups and corporations as part of an offensive intelligence strategy. This approach will:

- provide early access to emerging technologies that can be integrated into national defence systems;
- allow intelligence agencies to gather strategic insights on adversarial countries' military and corporate advancements; and
- enable economic influence and technological dominance, ensuring that national corporations maintain leverage over global competitors.

Example: Chinese venture capital firms have invested in Silicon Valley AI startups, allowing China to acquire critical technological insights that inform its national AI and cybersecurity policies. Similarly, Western intelligence agencies have used corporate partnerships to monitor technological developments in rival states.

3. Establishing State-Controlled Cyber and AI Defence Units

With corporate actors playing an increasing role in intelligence operations, states must:

- develop cyber-intelligence units within national security agencies that work alongside (but are independent from) private firms;
- mandate strict cybersecurity protocols for corporate entities that handle sensitive government data; and
- create AI-driven defence infrastructures that minimise vulnerabilities from foreign-controlled technology firms.

Example: Israel's military intelligence agency, Unit 8200, has successfully integrated state and private-sector intelligence efforts while maintaining strict government oversight. Other nations can adopt similar models to prevent intelligence outsourcing from undermining national security.

4. Regulating Private Military Security Companies (PMSCs) to Ensure State Control

Given the increasing role of PMSCs in global security, governments must:

- implement strict licensing and operational oversight for all private military contractors operating within national borders or under government contracts;
- restrict foreign corporate ownership of PMSCs to prevent external influence over national security operations; and
- establish international frameworks for accountability, ensuring that private military firms adhere to human rights and conflict regulations.

Example: The European Union has proposed new regulations on PMSCs to limit their influence in conflicts, setting a precedent for other regions to follow.

5. Strengthening Geoeconomic Warfare Capabilities

To counterbalance corporate intelligence threats from rival nations, states should:

- enhance economic counterintelligence units that monitor foreign corporate activities and prevent economic espionage;
- leverage economic sanctions strategically to disrupt adversarial corporate-military alliances; and
- use sovereign wealth funds to acquire stakes in key industries, ensuring that critical sectors remain under national control.

Example: Russia and China have used state-controlled economic intelligence strategies to influence global markets and enhance their geopolitical leverage. Western nations can adopt similar economic intelligence frameworks to remain competitive.

Final Thoughts: The Road Ahead for Corporate-Military Intelligence

The findings in this book confirm that corporate intelligence will be a decisive factor in future warfare. Nations that fail to integrate corporate intelligence into their security strategies will find themselves vulnerable to economic coercion, cyber warfare, and intelligence manipulation. The future of warfare will be characterised by:

1. the increasing privatisation of intelligence and military operations;
2. the dominance of AI, big data, and cyber capabilities in intelligence warfare;
3. the emergence of corporate-led intelligence competition with the ability to influence the world order; and
4. a redefinition of national security strategies to balance state and corporate power.

For policymakers, security professionals, and intelligence analysts, *Corporate Military Intelligence* serves as a critical resource for understanding the shifting nature of global power. As warfare evolves, success will depend on a nation's ability to harness corporate intelligence as a pillar of Comprehensive

National Power (CNP) while ensuring state control, ethical oversight, and strategic dominance.

The challenge ahead is clear—nations and institutions must innovate, regulate, and compete in the corporate intelligence domain or risk falling behind in the geopolitical struggle of the 21st century.

Editors and Contributors

Editors

Shantanu K. Bansal is a Delhi-based strategic analyst and the founder of Indian Aerospace Defence News (IADN), India's leading defence and strategic news portal. He has more than 10 years of experience in research and analysis. His research endeavour covered reforms in India's external intelligence, including Research and Analysis Wing (R&AW) and Defence Intelligence Agency (DIA). He has been a senior consultant to the Army Training Command (ARTRAC), Indian Army and Helicopter Training School (HTS), Indian Air Force. He wrote the most illustrious book of the Indian Army, *The 75 Indian Stratagems and 60 Years of Chetak*, for the Indian Air Force.

Dr Monojit Das specialises in geopolitics and national security. He is Executive Editor at Indian Aerospace and Defence News (IADN), India's leading magazine on defence since 2012, and has publications on national security and geopolitical affairs added in the curriculum of multiple institutions. Besides academics, he also has experience in promoting academic exchanges and Indian education through institutional collaboration and coordination with ICCR, MEA, GoI.

Contributors

Hasim Turker was born in 1976 in Antalya, Turkey. He graduated from the Turkish Naval Academy in 1998 and served at various units of the Turkish Navy for 19 years. Between 2014 and 2016, he commanded TCG Giresun, a guided missile O.H. Perry class frigate. In 2017, he retired with the rank of commander. In 2005, Dr Turker graduated from the National Defense University Atasaren, with an MA degree in 'International Relations' and in 2008 from the Turkish Naval War College, with an MA degree in 'National and International Security Strategies Management and Leadership'. He is an alumnus of the NATO Defense College (SC-118 of 2011). He received his Ph.D. from Kocaeli University in 2018.

Oloke Moses Olalekan is a data analyst at VerionX, Nigeria.

Sasha Gillies-Lekakis is a Ph.D. researcher in the Faculty of Languages and Linguistics (Spanish and Latin American Studies) at the University of Melbourne, Australia. His research focuses on Cuba-Pacific Islands cooperation in education and healthcare, development in the Global South, and South-South cooperation. He has travelled extensively throughout Cuba, Fiji, the Solomon Islands, and Tonga for research and institutional collaborations, with a focus on fostering exchanges between Pacific Island countries and Cuba.

Dr Sureyya Yigit is a Professor of Politics and International Relations at the School of Politics and Diplomacy at New Vision University in Tbilisi, Georgia. He has lectured at several universities in Scandinavia, Turkey, and Central Asia. He is an Editorial Board member of the IGI Book Series Conflict Management-3 Volumes, an International Academic Board member of RIPEA—Journal of Argentine Foreign Policy Research—an Associate Editor on the Editorial Board of the International Journal of Green Business, a member of the Editorial Board of AcademCraft—Open access journal of education research and case studies—and an Editorial Advisory Board Member for IGI Global Cases on Security, Safety, and Risk Management. He is also the senior consultant to ZDS—Women's Democracy Network Public Fund, a non-governmental organisation based in Bishkek, the Kyrgyz Republic—and a consultant to Aeropodium, a London-based business.

Dr Mohamad Hassan Soueidan is an academic and researcher specialising in International Relations, Strategy, and Security. He holds a Ph.D. in Business Administration and is currently pursuing a second Ph.D. in International

Politics and Diplomacy in France, Paris. Dr. Soueidan regularly contributes insightful analysis on international politics as a columnist for *The Cradle Magazine*. His scholarly contributions include numerous publications, authored books, co-authored books, and active participation in international conferences. He previously consulted on infrastructure projects for the Iraqi government, conducted research at the Moscow State Institute of International Relations in Russia, and actively participates in international conferences, emphasising geopolitics, cognitive warfare, and strategic alliances.

Dr Sampa Kundu joined the ASEAN-India Centre (AIC) at RIS in October 2021 as a consultant. She has completed her Ph.D. from the Centre for Indo-Pacific Studies, School of International Studies, Jawaharlal Nehru University, New Delhi. She is working on various nuances of ASEAN-India relations at the AIC. She has previously worked with MP-IDSA, Amity University, and Symbiosis International (Deemed) University. She has written peer-reviewed articles, commentaries, and book chapters for nationally and internationally reputed publishers.

Dr Shushant Vc Parashar is an independent researcher. Previously, he worked as a research fellow at the Centre for Land Warfare Studies (CLAWS) and as an associate fellow at the National Maritime Foundation (NMF). He has completed his Ph.D. in Political Science from Amity University (thesis titled "Environmental Security Policy in South Asia: A Case Study of India and Bhutan"). His research interests include national security, nuclear deterrence, internal security, non-traditional threats, statecraft–non-military, and the history of India's relations with its neighbours. Apart from his doctorate, Dr Parashar holds an M.Phil. degree in South and Southeast Asian Studies from the University of Madras, an MA degree in South Asian Studies from Pondicherry University, and a bachelor's degree in journalism and mass communication from Amity University, along with a PG Diploma in English journalism from the Indian Institute of Mass Communication, Delhi.

Greg Simons, Associate Professor, has a Ph.D. from the University of Canterbury in New Zealand and has been awarded an Associate Professor title in Political Science by Uppsala University in Sweden. He is an Associate

Professor at the Department of Communication Science at Turiba University in Riga, Latvia, and an Associate Researcher at the Department of Journalism, Media and Communication at Daffodil International University in Dhaka, Bangladesh. His research interests include the changing political dynamics and relationships, mass media, public diplomacy, political marketing, crisis management communications, media and armed conflict, and the Russian Orthodox Church. He also researches the relationships and connections between information, politics, and armed conflict more broadly, such as the GWOT and Arab Spring.

Dr Simant Shankar Bharti is a lecturer at the University of Economics and Human Sciences in Warsaw. He has also been affiliated with the Faculty of Political Science and International Studies at the University of Warsaw. He also holds the esteemed position of Honorary Fellow at the Forum for Global Studies in New Delhi. Dr Bharti received his Doctorate in Political Science and Public Administration in the field of International Relations, specialising in EU Development Diplomacy and Soft Power, from the Faculty of Political Science and International Studies at the University of Warsaw, based in Warsaw, Poland. His impressive academic contributions are evident in his prolific publication record, with over 25 articles published in peer-reviewed journals, book chapters, commentaries, and media reviews. Dr Bharti's research interests include European Union politics, regional geopolitics of South Asia, post-colonialism, developing countries; evolving role in the world order';s geopoliticsand the Global South.

Dr Saroj Kumar Aryal is an Adjunct Professor at the Faculty of Political Science and International Studies, University of Warsaw, Warsaw, Poland.

Aaryaman Nijhawan is an international relations researcher and a political commentator. He is a postgraduate from University of Delhi and also from the Moscow State Institute of International Relations (MGIMO), under the aegis of the Ministry of Foreign Affairs, Russian Federation. He is a regular contributor to global outlets, such as Russia Today, India Narrative, and Sputnik India, on contemporary geostrategic issues.

Antoine Renaux is a French analyst based in Poland, holding a bachelor's degree in Political Science and a master's in European Affairs from Sciences Po Grenoble, with specialisation in European Security and Central European Politics. A former reservist in the French armed forces with the 93rd Mountain Artillery Regiment (2016–2018), his professional experience spans roles at Nexter Systems in the defence industry, the Casimir Pulaski Foundation, an international security think tank, and military representation at the French Embassy in Austria. He is currently working as an analyst in the IT industry.

Niranjan Marjani is an independent political analyst and researcher based in Vadodara, India, specialising in international relations and geopolitics. He collaborates with Indian and international publications and think tanks. He has written over 300 opinion/analytical articles. He has also written research papers and book chapters and has presented papers at national and international conferences. Currently, he is pursuing his Ph.D. from the Maharaja Sayajirao University in Vadodara. His research topic is 'India-Spain Relations in the 21st Century: Dynamics and Prospects'. He is associated with the New Delhi-based magazine, *The Kootneeti Español*, as Consulting Editor and with Pune-based think tank, Tatvita-Analysts, as Country Specialist-Spain. He also offers consultation as a political risk analyst to Indian and foreign corporate entities.

Dr John Mwangi Githigaro, is an academic and holds a Ph.D. in International Relations from the United States International University (USIU-A), Nairobi, Kenya. In Autumn 2023 (October-December), he was a visiting fellow at the Moscow State Institute for International Relations (MGIMO University), Russia. Some of his works have been published in the *Terrorism and Political Violence Journal*, *Critical Studies on Terrorism*, the *Journal of Third World Studies, African Conflict and Peacebuilding Review, African Peace and Conflict Journal, and the Journal for Deradicalization.* His most recent book is titled *Countering Violent Extremism in Kenya: Community, State, and Security Perspectives*, Lanham, MD: Rowman and Littlefield, 2024.

David Shakarishvili is a Ph.D. candidate in Political Science from Klaipeda University. He is an invited lecturer at OSCE Academy and Batumi Shota Rustaveli State University. Additionally, Mr. Shakarishvili takes economics classes at the American International School-Progress. He holds academic degrees in International Relations and Diplomacy (Estonian School of Diplomacy), Business Management (Klaipeda University), Intelligence and Global Security (Charles University), and Public Administration (IBSU). Mr. Shakarishvili was a research fellow at the Johan Skytte Institute of Political Studies at the University of Tartu and at the Documentation Center of the Organization for Security and Cooperation in Europe (OSCE). He previously worked in international politics for private, government, non-governmental, and international organisations, such as the Ministry of Economy and Sustainable Development of Georgia, the State Employment Support Agency, the Georgian Parliament, the Thomas Jefferson Research Center, and the Foreign Policy Council.

Dr Anuradha Oinam is an Assistant Professor at Imphal College, Imphal. She completed her Ph.D. from the Diplomacy and Disarmament (DAD) division of the Centre for International Politics, Organization and Disarmament (CIPOD), School of International Studies (SIS), Jawaharlal Nehru University, New Delhi, on the topic 'Weak States and Private Military and Security Companies (PMSCs): Case Studies of Afghanistan and Sierra Leone'. Her M.Phil. dissertation focused on 'Privatisation of Security in Contemporary International Relations: A Study of Motivations, Legality and Implications'. She is also the recipient of the British International Studies Association (BISA) Founder Fund for Ph.D. Scholars in 2019-20. Previously, she was associated with the Centre for Land Warfare Studies (CLAWS) and the Foundation for National Security Research (FNSR), Delhi-based think tanks. In addition, she was a guest faculty, teaching Political Science at Jesus and Mary College, University of Delhi (NCWEB), for two and a half months. Dr Oinam has presented her research works at various national and international conferences, both within India and abroad. She is also a co-editor of the books '*Counterterrorism and Global Security*' and '*Securing the Future: Youth Perspective on National Security Challenges*'. She contributes articles, issue briefs, and book reviews for *CLAWS, Contemporary Asia, Strategic Studies Quarterly, Asian Confluence, South Asian Voices* and the *Diplomat*. Her areas of interest cover Changing Character of Warfare, Private Military and Security Companies (PMSCs), India's Act East Policy, Insurgency, Northeast Region of India, Myanmar, and Bangladesh.

Bibliography

Aldrich, R. (2009), *Secret Intelligence.* Washington: Routledge.

Alexander, K. (2009), Introduction in *Economic Sanctions.* Palgrave Macmillan, London.

Bajoghli, N., Nasr, V., Salehi-Isfahani, D., & Vaez, A. (2024), *How Sanctions Work: Iran and the Impact of Economic Warfare.* Stanford University Press.

Bakir, V. (2018), *Intelligence Elites and Public Accountability: Relationships of Influence with Civil Society.* Washington: Routledge.

Baykov, A. & Shakleina, T. (2023), *Polycentric World Order in the Making.* Singapore: Palgrave Macmillan.

Beck, U. (2006), "Risk Society Revisited: Theory, Politics and Research Programmes".

Bellaby, R. (2014), *The Ethics of Intelligence: A New Framework.* Sheffield: Routledge.

Bradford, A. (2023), *Digital Empires.* Oxford University Press.

Brooks, S.G. & Wohlforth, W.C. (2016), *America Abroad: The United States' Global Role in the 21st century.* New York: Oxford University Press.

Buzan, B. (1983), *People, States, and Fear: The National Security problem in International Relations.* North Carolina : University of North Carolina Press.

C. Wright Mills, *The Power Elite*, Oxford University Press, 1956.

Chapman, B. (2004), *Researching National Security and Intelligence Policy.* London: CQ Press.

Cooley, A. & Nexon, D. (2020),*Exit from Hegemony: The Unravelling of the American Global Order.* New York: Oxford University Press.

Desch, M.C. (2001), *Civilian Control of the Military: The Changing Security Environment.* Baltimore: Johns Hopkins University Press.

Dunne, T., Kurki, M. & Smith, S. (2007), *International Relations Theories: Discipline and Diversity.* Oxford: Oxford University Press.

Dupont, A. (2013), "Intelligence for the twenty-first century". In *Twenty-First Century Intelligence*, pp. 15–39. Routledge.

Eichler, M. (eds.) (2015), *Gender and Private Security in Global Politics*, Oxford University Press, Oxford.

Finkel, M. (2011), *On Flexibility: Recovery from Technological and Doctrinal Surprise on the Battlefield.* Stanford University Press.

Flint, C. (2017), *Introduction to Geopolitics* (3rd ed.). London: Routledge.

Franklin, B., Hamer, M., Hanna, M., Kinsey, M.,& Richardson, J.E. (2011), *Key Concepts in Journalism Studies*. London: Sage.

Freedman, L. (2015), *Strategy: A History*. Oxford University Press.

Gaskarth, J. (2020), *Secrets and Spies: UK Intelligence Accountability after Iraq and Snowden*. Washington: Brookings Institution Press.

George, R.Z. (2020), *Intelligence in the National Security Enterprise: An Introduction*. Georgetown: Georgetown University Press.

In *Corporate Espionage, Geopolitics, and Diplomacy Issues in International Business*, pp. 1–12. IGI Global.

In *Leaders and Intelligence*, pp. 3-39. Routledge.

In *Research Handbook on International Law and Cyberspace*, pp. 231–252. Edward Elgar Publishing.

In *The Military Intelligence Community*, pp. 149-168. Routledge.

In *The Sociology of Risk and Gambling Reader*, pp. 68-90. Routledge.

Jervis, R. (2005), *American Foreign Policy in a New Era*. Routledge: New York.

Johnson, L.K. (2017), *Spy Watching: Intelligence Accountability in the United States*. Oxford: Oxford University Press.

Keohane, R.O. & Nye, Jr, J.S. (eds) (1972), *Transnational Relations and World Politics*. Harvard University Press.

Kissinger, H. (2015), *World Order*. New York: Penguin Books

Klieman, A. (Ed.) (2015), *Great Powers and Geopolitics: International affairs in a Rebalancing World*. Cham (Switzerland): Springer.

Knight, F.H. (1960), *Intelligence and Democratic Action*. Harvard University Press.

Leary, W.M. (2014), *The Central Intelligence Agency: History and Documents*. Alabama: University Alabama Press.

May, R.J., Regan, A., and Dinnen, S. (1997), *Challenging the state: The Sandline Affair in Papua New Guinea*, ANU Press, Canberra.

Pfeffer, J. & Sutton, R.I. (2006), *Hard Facts, Dangerous Half-truths, and Total Nonsense: Profiting from Evidence-based Management*. Harvard Business Press.

Piaget, J. (2005), *The Psychology of Intelligence*. Routledge.

Roselle, L., Spray, S., & Shelton, J.T. (2020), *Research and Writing in International Relations* (3rd ed.). London: Routledge.

Silverman, D. (2020), *Interpreting Qualitative Data*. London: Sage

Sinek, S. (2011), *Start with why: How Great Leaders Inspire Everyone to Take Action*. Penguin.

Smith, S., Hadfield, A., & Dunne, T. (2008), *Foreign Policy: Theories, Actors, Cases*. Oxford: Oxford University Press.

Snyder, R.C., Bruck, H.W., Sapin, B., Hudson, V., Chollet, D., & Goldgeier, J. (2002), *Foreign Policy Decision Making*. New York: Palgrave Macmillan.

Tidd, J. & Bessant, J.R. (2020), *Managing Innovation: Integrating Technological, Market and Organisational Change*. John Wiley & Sons.

Till, G. (2013), *Seapower: A Guide for the Twenty-first Century* (Vol. 51). Routledge Oxon.

Waltz, K.N. (1954), *Man, the State, and the State System in Theories of the Causes of War*. Columbia University.

Willink, J. & Babin, L. (2017), *Extreme Ownership: How US Navy Seals Lead and Win*. St. Martin's Press.

Index